Tom Stoppard's Plays

Works by Tom Stoppara
Published by Grove Press

ALBERT'S BRIDGE AND OTHER PLAYS (IF YOU'RE GLAD, I'LL BE FRANK; ARTIST DESCENDING A STAIRCASE; WHERE ARE THEY NOW?; A SEPARATE PEACE)

DIRTY LINEN *and* NEW-FOUND-LAND

ENTER A FREE MAN

EVERY GOOD BOY DESERVES FAVOR *and* PROFESSIONAL FOUL

JUMPERS

LORD MALQUIST AND MR. MOON

NIGHT AND DAY

THE REAL INSPECTOR HOUND

ROSENCRANTZ AND GUILDENSTERN ARE DEAD

TRAVESTIES

Tom Stoppard's Plays

JIM HUNTER

GROVE PRESS, INC./NEW YORK

First published in 1982 by Faber and Faber Limited, London.

First Evergreen Edition 1982
First Printing 1982
ISBN: 0-394-62414-9
Library of Congress Catalog Card Number: 82-47988

Library of Congress Cataloging in Publication Data
Hunter, Jim.
    Tom Stoppard's plays.

    Bibliography
    1. Stoppard, Tom—Criticism and interpretation.
I. Title.
PR6069.T6Z68   1982   822'.914   82-47988
ISBN 0-394-62414-9

Manufactured in the United States of America

GROVE PRESS, INC., 196 West Houston Street,
New York, N.Y. 10014

CONTENTS

PREFACE

I hope that both fans and sceptics will find useful this attempt to look fairly closely at Tom Stoppard's plays so far. The book is meant for performers, directors, and audiences, who I hope won't find it 'academic'; and for students, who I hope won't forget to laugh.

After a short opening chapter of biography, which summarizes unpublished plays but refers only briefly to those published, there follow seven chapters studying the published plays, with a different emphasis in each chapter. It is possible to select the treatment of a single play by means of the Study-guide at the end, which combines the functions of bibliography, synopsis, annotation, and index.

The longer titles of plays are consistently abbreviated, to *Earnest*, *If You're Glad*, *Rosencrantz*, *Hound*, *Artist Descending*, and *Every Good Boy*.

I have been helped by conversations with Rajan Chetsingh, Frank Pike, and Hedley Stone; by BBC staff who allowed me access to transcripts, tapes, and videotapes; and by Hugh Brazier of Trinity College Library, Dublin, who made available to me a great amount of newsprint and academic criticism of Stoppard.

I am grateful to the playwright and to Faber and Faber for permission to quote from the plays.

J.H.

1 · BIOGRAPHY

The quotations from Tom Stoppard referring to his early years are here taken freely from interviews with *Theatre Quarterly* (June 1974) and the *Sunday Times* (June 1974); from an article Stoppard wrote for *The Author* (Spring 1967); and from letters or conversation quoted by Kenneth Tynan in the essay on Stoppard in his book *Show People* (1980). Only brief mention is made here of the *published* plays, which are summarized in the Study-guide (pp. 218ff.).

1937

Thomas Straussler was born on 3 July in Zlin, Czechoslovakia, the second son of Dr Eugene Straussler, a doctor employed by Bata, the shoe company.

1939

Either Dr Straussler or his wife was of partially Jewish descent; when the German invasion of Czechoslovakia was imminent, the family was transferred by Bata to Singapore.

1942

The Japanese invaded Singapore.

It was women and children first, and [my father] remained behind, while my mother and my brother and I were evacuated to India. . . . My father died in enemy hands, and that's it.

1943–6

Thomas's mother managed the Bata shoe shop in Darjeeling.

> We never seemed to be particularly short of money. . . . I think of those four years in India as happy and interesting. . . . I have a huge nostalgia. But I've never been back. I imagine I'd be fairly disillusioned and despairing if I did, with the population increase, for one thing.

He attended an American multi-racial school in Darjeeling.

1946

Tom's mother married Kenneth Stoppard, a major in the British army in India. The boys took his surname and the family moved 'home' to England, where Kenneth Stoppard became a successful machine-tools salesman.

Stoppard seems uncertain at what time English became his first language. To different interviewers he has suggested it may have been at the ages of three, four, or five-and-a-half, and he told *Theatre Quarterly* that 'English had always been my own language'. On arrival in England he was sent to a prep. school in Nottinghamshire, where he was

> teased a certain amount . . . I was foreign, but I did not know it. I pronounced 'th' like 'd' and made a soft 's' into a hard 's'. All that remains is that I have a very slightly idiosyncratic 'r'. . . . But I was very happy. . . . It really was a privileged education, a lovely house, acres of parkland, we had a lovely time.

1948

Stoppard transferred to Pocklington School in Yorkshire.

1954

At seventeen, Stoppard left school

> thoroughly bored by the idea of anything intellectual, and gladly sold all my Greek and Latin classics to George's Bookshop in Park Street [in Bristol, where the family now lived]. I'd been totally bored and alienated by everyone from Shakespeare to Dickens.

He joined the *Western Daily Press* as a journalist, dreaming of becoming a 'big-name, roving reporter' in international trouble-spots. Dick Wagner and Jacob Milne in *Night and Day* clearly link with this dream. He wrote news reports, features, humorous columns, and reviews of plays and films, getting to know people at the Bristol Old Vic.

1958

Stoppard joined the *Bristol Evening World*. His interest in writing rather than journalism was growing, and particularly, though far from exclusively, his interest in theatre. Kenneth Tynan attributes this to Peter O'Toole's 1957–8 season at the Bristol Old Vic; Stoppard attributes it to Tynan's own reviews on the *Observer* and to Peter Hall's directing at Stratford; and both attribute it to the general new vitality of British theatre associated with John Osborne's *Look Back in Anger* (1956, included in the Bristol 1957–8 season).

1960

In July 1960, sitting gloomily in the turquoise sea, waiting for the mainland boat to rescue me from the crush of Capri, I remembered that it was my twenty-third birthday; twenty-three and still unpublished, still unstaged—still, as a matter of fact, unwriting. . . . So getting back to Bristol from my annual three weeks, I handed in my notice after six years of reporting, subbing, reviewing and interviewing and, having contracted to write two weekly columns for a total of six guineas, started writing a stage play, *A Walk on the Water*. . . . I took it round to the Bristol Old Vic. Nothing happened for nine months. I wrote 72 more columns, and a one-actor not unlike *Waiting for Godot*.

1961

A Walk on the Water was sent to the literary agent Kenneth Ewing, who had been recommended by someone at the Bristol Old Vic.

I had one of those Hollywood-style telegrams that change struggling young artists' lives . . . An option was bought almost immediately, and, drunk with riches (£100), I went out and bought 20 books and a Picasso print.

There was talk of the play opening in April 1962 with one or other famous actor in the lead. Nothing happened and at the end of a year the option ran out.

1963

Stoppard worked in London as theatre critic for the short-lived *Scene* magazine. He was commissioned by the publisher Anthony Blond to write a novel (which emerged in 1966 as *Lord Malquist and Mr Moon*). *A Walk on the Water* was bought and transmitted by ITV in November. It was staged in Hamburg in 1964 and, partly rewritten, in London in 1968 as *Enter a Free Man*, the earliest-written of Stoppard's published plays.

1964

In February BBC Radio broadcast a fifteen-minute play:

The Dissolution of Dominic Boot

Dominic drops off his fiancée from his taxi and then, realizing he has too little money to pay the fare, travels about London trying to raise it, all the time incurring a higher debt on the meter. At the end, penniless and in his pyjamas, he is sacked by his employer, whose secretary hails a taxi and cries, 'Come on, you can drop me off'. The writing is extremely deft, wasting no time and using running jokes and small surprises to keep up the interest; and it is pure radio in its suggestions of a constantly changing scene and cast.

In April the companion fifteen-minute radio play was broadcast:

M is for Moon among Other Things

It is August 5th, 1962. Alfred and Constance, middle-aged, middle-class, and childless, are reading independently—Alfred his

*paper, Constance the M to N instalment of her mail-order encyc-
lopaedia. We hear their thoughts. They turn on the television in time
to catch the final credits of Dial M for Murder. Constance reveals
that she used to be known by her middle name, Millie, and that she is
dissatisfied with her life, though she doesn't 'want the Moon'. The
news is broadcast of Marilyn Monroe's death. Alfred tells Constance
'it's such a cold shallow world she was living in. No warmth or
understanding'—an accurate though unaware description of his own
wife's life. Constance yearns for the simple world of her childhood
ABC: 'M was for Moon. It was ages before I knew that M was for
anything else.' She retreats to bed with M's from her encyclopaedia
rattling in her brain. Alfred, having given his wife no comfort,
retreats into a fantasy of being Marilyn Monroe's comforter.*

Three stories by Stoppard were published by Faber in *Introduction 2*, the second in a series of anthologies introducing new
writers. In *Reunion* the unnamed man has yearnings and problems later to become familiar in Stoppard's characters. Instead
of Mr Moon's bomb (see below) he dreams of 'a certain word . . .
which, if shouted at the right pitch and in a silence worthy of it,
would nudge the universe into gear.'

Life, Times: Fragments consists of ironic notes on being an
apprentice writer and journalist. *The Story* is about a reporter's
guilt at the suicide of a man whose minor conviction in a provincial court he allowed to become national news.

From May to October Stoppard joined 'a kind of cultural
picnic in Berlin' paid for by the Ford Foundation. Young playwrights were 'fed and housed in great comfort and just asked to
get on with it'.

What I wrote in Germany, if I remember—and I'm trying to
forget—was just a sort of Shakespearean pastiche. It was Kenneth
Ewing who gave me the idea. . . . I remember writing a version in which
[Rosencrantz and Guildenstern] got to England, and King Lear was on
the throne. . . . I mean, the whole thing was unspeakable.

Also in 1964 Stoppard wrote five episodes of the daily family
radio serial *The Dales*, and a (still unperformed) television play

called *This Way Out with Samuel Boot*. Kenneth Tynan summarizes it: 'Samuel Boot, a fortyish man of evangelical fervour, preaches the total rejection of property. Jonathan, his younger brother, is a compulsive hoarder of objects.' By the end of 'an uneasy blend of absurdist comedy and radical melodrama' both are dead.

1965

The BBC hired Stoppard to write the diary of an imaginary Arab student in London, which was then translated into Arabic and broadcast on the Overseas Service. This brought in £20 a week for about nine months. Early in the year the Royal Shakespeare Company took a twelve-month option on *Rosencrantz*. The option expired in 1966 and several other managements also rejected the play.

'Round about 1965' the Bristol University Drama Department staged *The Gamblers*, described by Stoppard to Kenneth Tynan years later as '*Waiting for Godot* in the death cell—prisoner and jailer—I'm sure you can imagine the rest.'

At the end the condemned man and the executioner have swopped places, but since they both wear masks no one will be able to tell which is which. Although Stoppard obviously has no wish to resurrect the play now it is in some respects more original and personally-felt than the earlier *Enter a Free Man* which had a London production and is still in print. Stoppard has called *The Gamblers* 'the first play I regard as *mine*, after I'd cleared the decks with *A Walk on the Water*' (*Enter a Free Man*).

In 1965 Stoppard's first marriage took place, to Jose Ingle, a nurse he had known since 1962.

1966

This was the year of Stoppard's real arrival as a writer. In February BBC Radio broadcast *If You're Glad*. In May Stoppard's adaptation of Slawomir Mrozek's play *Tango* was presented by the Royal Shakespeare Company in London (it was published in 1968 by Cape). And within a few days in August the television play *A Separate Peace* was transmitted, *Rosencrantz* received its first performance, by the Oxford Theatre Group, as part of the Edinburgh Festival fringe, and the novel *Lord Malquist and Mr Moon* was published.

Lord Malquist and Mr Moon

Any study of the plays is likely to cross-refer to this novel occasionally. A highly original black-comic book, it deserves to stay in print as an unusually good example of the exuberant absurdism of its time, as well as for Stoppard's superb writing. The novel is dense with cultural allusion, and any extract is likely to cause open laughter in a reader of a certain literary-cultural background. Taken as a whole it becomes exhausting to read and lacks real onward drive, a problem the plays don't always escape. The book is theatrical (or dramatic, or filmic) in its assembling a series of funny encounters or panoramic sequences; novelistic in being centred on the unbalanced consciousness of Mr Moon, a young free-lance historian offering himself as Boswell-like recorder of the lives and sayings of the great. Moon carries about a bomb inherited from an eccentric uncle, and has every intention of exploding it somewhere soon, as a despairing gesture against the 'rottenness' of things, which has something to do with over-population, the seething mass of people, the fragility of social and communal systems—themes recurrent at this time in Stoppard—and also, more significantly for his later work, with Moon's failure to find goodness or complete honesty. His unrest may more cynically be traced to the refusal of his wife Jane (whom he has known since childhood) to allow the marriage to be consummated; and indeed after eventually losing his virginity with the Lady Malquist, wife of his present client, Moon 'thought that he might after all get through life if he could periodically (two or three times a day) rendezvous with Lady Malquist for his sexual fix'.

Lord Malquist himself is a mixture of Chesterfield, Wilde, and Sir Archibald Jumper, utterly callous to the most obvious suffering where Moon is 'wide-open' to everything from the starving in Asia to the wiping-out of the white rhino. The possible consolations of Christianity are harshly treated by the repeated appearances of The Risen Christ, a donkey-riding Irishman who appears to have superficially-healed stigmata but who 'wrote off nearly two thousand years of Pauline dogma with a single observation: "That Lady Whosis, I wouldn't kick her out of bed."' Further comic interest is added by a black Irish Jewish Cockney coachman called O'Hara, two cowboys on horseback, a murdered French maid, a lion, and another *mad bomber.*

As a result of Ronald Bryden's enthusiastic *Observer* review of the Edinburgh *Rosencrantz*, Kenneth Tynan brought the play to London in April 1967, performed at the Old Vic by the National Theatre.

1967

In February BBC Television transmitted a thirty-minute unpublished play:

Teeth

George Pollack is having an affair with the wife of his dentist, Harry Dunn, whose receptionist is George's wife, Mary. Once George is captive in the dentist's chair, Harry probes both his teeth and his liaison; stains his gums green, gasses him, makes love to his wife, and removes his middle tooth. At the end, as George leaves, he discovers that all Harry's patients in the waiting-room have missing front teeth; the best line in a disappointing script is the last: 'All round him there are smiles like broken-down brooms.'

In June BBC Television transmitted another thirty-minute comedy:

Another Moon Called Earth

An early version of Jumpers. *The historian, Bone, is working on a great thesis: that nothing happens at random (that, one might say,*

*there is a fixed logic to everything—see pp. 167–81 below). His
wife Penelope became unbalanced the day the first man landed on the
moon, and it seems likely she is responsible for the death of her maid,
Miss Pinkerton, though she feels no guilt. The closeness of her
doctor's attentions to her worries Bone as Archie's worry George in*
Jumpers *(where Bone's name is transferred to the policeman).*

In July the BBC transmitted *Albert's Bridge*, the fifty-eight-
minute radio play which won the Prix Italia the following year.
Also in 1967 Stoppard won the John Whiting Award and the
Evening Standard drama award; *Rosencrantz* was a hit success
both in London and New York.

1968

The Real Inspector Hound was Stoppard's first play to originate
in the West End, in June 1968; a second production and a New
York production followed in 1972 and the play soon became
popular with amateurs.

In December Granada television transmitted a sixty-minute
thriller, *Neutral Ground*, a neat transference of the classical myth
of Philoctetes to the agent/double-agent-behind-the-Iron-
Curtain field of John Le Carré.

1970

In April *After Magritte* was presented at a lunch-hour theatre
club in London. With *Hound* it made a West End double bill in
1972.

Where are They Now?, written for BBC Schools Radio, was
broadcast in December and repeated in general listening hours
the following year.

1971

In December at the Almost-Free Theatre in Soho, Inter-Action
presented *Dogg's Our Pet*, a short play which later became

substantially the first part (pp. 15–30) of *Dogg's Hamlet*. Ed Berman—pseudonym Professor Dogg—founded Inter-Action in 1968 to stimulate community theatre; *Dogg's Our Pet* is an anagram of Dogg's Troupe.

1972

In February *Jumpers* opened, performed by the National Theatre Company at the Old Vic, and was highly acclaimed. In July Stoppard presented for BBC Television's series 'One Pair of Eyes' his own verbal and visual statement, *Tom Stoppard Doesn't Know*. In November the BBC broadcast *Artist Descending*.

Also in 1972 Stoppard's second marriage took place, to Miriam Moore-Robinson, the first having ended in divorce. Miriam Stoppard is a doctor and a television 'personality'.

1973

In March Stoppard's adaptation of Lorca's *The House of Bernarda Alba* (unpublished), based on a literal translation by Katie Kendall, was presented at the Greenwich Theatre; and at the same theatre Stoppard himself directed Garson Kanin's *Born Yesterday*.

1974

Stoppard was contracted to work on the screenplay of Thomas Wiseman's *The Romantic Englishwoman*, directed by Joseph Losey.

In June *Travesties* was presented at the Aldwych Theatre by the Royal Shakespeare Company.

1975

Stoppard adapted Jerome K. Jerome's *Three Men in a Boat* for BBC Television.

In July BBC Television transmitted live a half-hour play, *The Boundary*, as one of a series of plays written, rehearsed and performed, from scratch, within a week. The writers were Stoppard and Clive Exton.

The Boundary

Johnson and Bunyans are compiling a dictionary. They find their workroom in chaos: a window is broken, and huge mounds of windblown paper obscure telephone, television set, and the body of Johnson's wife and assistant, Brenda. We gather during the play that Brenda has also been intimately related to Bunyans; and that her influence on the dictionary has been a mixed blessing, since she has a genius for malapropism. As the lexicographers attempt to restore the scattered dictionary items to their correct files, each in turn glimpses Brenda's body, assumes her to have been killed by the other, and does not comment; in due course, indeed, 'the two men cravenly attempt to establish that each is willing to condone the other'. *At intervals, meanwhile, we see signs of a cricket match in progress outside.*

Eventually Brenda, who has regained consciousness minutes earlier and has overheard the men condoning her 'murder', stands and hurls 'malaprop' abuse ('Philatelist!') at her husband, whom she believes to have clubbed her down. Another windowpane breaks and Brenda is struck (for the second time, we realize) by a cricket ball. This time she is killed instantly.

Whatever Clive Exton's share in it, the play reads like a reprise of many of Stoppard's own best tunes: the snowfall of words, the malapropisms, the lexicographers' own stumbling over language; the false assumptions about, and the eventual grotesque explanation of, an opening tableau; the two men both involved with one woman; and a 'grid' of language familiar to most of us but not to the learned lexicographers: the typewriter 'has letters of the alphabet . . . But not in order. "qwertyuiop". Dear God in Heaven, a faulty machine!' This very funny play, which is unpublished, cries out for a second production.

1976

Inter-Action presented Stoppard's *The Dogg's Troupe 15-Minute Hamlet* 'which was written (or rather edited) for performance on a double-decker bus.' And *Dirty Linen* and *New-Found-Land* were written for Ed Berman and their first performance, which he directed, was on 6 April, the date of his British naturalization—the sort of complex, wittily appropriate gesture said to be characteristic of Stoppard as a friend. The first performances were in an Ambiance Lunch-Hour Theatre Club at the Almost-Free Theatre. The plays transferred to the Arts Theatre in June and, in spite of the brevity of the evening, became a great box-office success.

By the beginning of 1976 Stoppard was reading about Russian dissidents, 'intending to use the material for a television play'. In April he met Victor Fainberg, who had emerged into exile in 1974 after five years in the Soviet prison-hospital system. Fainberg was campaigning on behalf of Vladimir Bukofsky (the campaign was successful in December 1976). In August Stoppard addressed a Trafalgar Square rally sponsored by the Committee Against Psychiatric Abuse, and joined in the subsequent march to the Soviet Embassy.

1977

Early in the year Stoppard visited Moscow and Leningrad with the assistant director of Amnesty International (who had designated 1977 'Prisoner of Conscience Year'). Meanwhile in Czechoslovakia three men were arrested for attempting to deliver their 'Charter 77' to their own government—'a request,' as Stoppard puts it, 'that the government should implement its own laws'. One of these three was the dramatist Vaclav Havel, whose work Stoppard may have come to know through the enthusiasm of Kenneth Tynan, who saw him as Stoppard's 'mirror-image'. Havel's play *The Increased Difficulty of Concentration* (1968) anticipates *Jumpers* in featuring an academic 'dictating a bumbling lecture on moral values which goes against the intellectual grain of his society' (Tynan).

In February Stoppard wrote in the *New York Times* about the repression of Charter 77 in Prague, and in the British *Sunday Times* about his visit to Russia. In the same month he worked out the scheme of *Professional Foul*.

On 3 June Stoppard reviewed Paul Johnson's book *Enemies of Society*, which defends 'the Western liberal democracy favouring an intellectual elite and a progressive middle class and based on a moral order derived from Christian absolutes'.

Johnson was described, with an implicit approval important to our knowledge of Stoppard, as 'an intellectual affronted by unreason, and a moralist affronted by relativism'. From the heart of his concerns in 1977 Stoppard noted that 'one does not have to be an expert on anything to know that in one of his themes—the defence of objective truth from the attacks of Marxist relativists—Johnson has got hold of the right end of the right stick at the right time'.

In June Vladimir Bukofsky attended a rehearsal of *Every Good Boy* in London. 'His presence was disturbing,' Stoppard writes in his Introduction to the play. Also in June Stoppard visited Czechoslovakia, for the first time since his family's departure in 1939. He met Havel, now released after four months' imprisonment, and they talked for five or six hours. Later Stoppard dedicated *Professional Foul* to him.

In July *Every Good Boy* was performed at the Festival Hall, with the London Symphony Orchestra under the play's co-author, conductor André Previn. Previn had first invited Stoppard in 1974 to write a play which employed a full-size symphony orchestra on stage.

In September *Professional Foul* was first shown. Of all Stoppard's plays it is perhaps the hardest to fault (of course it is less ambitious than some of the stage plays), yet Stoppard says the first draft was written in 'about three weeks'.

1978

In November *Night and Day* was first performed at the Phoenix Theatre, a Michael Codron presentation. Stoppard told Ronald Hayman in 1976:

> I think people like Codron are as important to the theatre as the National and the Royal Shakespeare Company. So I said, 'Yes, I'll try and do you a play, Michael'. The silly thing is that even I am thinking in terms of a 'Codron-type play' instead of a 'play'. It would be absurd to write a play for Michael Codron that had twenty-eight characters, but that's merely a commercial consideration. What I mean is that I think: 'Oh well this is a chance to write my West End play, to write *The Linden Tree* or *The Rattigan Version*.'

1979

The first performance of *Dogg's Hamlet, Cahoot's Macbeth* was given in May at the University of Warwick by the British American Repertory Company, directed by Ed Berman. It opened in London in July.

In June the National Theatre gave the first performance of Stoppard's English version, *Undiscovered Country*, of Arthur Schnitzler's *Das Weite Land*, a sharp-eyed, sharp-tongued realist four-acter about Viennese society at the turn of the century. The text was published by Faber in 1980.

1981

In August the National Theatre gave the first performance of *On the Razzle*, which Stoppard presents as his own play adapted from its Austrian original, Johann Nestroy's *Einen Jux will er sich machen*.

Most of the world's best dramatists have done much hack work, work to commission, and adaptation of other people's plays, at least in the earlier part of their careers. Later some of them have become highly selective and concentrated only on their own most serious output. Stoppard shows no sign of wanting to move into an ivory tower: he continues to work on screenplays and adaptations and to be a man of the theatre, not only of the desk. He described himself in 1974 as a writer 'for hire' and is clearly proud of this kind of professionalism. And he delights in the word 'showbiz' and all it suggests. He is successful and prosperous enough to be able to withdraw; but he is unlikely to do so. He spoke well about himself to Ronald Hayman in 1976:

I have a love–hate relationship with this mythical figure of the dedicated writer.... About 51 per cent of me views this figure with utter contempt and about 49 per cent with total admiration. I also have 51 per cent contempt for the artist who is very serious about himself and ploughs a lonely furrow and occasionally a few pages are released to the millions, and 49 per cent admiration. Conversely, I've got a weakness or a commendable admiration for rather shallow people who knock off a telly play and write a rather good novel and go and interview Castro and write a good poem and a bad poem and give a silly interview and every five years do a really good piece of work as well. That sort of eclectic, trivial person who's very gifted. In a way I catch myself liking these people too much, as if they were sirens on a rock saying, 'Come on, come away from the serious artists'. I never quite know whether I want to be a serious artist or a siren.

and again to *Gambit* (1981):

I've got a cheap side and an expensive side. I mean rather like a musician might stop composing for a few days to do a jingle for 'Katomeat' because he thinks it's fun. And I honestly can't believe that because of something that happened to the world or to England I'll never write a 50-minute rompy farce for Ed Berman.

2 · PLAYING

The uncertainty whether to be a serious artist or a siren is one intrinsic to the nature of theatre and film. Stoppard is merely a rather remarkable example of it. This needs grasping, so as to avoid the foolishness of trying to take the jokes too seriously, and equally to avoid missing the richness on offer. With all theatre, but especially with Stoppard, playing is where we start and finish.

'If rationality were the criterion for things being allowed to exist,' George heatedly tells Dotty (*Jumpers*, p. 40), 'the world would be one gigantic field of soya beans!' Art is 'a monument to irrationality'.

The irrational is often funny or lightweight, and often subversive: it is likely to be disapproved by those who (like the First Lord in *If You're Glad*) think they are God. We shall see later how often Stoppard identifies the fatal attractiveness of rational rigidities applied to experience and behaviour, and how consistently his plays urge us to keep jinking, on the move, sceptical and free. Irrationality, in Stoppard, becomes heroic: it even becomes the best hope for the survival of reason. (Compare—especially if you have missed it so far—Charles Dickens's *Hard Times*.)

Art is, of course, often wise, lucid, and carefully reasoned. But it is always irrational (like its more transient brother, sport) in so far as it is not productive, not purposeful. Like the majority of artists, Stoppard has a low opinion of art with a 'message': 'if you are angered or disgusted by a particular injustice or immorality . . . you can hardly do worse than write a play about it. . . .

That's what art is bad at.' (*Theatre Quarterly*, 1974.) We also need to be on guard against those who praise art as helpful, therapeutic, informative: they are really rationalizing art away, valuing it for its spin-off rather than for itself. The Schubert String Quintet is not there to help us to lead our lives: it is something we *do* with our lives, something (we may even feel) that the rest of our life has led up to.

Having said that art is 'bad at' messages, Stoppard goes on to say that art 'is important because it provides the moral matrix, the moral sensibility, from which we make our judgements about the world'. (But note that it is *we* who are to make the judgements.) Art is playing: plays are a particular kind of playing. And as we play we live, and learn to live: this is generally known to be true about children, and there is good reason to think it true for adults. The way a farce is created is as relevant here as the theory of tragedy.

A Puritan might not have accepted this, and neither, perhaps, does a Marxist. Modern Puritans or Marxists are unlikely to enjoy Stoppard's plays, or to get far with this book: they look at the world—often with great shrewdness and integrity—in a different way. It is fundamental to the Stoppardian view that playing needs no ticket to make it respectable: that it is, rather, *not* playing which may be ruinous.

This doesn't mean that anything goes. Stoppard writes with a considerable decorum, based not only on his sense of the West End box-office but also on a natural gentleness. It is interesting to see, in a pre-production typescript, Stoppard deleting several 'blue' jokes because they are crudely forced—not because they are 'blue': other equally risqué lines survive because they are naturally—elegantly—integrated with the dialogue. An *artistic* judgement is at work. And it points to another important concern:

I think it's right to take pride in one's craftsmanship, as much as in one's originality.

(Stoppard to *Gambit*, 1981)

[About Magritte] I like the way he did things very carefully and perfectly.

(Stoppard to Joost Kuurman, March 1979)

As in sport, the *quality* of the playing is vital—is, perhaps, part of 'the moral sensibility from which we make our judgements'.

I really hate gratuitousness. On television—and I have enough technical knowledge about how plots work—if I see something which is a cheat on the one hand or a left-over on the other, or a little loose end, it destroys the entire edifice, as far as I'm concerned. To me it's like a bridge which is going to fall down in minutes.

(to Hayman, 1976)

A more specially Stoppardian aspect of playing is the juggling of different explicit perceptions. This can put some people off. It is one thing, they feel, for sports, or non-verbal arts, to be self-defining, purposeless, or frivolous; another when serious debate is staged convincingly and then dismantled, or just unresolved. A writer, they will tell us, should 'deal responsibly' with his material. Such people tend to seek (or worse, think they are expected to seek) some overall and explicit synthesis. Not finding it in the early Stoppard, a good many were troubled.

Nor was the early Stoppard helped by misguided classifications of his plays as 'Absurdist' or 'Surrealist'. Absurdism *is* based on a sort of synthesis: everything is meaningless when viewed against the certainty of death. Stoppard's own convictions are far from this and the nearest he comes to it is the sad, clown's nod of *Rosencrantz*. Surrealism is an anti-rational genre heavy on psychology; Stoppard loves reasoning and (with the partial exception of *Night and Day*) will walk a long way round about to avoid stepping in psychology. Surrealism tells us that our reality is stranger than we thought, and to trust nothing; Stoppard that its strangenesses are often explicable and comical, and to trust life itself.

Those readers already familiar with Stoppard interviews will recognize in his refusal to offer detachable 'morals' not apathy but scruple. His 'not knowing' is discussed later (Chapter 7). It means that what he attempts in his more 'intellectual' plays (the word is his) such as *Jumpers*, *Artist Descending*, *Travesties*, *Professional Foul*, or *Night and Day* is a lighter-weight version of what is available to us in some of the greatest writers: in Shakespeare, or in the nineteenth-century novelists. There it would be small-minded of us to expect endorsement of one single point of view; and there can be no explicit synthesis of all the conflicting values and emotions in *King Lear* (or even, perhaps, *Coronation Street*). What art can attempt to do is make a structure in which synthesis becomes to some extent *implicit*: in which, though the electrons can dash madly about, the overall chemical structure is stable. We can't pick up a chunk of life; we can pick up *The Cherry Orchard*. About some great works there seems nothing explicit to say: it would be like commenting on life itself. (Emily Dickinson in a letter: 'What do I think of *Middlemarch*? What do I think of glory?') This sense of picking up life itself is connected with the artist's refusal to endorse one single thesis (otherwise you could pick that up instead).

More obviously than these major artists, Stoppard is at play; but more obviously than most comics he deals with human values, and with alternative philosophies. His refusal to arrive at a single view is not necessarily an opting-out: it can be an inclusion. 'The objective is the universal perception,' he told *Theatre Quarterly*; adding, as if it were self-evident, 'isn't it?'

Clive James's way of putting it, a year later, was 'that no readily appreciable conceptual scheme can possibly be adequate to the complexity of experience'.

James's *Encounter* essay has some of the nerve of Stoppard's own ingenuities, sketching an extravagant parallel between Stoppard and Einstein. Einstein, James says, produced his baffling relativity not to confuse people but to clarify reality—to clarify the fact that reality cannot be pinned down. Stoppard's 'not knowing' is a determination to tell the truth; his 'impulse to clarify' leads him 'to create a dramatic universe of perpetual transformations'. James sells all this hard but well ('The chill which some spectators feel at a Stoppard play is arriving from infinity'); and he is certainly taking up explicit indications in the novel *Lord Malquist and Mr Moon*:

> How can one be consistent about anything, since all the absolutes discredit one another? . . . . I take both parts . . . leapfrogging myself along the great moral issues, refuting myself and rebutting the refutation towards a truth that must be a compound of two opposite half-truths. And you never reach it because there is always something more to say.
>
> (pp. 52–3)

Perhaps some form of *playing* is the only way to accommodate such restless fidelity to apparently conflicting 'truths'; and Clive James concludes by telling us that 'Einstein's life-long search for the Unified Field was the same game'.

At the outset I suggested an affinity between art and sport. Kenneth Tynan, incidentally, has an enjoyable anecdote of Stoppard as winning scorer for Harold Pinter's cricket team; and goes on to say that 'for Stoppard art is a game'—but then adds, with characteristic loading, 'within a game—the large game being life itself, an absurd mosaic of incidents and accidents'. (Tynan's whole essay should, in my view, be enjoyed and mistrusted.) One of the major contrasts between art and sport, of course, is that art tends to be built to last, and is certainly *built*, while sport is, in spite of the Wisdens and the track records, very much a momentary happening. No sporting event, not even Boycott playing a maiden over, happens twice; and the kinds of intention, as well as the kinds of activity, of sport and art differ widely. Where sport comes closest to the arts is in *performance*. Strictly speaking, no theatrical event happens twice, either.

As a performance art, theatre has good and bad productions, actors, audiences, and nights. The dramatist is in a looser, less authoritative, but perhaps more exhilarating relationship to his work (his play) than a poet or a painter or (the most absolute master) a novelist. He is often readier to take risks, partly because what seems to him extravagant or difficult may not seem so to his actors, partly because the actors are expert in salvaging clumsy scenes and papering over weaknesses, and partly because the rehearsals offer some chance for reconsideration and rewriting. Stoppard makes the most of this relationship to his work. He takes abundant risks; and although he likes to be involved in the first production of a play, and has admitted a Beckettian fantasy of being able to score every detail and gesture, he also admits the fantasy is misguided, and he hands his director and actors an unpredictable, restless text with many changes of mood, many theatrical set-pieces, and a number of options. Even in those published texts which he has corrected with hindsight he still writes 'there may be—', 'It could be . . . or it might . . . might well be visible', 'hopefully', 'it might be an idea', 'another possibility', 'not necessarily', 'it is not important how this transference is achieved, only that it is seen to occur'.

The criterion of theatrical success tends to be whether the play *works* (a linguistic wriggle which might interest Stoppard). It works if it is absorbing, exciting, moving or funny to watch, so that we would like to watch it again; or, in the case of a scene-change or transition, if it gets us from one section of the play to another without irritation. Some people who set a high value on art in general have a low opinion of theatre, for this reason. They point out that to talk of a scene 'working' implies mechanism and possibly deception, appropriate enough to juggling and conjuring but (they claim) fatal to the integrity of the artist's study of life.

In its working on audience-reaction theatre is always potentially in decline towards sensationalism. Equally, though, it has always still the potential force of its origins, which—in all societies—are in religion and superstition. Early drama has its roots in ceremony, in going not to see *what* will happen, but to see it happen. And to see it *together*.

Writing for such corporate response is still possible in

today's pluralism. Beckett's *Waiting for Godot*, the great post-war European play, could be easily adapted into the idiom of a primitive society, yet in some respects is intellectually sophisticated. It overlaps with, say, Oedipus on the road to Colonus, Everyman on his journey, or Faustus seeking diversion to forget his doom—but also with Will Kempe and Charlie Chaplin; it enabled Harold Pinter, but also Tom Stoppard. The potentially religious force of theatre, like the potentially sensationalized, is there in *Jumpers* and *Travesties* as well as in more solemn plays; and they are performances, for us to watch together.

What we watch is a deception in the interests of discovery. The actor feigns grief for Hecuba; yes, it is false. But his 'playing' offers a circumstance for us to appraise in more detachment than we could feel if the man stood on stage overcome with real grief. Theatre is particularly suited to enriching our experience, vicariously and acceptably, by such representations; it is also particularly good at the study of deception itself.

Near the end of Stoppard's *Rosencrantz* an actor gives a convincing rendering of death in agony. The audience know it is only acting; acting, what is more, the one event which can never be acted from personal experience. So we play, or watch others play, things which frighten or disturb us. Whether it is tasteful or crudely sensational to feign death is a long and old debate; certainly the classical and neo-classical theatre avoided it. Something of the debate goes on in our stomachs as we watch. Since the actor is in this case acting an actor (Player) who has previously boasted that his team can die 'heroically, comically, ironically, slowly, suddenly, disgustingly, charmingly, or from a great height', we are also not sure whether he is acting death, or only acting an actor acting death. It partly depends on whose reaction we watch: if we watch Guil's, we see he is sure he has killed the Player; so is Ros; if we watch the tragedians, we see on their faces only 'interest'. So, theatre shows us different reactions, which become different *versions* of the event. If Guil has 'really' killed the Player, then the significances flash across one another in a blur: it means the tragedians are wrong this time (the deceivers deceived—that'll teach them to muck about with death); it means the gentle, fastidious Guil has committed murder; and it means that he has proved himself able to interfere in the fixed destiny of himself and the tragedians as characters in the play *Hamlet*. (Or has he?—their function in that play is now over.)

The theatre is tensely still after the body has ceased to move. Very faintly, immediately rejected by our intellects, is the astronomically remote possibility that the actor is genuinely dead (the idea is used in several classic English detective stories, including one called *Hamlet, Revenge!*). Much more substantially present in our minds is the possibility that in the Stoppard play the Player is genuinely dead; something of the kind happens at the end of Pirandello's *Six Characters in Search of an Author*. Now the tragedians begin to applaud fervently; and for a second we are flooded with embarrassment at that remote possibility that the actor will not get up. . . . (In theatre, we feel a character's potential embarrassment before he does—and we can do nothing about it.) Then the Player gets up, the audience is relieved or 'drained', depending partly on how much they identify with Guil, and, harshly rubbing salt into open wounds, the Player proceeds to direct like a ringmaster a cavalcade of violent deaths, mocking our discomfiture and mocking particularly, of course, the undying Ros and Guil. Yet this time the tragedians *are 'really' dying*. Again the significances overlap: the deaths are theatrically compelling; they also present (for the second time—see Act Two) a travesty of the end of *Hamlet*; they include, which Shakespeare does not, stabbings of Ros and Guil's travesty-substitutes (cloaked 'Spies'). Ros and Guil, however, do not themselves die (they disappear, a few moments later), in spite of the fact that the play's title announces that they are dead.

And so on. Whether or not it is a weakness that a good deal of this has already been teased through in Act Two, it is good theatre, at which the playwright's laughter can almost be heard. Trying to analyse what's going on in a few moments like this takes some time—which is, of course, the mark of theatre's distinctiveness.

Take another example: Lenin's harangue, relatively late (p. 85) in *Travesties*. Imagine the first performance: in one of the most prestigious theatres in Europe, in the heart of London, a smart and probably rather self-satisfied audience, rosy from warmth, interval drinks, and nearly two hours of communal laughter, watches an actor simulating a famous photograph of Lenin in 1920. He harangues the theatre with great ferocity.

> Your talk about absolute freedom is sheer hypocrisy. There can be no real and effective freedom in a society based on the power of money. . . . The freedom of the bourgeois writer, artist or actor is simply disguised dependence on the money-bag, on corruption, on prostitution.

The audience listens attentively without apparent emotion, some perhaps nodding, some smiling in a glazed way, waiting for the next obvious laugh.

Most clearly, this is an example of another natural facility of theatre: the presentation of conflicting ideas, in debate, legal process, or rhetoric. We have had various aesthetic versions earlier, now we have Lenin's. *Travesties*, then, is a comedy of ideas. But this will not do as an account of what is going on here. In Bernard Shaw, the best-known and most prolific writer of the comedy of ideas, we are intended to feel a progression of thought: characters and audience are wiser at the end than at the beginning. At best, the plot itself compels—or derives from—the progression; thus by the end of *Major Barbara* Cusins, the Professor of Greek, and Barbara the aristocratic Salvationist, have given up their Greek, their social position, and the Salvation Army in order to manage a cannons factory. (It is a sufficiently Stoppardian situation!) Shaw has in fact developed a definite message: that art, culture, society and religion must grapple with and control the brutal realities of the world, or be controlled by them. The study of Greek, the graces of society, the good works of religion are all (we are meant to feel) 'placed' in the developing debate. Theatrically the play is of little interest beyond the energy of its arguments, though a large bass drum and some comic Cockneys mildly enliven Act Two. The arguments, though, are forceful and witty (and, incidentally, echoed by Stoppard on p. 39 of *Travesties*).

The ideas in *Travesties* scarcely progress. The play is a flashback and a farrago, and Stoppard carefully shows us, in the last moments, not only that we have got nowhere but also that we have gone by the way of historical inaccuracy. This doesn't mean the ideas aren't 'important'. It means that, unlike Shaw, Stoppard does not press them into linear development, with the judgements that would involve. This may be seen as laziness, opting-out, or having it both ways; or as humility, beside the blarneying self-assurance of Shaw; as going, moment by moment, for whatever 'works' theatrically, or as the 'inclusive' delicacy of a good novelist, allowing different and apparently conflicting versions to live together.

In fact each dramatist is doing what he does best. Shaw works as a barrister presenting a case, always towards an end, a last word, a judgement; even if his tongue is in his cheek, and the final proof of his case not as important to him as he makes out, still he believes sincerely in truth arrived at by process of argument. Theatre, though enjoyable enough, is merely the rhetoric he uses to win the jury, and indeed to get himself heard at all. (I am sure music meant more than theatre to Shaw.) Stoppard is intensely concerned with the ideas of *Travesties*; but he has the artistic sense to present them through his own outstanding gift for theatrical surprise. He is the juggler of Notre-Dame, offering what he does best. The development of *Travesties* is theatrical: the full impact of Lenin's harangue is understood only in the context of the theatrical exchanges of philosophies which precede it.

To study these exchanges in sequence is to study the very nature of Stoppard's playing: it is a direct approach to his achievement at its best, and will take up the rest of this chapter.

* * * * *

The prologue of *Travesties* shows us the three revolutionaries in the Zurich Public Library: the political revolutionary Lenin; the literary revolutionary Joyce, dedicated to the great traditions of art and radical only in his methods; and the Dadaist Tzara, flirting with Communist ideology but artistically anarchist. The play begins in silence. Then Tzara reads aloud his cut-up poem: it is gibberish (except that it happens to make sense in *French*—see p. 240 below). Joyce dictates his own gibberish, the earliest words of chapter XIV of *Ulysses*. Tzara leaves. Lenin's wife appears and they speak in Russian, while Joyce finds scraps of paper and reads them aloud: still the effect, for an English-speaking audience, is gibberish. Lenin drops *his* scrap of paper, which Joyce reads aloud and then surrenders to him after an exchange in which Lenin tries various languages on him and Joyce responds in each in turn. The Lenins leave and the prologue ends with a limerick and a song, the limerick being a trap set by Joyce for the librarian Cecily, who completes it when intending to curtail it (pp. 20–1).

The prologue is like a whole Stoppard play in miniature. There is the mischief of teasing an audience: an opening silence, followed by a varied flow of language which is incomprehensible. Though actually practising their 'serious' art, Joyce and Tzara appear in many respects like clowns; and Gwendolen and Cecily as their foils. Lenin, on the other hand, though the butt of one Joycean joke, appears an intensely serious student, and there is no invitation to laughter in the urgency with which he and his wife converse and leave. Yet he is linked to the 'clowns' by the scrap-of-paper motif as well as by sharing the library. This uneasy interlocking of Lenin's earnestness and occasional unwitting absurdity with the artists' serious play is much of what *Travesties* is about. The first line partially intelligible to an English-speaking audience cuts through with a metallic realism: it is Lenin's dropped note: 'G.E.C. (USA) 250 million marks, 28,000 workers ... profit 254 million marks.'

In much the same way Cecily's lecture, and Lenin's harangue, will disturb in Act Two our comfortable expectations of erudite laughter. Finally, of course, the dramatic event shown in the Prologue—the announcement to Lenin of revolution in St Petersburg—is the key event of the play and one of the key events of our century.

There follows Carr's long monologue, with more explicit overlap of grim history and zany parody; and then the launch into the travesty *Earnest*, still with substantial chunks of Russian history thrown in. After a 'manic' interlude of limericks (the *content* of which, though the audience can hardly register it fully, is entirely in character with the participants), we return to *Earnest* with a Tzara/Carr conversation, the first of a series of heated exchanges on the nature and role of art. The climax of each such set-piece is when one participant boils over into straight abuse, as thus Carr to Tzara: 'My God, you little Rumanian wog—you bloody dago—you jumped-up phrase-making smart-alecy arty-intellectual Balkan turd!' (p. 40)— a momentary release from a highbrow tension, though always followed by a particularly forceful continuation of the argument.

Stoppard enlists our sympathies for each point of view, and the strip-cartoon simplification of the characters doesn't matter—it may even help—when the balloons which come out of their heads are so eloquent. The exaggerations, the clowning and the echo-pattern effect of the encounters amuse us, confirming the sense of play; but the arguments are about major matters and the debate seizes our attention.

The first strong grip on our consideration is the horror of the trenches, remembered by Carr. His exchanges with Bennett (pp. 26–32) are funny, in their time-slips, their travesty of Wilde, in their incidental gags ('Dada dada dada. Did he have a stutter?') and in Bennett's exhaustive political and historical knowledge. But the *content* is nothing less than a popularized refresher-course in the background to the 1917 Revolution: not the sort of thing Auntie goes to the theatre to laugh at. The discord already sounded in the Prologue is heard again in Carr's tailpiece:

Bennett seems to be showing alarming signs of irony. I have always found that irony among the lower orders is the first sign of an awakening social consciousness. It remains to be seen whether it will grow into an armed seizure of the means of production, distribution and exchange, or spend itself in liberal journalism.

(p. 32)

—where, before the final dig, the phrase 'an armed seizure . . . exchange' grates and clatters within the Wildean elegance.

The limericks release us for a few moments. In the following set-piece Tzara asserts that 'everything is Chance, including design. . . . And it is the duty of the artist to jeer and howl and belch' at the contrary delusion. Carr responds with the orthodox Edwardian view that 'It is the duty of the artist to beautify existence', but reveals that he regards the artist as a kind of dubious luxury. Nevertheless, 'The easiest way of knowing whether good has triumphed over evil is to examine the freedom of the artist.' To defend this freedom he went to war.

Another frightening trench-memory, this time in fading light, suspends the dialogue, and when we emerge from it we have a second stab at the Jack–Algernon scene, this time following Wilde more closely but returning eventually to the debate about art (p. 46) with Carr's fundamental distaste for the artist becoming more apparent. 'For every thousand people there's nine hundred doing the work, ninety doing well, nine doing good, and one lucky bastard who's the artist.'

Tzara is stung into a defence of the artist as 'priest–guardian of the magic that conjured the intelligence out of the appetites' of early man. Carr insists that early man was artist *as well as* man of action; he objects to the modern theory of artist as special kind of human being. Tzara's continuing defence of art suddenly collapses into the Dada-ist orthodoxy that art has now sold itself, beginning 'to celebrate the ambitions and acquisitions of the paymaster'.

'What I'm always trying to say,' Stoppard told Ronald Hayman in 1974, 'is "Firstly, A. Secondly, minus A." ' This is very much the pattern of the debate in *Travesties*: one can find oneself nodding at each epigram as it flashes by, recognizing some truth in it. In the final reversion by Tzara to Dadaist theory we also begin to approach Lenin's territory. The back-cloth is the Great War, which 'had causes' (perhaps an ironic allusion to a cliché of modern European history study, as well as introducing the alternative theories of Carr's patriotism and Marxist economics). The view forwards is to the late twentieth-century Europe of the audience, a large part of which is dominated by a super-power 'fathered' by Lenin. The gravity of this context sets off the debate about art. Perhaps already in the backs of our minds is the question of the place of the artist in a Leninist state.

Joyce (p. 49) is allowed to recite (grotesquely, in mid-sentence!) his 'Mr Dooley' poem about opting-out. After more twists in and out of Wilde, the Lady Bracknell/Jack interview sketches the ambivalence and incoherence of Dadaism, explod-ing suddenly into climax—in the pattern we now clearly recog-nize. Tzara's charge against Joyce is still endorsed by many who are not Dadaists: 'You've turned literature into a religion and it's as dead as all the rest, it's an overripe corpse and you're cutting fancy figures at the wake.'

What follows is the one point at which Stoppard allows the caricature Joyce something of the eloquence of the real Joyce (this speech was added at Peter Wood's suggestion): 'The temples are built and brought down ... from Troy to the fields of Flanders. If there is any meaning in any of it, it is in what survives as art. ... What now of the Trojan War if it had been passed over by the artist's touch?'

The grandeur of this is endorsed by a comic stroke a few minutes later, at the end of the Act:

'And what did you do in the Great War?' 'I wrote *Ulysses*,' he said. 'What did you do?'
Bloody nerve.

(p. 65)

By the interval we have laughed much and in many ways—at the simplest gags, at conjuring, at epigram, and at the travesty of a popular play. We have also winced: mildly, perhaps, at Tzara's smashing of crockery on stage, genteelly at Tzara's reduction of man to a coffee-mill ('Eat-grind-shit'), wryly at Bennett's prediction that 'if one can be certain of anything it is that Russia is set fair to become a parliamentary democracy on the British model' (p. 30), and more sharply at the cries of horror as Carr remembers the trenches. And our minds tingle from the altercations about art. We are, very probably, delighted. We drink whatever makes us still more delighted, we compare reactions with friends, we see others in the distance, we see the tingle still in their faces as we share a flush after a day of sun and wind. No apologia for playing seems necessary: emotionally we are sure at this moment of its value in our lives. Few plays, perhaps, so beautifully link diversion and challenge, and in so poised a manner; always just when things are getting a bit heavy, something 'dramatic' happens to refresh us and, in most cases, give us a big laugh. Besides, have we not heard in the course of the play some eloquent defences of playing? Here in the theatre, by paying for our seats, we are confirming our allegiance to the glory of art as outlined by Joyce. We can be a little bit pleased with ourselves.

The interval is quite significant, in modern theatre. . . .

We return: to a lecture. Most of the stage is unlit. Cecily, who has not appeared since the prologue, stands at the front of the stage like a teacher waiting for us to settle down: she puts us at once at a disadvantage. She begins 'To resume' and continues with a brisk, crisp, but humourless historical account of Lenin's life before 1917. The lecture is meant to make a stiff impact; outside the dullest of post-Brechtian drama it is difficult to imagine another play risking it; and making an audience take it is part of the point for Stoppard.

In spite of Bennett's knowledgeability and Tzara's references to the Communist beliefs of Huelsenbeck, Marxist or Leninist views have not really threatened Act One. Here at the start of Act Two there is obviously a shift. Theatrically it is audacious, though simple; it also upsets our previous understanding that the play is made up of the blurred and exaggerated recollections of Henry Carr. It steps outside the comfortable structure, quite deliberately; partly for Brechtian reasons, and partly because the comfortable comedy may have been largely used up in Act One. None of this seems to me the weakness that some critics have judged it: I think it simply makes the play more serious, a more remarkable evening generally.

Suitably chastened, then, we are attentive to further debate about art, between Cecily and Carr. Where Algernon as Ernest flirts quite successfully with Cecily, Carr as Algernon/Ernest/Tristan gets into heated argument. This time he represents the traditional case for art as non-utilitarian playing, gratifying 'a hunger that is common to princes and peasants'.

CECILY: The sole duty and justification for art is social criticism. . . . We have the responsibility of changing society.
CARR: No, no, no, no, no—my dear girl!—art doesn't change society, it is merely changed by it.

(p. 74)

Clearly Carr is shocked by the suggestion that society should be changed; clearly, too, his allegiance to art is really somewhat lukewarm. His enthusiasm for Gilbert and Sullivan is turned into a funny climax of anger, after which the action clicks back into a further attempt at the Algernon–Cecily dialogue, this time on the subject of Marx. After a further climax of abuse, complicated by a coloured fantasy of Cecily dancing a striptease, a further click-back produces a brisk third-time-lucky capitulation on Cecily's part (dragging Carr down behind her desk). To the full flow of the audience's laughter, Nadya Lenin enters and we return, sheepish and confused, to history.

For some time the Lenin story and the Wildean travesty operate independently and concurrently in different parts of the stage. The uneasiness already present in the prologue is now visually explicit. Aside from the deadpan reportage of the Lenins' historical narrative, Carr challenges Tzara, convincingly:

All this dancing attendance on Marxism is sheer pretension. You're an amiable bourgeois with a chit from Matron and if the revolution came you wouldn't know what hit you. You're nothing. You're an artist. And multi-coloured micturition is no trick to those boys, they'll have you pissing blood.

(p. 83)

A page later Lenin's train leaves: the moment, as prepared in the Prologue, to which the rest of the play has been leading. '*The train noise becomes very loud. Everything black except a light on Lenin.*' The further stage direction includes the revealing sentence: '*It is structurally important to the Act that the following speech is delivered from the strongest possible position with the most dramatic change of effect from the general stage appearance preceding it.*'

The speech is powerful in itself; but it gains immensely in force from the arguments, the ironies, and indeed the frivolities which have preceded it. Which is not to say that there has been a Shavian 'progress' of ideas: perhaps there has been a sinister shrinking.

The play continues sombrely after the harangue, with extracts from the Lenins' writing—the most difficult section to bring off. Lenin changes before our eyes, from the fanatic orator to an emotionally conservative human being. Lenin's last speech makes—for *us*—something near to a synthesis: 'I don't know of anything greater than the Appassionata. Amazing, superhuman music. It always makes me feel, perhaps naïvely, it makes me feel, proud of the miracles that human beings can perform. But . . .'

This is perhaps the most expressive testimony to art in the play; and as the music of the *Appassionata* 'swells in the dark' we leave Lenin as something like a tragic hero—yet not purifying his community but taking it to tragedy with him. Nadya's last words are 'Something went wrong. I forget what.'

Most of the rest of the play is hilarious, a wind-up of the *Earnest* material which comes refreshingly after its enforced rest. It is like the final *presto* of a pre-Romantic symphony whose weightier thinking has been accomplished earlier. There is no question of finding synthesis here, unless it is in Carr's very last words, which manage to be both appropriate and theatrical:

> I learned three things in Zurich during the war. I wrote them down. Firstly, you're either a revolutionary or you're not, and if you're not you might as well be an artist as anything else. Secondly, if you can't be an artist, you might as well be a revolutionary. . . .
> I forget the third thing.

We have laughed together, thought together, felt uneasy together. We have no answers, but in the *play*, as actors and audience, we have come closer to inclusion—to spanning a wide range of human possibility, and bringing our conflicting responses together—than we come in most activity. Now if we wish we can go home and read the play and relish more slowly its intricacies, but in doing that we are only reviving that shared experience; and very possibly planning to go and share it again.

3 · STAGING

Plays in general, and comedies in particular, tend to date; and we are sometimes told that Stoppard's plays will date badly, once their distinctive zip of verbal and theatrical excitement has become familiar. This prediction is based on two main criticisms: that all the plays really offer are 'squibs'—briefly amusing trick-effects, with no heart and no development; and that the plays are too literary, too wordy, even too static.

Clearly the plays *are* full of squibs, but I hope this book will show there is more than that going on. The second charge—and its apparent refutation (that, on the contrary, Stoppard is theatrically highly *imaginative*)—between them almost pluck out the heart of his mystery. There are potentially opposing richnesses here; and their mixture has made Stoppard attractive to many of us in his own day. Future spectators may find that increasingly the two richnesses break awkwardly apart and appear less interesting. Much of the linguistic comedy will certainly date and may already fall flat for audiences not familiar with the British mass-media since the war; but the most loss here may be suffered by work which Stoppard has always regarded as ephemeral—the 'nuts-and-bolts' farces.

The brilliance with words is undoubted. Two substantial pieces of 1966—*Rosencrantz* and the novel—both displayed, when Stoppard was twenty-nine, mastery of many kinds of pastiche, including 'literary' descriptive writing of some subtlety. Twelve years of journalism and journeyman work had developed a gifted young man into an outstandingly accomplished professional. He could have become a distinctive success in any of a number of fields, and his own account (*Theatre Quarterly*, 1974) tends to treat his choice of theatre as a matter largely of historical accident. This doesn't ring very true. Stoppard's 'literariness' has little to do with prose fiction, even that of the early Beckett, not much to do with poetry outside Shakespeare and the early Eliot, and a great deal to do with journalism and with theatre. The moments in his plays at which audiences may begin to fidget are not prose-fictional or poetic; they are didactic-journalism or are spinnings-out of already-used material. The real literariness of Stoppard (and I see it as a characteristic rather than a weakness) is his allusiveness: to get a lot of his jokes you have to share a certain cultural background. It is not the limp literariness of, say, Christopher Fry, where verbal decoration tended to be offered instead of theatrical vitality.

Nevertheless, the risk that a writer so verbally fluent, and so interested in words, will talk us all to sleep is a real one.

The chief thing that added one line to another line was that the combination of the two should retain an audience's interest in some way ... my preoccupation as a writer, which possibly betokens a degree of insecurity, takes the form of contriving to inject some sort of interest and colour into every line, rather than counting on the general situation having a general interest which will hold an audience.

(*Theatre Quarterly*, 1974)

This suggests that Stoppard has not seriously doubted that he can put words together, but has been less sure that he can make theatre. The result, since he is a hard-working ingenious craftsman with a vivid appreciation of other people's 'theatrical events', is that he tends to 'break his neck' (his own phrase) to be theatrical: if his use of theatre has a fault, it is that of trying too hard. In the later seventies there have been signs of a readiness to chasten his theatrical writing, and to move into realist territory. In plays yet to come Stoppard may work less in moments and special effects, and more in long scenes and gradually generated power.

What follows is a descriptive analysis of the achievement so far—of the squibs, but also of the fundamentally theatrical thinking which forms the structure of the plays. Finally there are separate notes on Stoppard's use of radio and television.

SQUIBS

The attraction of unexpected, unnatural, or 'unnaturalistic' things happening on a stage is precisely that they *are* happening on a *stage*. The surprising effects depend partly on the audience's barely conscious knowledge of the limitations of a stage.

(Stoppard to *Gambit*, 1981)

The most immediately striking quality of Stoppard's stage-craft is sheer nerve, a perpetration of theatrical outrage in pseudo-surrealist modes. The stage runs with water at the end of *Enter a Free Man*; in *Hound* we find ourselves looking at a mirror-image audience across the stage; *After Magritte* scrambles from a ludicrous tableau to something like normality and then on to a different ludicrousness. *Jumpers* opens with a singing act which immediately fails, followed by a circus/strip-tease act which collides with a realistic-looking drinks waiter; next a circus-acrobatic act is interrupted by a man in flannels and smoking jacket who is writing a philosophical lecture; it continues into a chaotic mixture of songs (the musicians being constantly led astray by the singer's muddle) accompanying a pyramid of acrobats, one of whom is suddenly shot. He dies crawling pitifully up the singer's body. The play continues with a television programme about a moon landing . . . and that is just the first five pages.

In *Travesties* nothing is intelligible at first; later a scene is spoken entirely in limericks and another sung to a music-hall tune; the dialogue and action keep slipping back on themselves; an actor performs conjuring tricks from a seated position throughout a spirited argument; and the public librarian of Zurich climbs on her desk to do a striptease act while chanting Leninist dogma. *Dirty Linen* sees a secretary steadily losing her clothing during the sitting of a Commons committee, and ends with an M.P. wiping his brow with her knickers; *Every Good Boy* uses a real symphony orchestra on stage and almost at once asks them to *mime*, while *On the Razzle* enlivens a Viennese waltz with a part for bagpipes. *Dogg's Hamlet, Cahoot's Macbeth* ends with a wall being built across the proscenium opening; and *Night and Day* opens with (apparently) a helicopter hovering in the flies and (actually) a jeep being driven onstage and turning full headlights on the audience, accompanied by the deafening sound of machine-gun fire.

All, Stoppard might say, excellent showbiz. But also, these audacities are justified, sometimes on the principle of *After Magritte* (they have rational explanations), sometimes as symbolism actually built into the plot (the Vice-Chancellor really does run a troupe of jumpers, the Inspector does solemnly intend to brick off the stage). Stoppard is also skilled at making more than one use of a device—he calls it 'trying not to miss opportunities'—and students of *Jumpers* should trace through the play the bow, arrow, hare and tortoise—stale examples given a comic new vitality; those with different predilections might like to follow the underwear through *Dirty Linen*.

THE OLD STOCK

Stoppard makes almost equal play with the only-too-expected, the clichés of the stage, and with the pleasantly familiar—old friends such as music-hall routines. The echoes are affectionate, though liable to date; Tony Hancock:

> RILEY: (*Hollow laugh*) Brown! Oh, dear, oh dear! An amateur! Brown!... (*Swings round and barks.*) You'll have to do better than that.
>
> (*Enter a Free Man*, p. 23)

or Eric Morecambe:

> INSPECTOR: I should hope not indeed. That would be acting without authority—acting without authority!—you'd never believe I make it up as I go along....
>
> (*Cahoot's Macbeth*, p. 56)

or Groucho Marx (*On the Razzle*, p. 55).

A few pages after Riley's Hancock reminiscence, he launches into cod courtroom cross-examination. Gwendolen and Cecily's expected grand confrontation towards the end of *Travesties* takes the amazing form of a classic double-act song *Mr Gallagher and Mr Shean*—an unexpected use of the familiar. Much of the original Wildean stage business can actually survive this ludicrous metamorphosis, as indicated in the package stage-direction: '*There is a certain amount of tea-pouring and tea-sipping to come, not to mention the cup suddenly clinked down on the saucer, and all that; but directions to this effect are omitted*' (*Travesties*, p. 91).

The words '*and all that*' express not weariness but a trouper's relish.

Rosencrantz follows Beckett and many broadcast comedy script-writers in affecting a good deal of difficulty in filling up time. The underlying joke here is a teasing of the audience for having paid money to come and watch, or even for bothering to stay tuned at home; in Beckett's case it ties in with a nihilist sense of the absurdity of everything, playing being one of the *less* absurd activities. So, after the first five 'heads' in the coin-tossing, Guil is allowed the give-away, tension-relaxing line: 'There is an art to the building-up of suspense.'

Later on: 'What are you playing at?/Words, words. They're all we have to go on' (p. 31)—both a disclaimer of any theatrical inventiveness and a glance at Hamlet's own 'words, words, words' in Shakespeare. And a moment later: 'I feel like a spectator—an appalling prospect. The only thing that makes it bearable is the irrational belief that somebody interesting will come on in a minute.'

This derives from a number of lines in *Waiting for Godot*; the effect in Stoppard is less subtle because we know we are in a play (though Ros and Guil may never know it) and meeting Players; but it also provides extra jokes.

GUIL: I'm trying to establish the direction of the wind.
ROS: There isn't any wind.

[We are, after all, in a theatre.]

ROS: *Draught*, yes.

[An in-joke for actors: stages can be notoriously chilly places.]

ROS: It's coming up through the floor. (*He studies the floor*). That can't be south, can it?

(p. 43)

A moment later, after a pause, Ros '*leaps up and bellows at the audience*, "Fire!"'

And so on. 'Somebody might come in./In Where?/Out here?/In out here?'—a joke at the relatively unconvincing nature of stage outdoor scenes: this one is on a ship, as has been established by a merciless send-up of cliché sound-effects and nautical cries (pp. 73–4). On p. 76 Ros thinks he's going to be sick (into the audience); Guil advises him 'Other side, I think.' In the same Act: 'Give us this day our daily cue' (p. 77); 'Now we've lost the tension./What tension?' (p. 80). The play is about being caught in a play and about the profession/art/prostitution of acting; and its jokes about having to fill stage time include the audience.

The introductory section of *On the Razzle*—the whole play is a homage to the farce tradition, of course—ends with a superb send-up of a clumsy dramatist's exposition or recapitulation. In many ways this (pure Stoppard, one guesses) is the funniest thing in the play. Note how the punctuation guides the timing.

ZANGLER: Well, that seems all right. Just the ticket. First class. Why do I have a sense of impending disaster? (*He reflects.*) Sonders is after my niece and has discovered the secret address where I am sending her to the safe keeping of my sister-in-law Miss Blumenblatt, who has never laid eyes on him, or, for that matter, on Marie either since she was a baby—while I have to leave my business in the charge of my assistant and an apprentice, and follow my new servant, whom I haven't had time to introduce to anyone, to town so that I can join the parade in a uniform I can't sit down in and take my fiancée to dinner in a fashionable restaurant.

One false move and we could have a farce on our hands.

(p. 19)

Hound is one sustained game with theatre clichés and their clumsy handling. Exposition by having the first character on stage answer the telephone was a lazy cliché of many 1930s realist plays; Stoppard makes a good attempt at killing it off finally, and also at satirizing the sheer technical inefficiency of some amateur productions, on p. 15:

> (*The phone rings.* MRS DRUDGE *seems to have been waiting for it to do so and for the last few seconds has been dusting it with an intense concentration. She snatches it up.*)
> MRS DRUDGE (*into phone*): Hello, the drawing-room of Lady Muldoon's country residence one morning in early spring?

Whenever the radio is turned on there is always, exactly timed, an interruption for a police message. The second time this occurs the imaginary dramatist's invention is already severely strained: '*A strange impulse makes Simon turn on the radio*' (p. 18).

The dialogue is as bad as Stoppard can make it and of course parodies the country-house detective story; four characters (but not the murderer) are heard threatening to kill Simon Gascoyne, and there is a comprehensive destruction of the 'significant' card-game: 'FELICITY: I've had my turn, haven't I, Simon? ... now, it seems, it's Cynthia's turn' (p. 24).

The tedium of eating and drinking in clumsily-written realist plays is sent up on pp. 28–9, provoking from the critic Birdboot the note: 'The second act, however, fails to fulfil the promise...'

Parody broadens into outright farce as Magnus, the crippled half-brother from Canada, careers at top speed across the stage in his wheelchair knocking people down; and as Inspector Hound enters (p. 30).

Meanwhile the clichés of theatre reviewing are also being parodied. The two parodies work alongside each other for two-thirds of the play, and then become grotesquely entangled, becoming a playwright's revenge-fantasy on the comfortable non-involvement of reviewers.

Inspector Hound is only one of a series of police inspectors, most of them owing something to Peter Sellers, who interrupt Stoppard's plays. The thread of plot in *Jumpers* is again that of a murder mystery, pursued by the level-headed, decent Inspector Bones. In *After Magritte* too an inspector calls (Stoppard has admitted to enjoying J. B. Priestley) with 'reason to believe that within the last hour you performed without anaesthetic an illegal operation on a bald nigger minstrel about five-foot-two or Pakistani and that is only the beginning!'

If Hound originates in the Goon Show ('I'll phone the police!/But you are the police!/Thank God I'm here!'), then Foot in *After Magritte* might have been written for John Cleese:

> FOOT: What we're looking for is a darkie short of a leg or two.
> HOLMES: (*Retiring*) Right, sir.
> MOTHER: Is it all right for me to practice?
> FOOT: No, it is not all right! Ministry standards may be lax but we draw the line at Home Surgery to bring in the little luxuries of life.
>
> (p. 33)

—though he is allowed also a parody of 1960s homely police television dramas:

> he's just a young man doing his job and doing it well—sometimes not seeing his kids—Dean, five, and Sharon, three—for days on end—often getting home after his wife's asleep and back on the beat before she wakes—tireless, methodical, eagle-eyed—always ready with a friendly word for the old lag crossing the road or sixpence for the old lady trying to go straight—
>
> (p. 28)

The Inspector in *Cahoot's Macbeth* represents a far more sinister State authority, but is allowed by Stoppard to be the fast-talking comic to whom all the other characters are straight-men, though the linguistic subversion of Dogg disconcerts him a little.

Another English tradition is that of the immensely suave and knowledgeable manservant, such as Wodehouse's Jeeves and any number of stage butlers including Lane in *Earnest*. The Admirable Crichton, in Barrie's play, is the natural master of the house. Stoppard with relish resurrects this social-class joke at the end of *Jumpers* when Crouch suddenly makes penetrating criticisms of George's philosophy, and in the Coda becomes the presiding dignitary—a theatrically refreshing shift, too, which makes sure that the actor playing Crouch feels the part is rewarding (part of the dramatist's skill). Bennett in *Travesties* is an even more rewarding part, from the Jeeves pastiche of 'It is more in the nature of a revolution of classes contraposed by the fissiparous disequilibrium of Russian society' into detailed historical exposition which, though deadpan, commands the stage. Bennett is later discovered to be a 'mole' in the Consulate, and, glancingly and as if idly, Stoppard allows it to be known at the end of the play that in reality the Consul *himself* was called Bennett (Carr being an assistant only)—so that the whole character of Bennett in *Travesties* is another version of the servant/master joke: a joke not irrelevant to the Communist revolution, of course.

On the Razzle follows one of the strongest of all traditions: the servant affecting his master's airs and place. Weinberl (p. 20) occupies the shop—when it is closed and Zangler is away—*'like a gentleman of leisure'*. He and the apprentice Christopher are 'the backbone of this country . . . the merchant class' and their razzle is to involve them in escorting two ladies—one of whom is their employer's fiancée—to dinner at an expensive restaurant. Again in the full line of tradition, they act with great speed and shrewdness in their mischief, where Zangler is a blunderer.

ACTOR-LOADING

Part of stagecraft, as I have just suggested, is writing reasonably for actors. Most of Stoppard's expectations and provision here are exemplary: profound characterization there may not be, but a strip-cartoon-character with good lines is rewarding to play, and there are plenty of those. Outside the 'Shakespearean' plays there are few spear-carriers (and in *Dogg's Hamlet, Cahoot's Macbeth* considerable doubling-up is allowed): there are excellent moments for every character in *Enter a Free Man*, *After Magritte*, *Jumpers* and *Travesties*, and although Francis in *Night and Day* is an old-fashioned servant (a penalty of realism) even he has one good laugh-line.

The commonest mode, as one might expect, is duologue, and in such passages Stoppard skilfully shifts the straight man/comic emphasis about from time to time—the most sustained example, which students of comedy script-writing might study, is of course *Rosencrantz*. Stoppard's plays are also distinguished by remarkably untedious long speeches and sometimes solos: he has described them (to Ronald Hayman), as 'the safe parts of a play'. The reason they work so well may be that they exercise in miniature the Stoppardian process 'of elaborate structure and sudden ... dismantlement' (Stoppard to Hayman, 1974). The metaphor of going off the rails, which Stoppard uses of Carr, applies equally well to George's preparation of his lecture. The King Charles's Head of Bertrand Russell repeatedly throws him off his stride; his sentences run to seed and wild, he has a donnish (and Stoppardian) facility in clever asides which tends to sabotage his credibility as well as his coherence (reminding me of Martello in *Artist Descending*: 'Oh God, if only I could turn it *off*!—no wonder I have achieved nothing with my life!')—and, of course, he is repeatedly and disastrously interrupted.

The longest of the monologues is Arthur's purple riot in *New-Found-Land*: this really is a separate act, in the line of Ruth Draper, Peter Sellers ('Balham, Gateway to the South') or Alan Bennett. It too has its King Charles's Head, the Redcaps whose expressions are usually 'cheerful' but who become 'phlegmatic' in Atlanta and 'surly' in Texas: finally, the Pacific ocean itself is 'flecked with cheerful whitecaps'. And it is mined with self-destructive clichés. A similar tone is struck early in *On the Razzle* when Weinberl pontificates about the merchant class; this time the monologue is 'fed' by Christopher at intervals (pp. 20–1).

The weighting of roles in Stoppard is generally reasonable.

Riley is active throughout Act One of *Enter a Free Man* but in textbook tradition is granted a rest at the start of Act Two. The successive set-pieces of *Travesties* offer something for everybody and also a break for everybody; and the burden of action in *Night and Day* is carefully budgeted. This of course cannot be true for Ros and Guil since it is the main point of their play that they cannot escape; until their final disappearance they are always on stage—but the emphasis is frequently shifted from them to the Player, or to Shakespeare's *Hamlet*. The really daunting role is that of George in *Jumpers*. He is onstage throughout (except the first moments and last moments of Act One) and nearly always involved in the dialogue; his only change of appearance is a beard of shaving foam and (by comparison with other huge parts) he has little variation of mode. This, quite apart from its physical demands, severely tests the actor's skill: how, for example, is he to get us to concentrate freshly, at the end of a long Act, on the crucial argument of p. 55? Heaven help an audience saddled with a weak George (for this reason as well as others the play is not suitable for amateurs). In spite of its pyrotechnics, *Jumpers* is in some respects a heavy and almost claustrophobic play, because what we see comes to us largely through the awareness of George. We don't know, as in most plays perhaps we would, how mad Dotty is; we don't know what she and Archie do in bed together; we don't know, till the end, about McFee's affair with George's secretary; we don't know (and it may worry us subconsciously throughout the play) where Thumper has got to—how does a hare get lost in a flat?—and we don't know what Dotty has done with Archie the goldfish when she uses his bowl for her spaceman charade. We do know what George doesn't, that McFee has been shot, but we don't know who by. What's more, though we are locked in George's awareness he is locked out from us. There is no passage across the footlights. With Ros and Guil we are all in the theatre together: we can almost feel the same draught; Carr spins the story of *Travesties* to us, yielding place to Cecily when he has to. Ruth's thoughts in *Night and Day* are often laughs direct to the audience, liberating us from the play's fourth-wall realism. *Jumpers* is a long play which lacks such easing of passage between characters and audience, and it is perhaps the more disturbing because for a good deal of the time George *appears* to be talking to us. He is, not, of course; he is rehearsing his lecture; and it is made clear early on that he is looking into a mirror (his squeezing of a blackhead 'at' the audience is a typical minor Stoppardian outrage).

We are, in fact, less intimate with George than with Ros and Guil, Carr, Ruth. Yet the play has to be centred in George's awareness, as the ⎓earest thing to moral sanity amid Rad-Lib jumping expediency. And if it seems claustrophobic that may well be intended: it is appropriate enough. By the end, as George lies on the study floor sobbing, and then dreams his nightmare of the Symposium, we may be relieved not to be more intimately identified with him.

The special distinction of Stoppard's theatre, however, is not in squibs, nor in efficient writing for actors, nor even in brilliant talk; but in its juxtaposition or overlapping of disparate realities. This is not new to Stoppard, of course: it is identified in modern theatre, and in Shakespeare, by such phrases as 'planes of reality' or 'colliding worlds'. But Clive James is interesting here:

> Critical talk about 'levels of reality' in a play commonly assumes that one of the posited levels is *really* real. By the same token, it would be reasonable to assume that although everything in a Stoppard play is moving, the play itself is a system at rest. But in Stoppard's universe no entity, not even a work of art, is exempt from travel.
>
> (*Encounter*, November 1975)

Stoppard's particularly fine use of simultaneity or bewildering sequence in the theatre may, James is suggesting, be an aspect of his overall openness to conflicting philosophies. Certainly his stagecraft shows a much more profound awareness of the possibilities of theatre than merely the embellishments of 'business', music, lighting, or gags.

THE DISPARATE REALITIES

Theatre is good at simultaneity: quite simply, different parts of the stage can be used for different purposes at the same time. See, for example, the play scene in *Hamlet*, discussed briefly on p. 135 below. It is equally good at very rapid sequential contrasts or at alternations between different modes. And since everything on stage is a pretence, there is no good reason why different pretences shouldn't overlap (academics may turn here to Johnson's *Preface to Shakespeare*). Octavius is in Rome, and Antony in Alexandria, within seconds; Atahuallpa watches from hundreds of miles away as Pizarro's men cross his land; Willy Loman is on his knees in a restaurant shouting to a woman in Boston twenty years earlier who is also on stage. Realist drama, of course, has to pass up this major opportunity, although the independent monologues of Chekhov's characters, littered about a room, are a subtle rediscovery of it within the rules.

This opportunity is tremendously important to Stoppard, for reasons of temperament as well as technique ('artistic differences,' he told *Theatre Quarterly*, 'are also liable to be temperamental differences in artistic disguise').

> There is very often *no* single, clear statement in my plays. What there is, is a series of conflicting statements made by conflicting characters, and they tend to play a sort of infinite leapfrog. . . .
> If the mixing-up of ideas in farce is a source of confusion, well, yes, god knows why I try to do it like that—presumably because I *am* like that. Plays are the people who write them. . . . My plays are a lot to do with the fact that I just *don't know*.
>
> (*Theatre Quarterly*, 1974)

Some of the quick shifts, or overlapping levels, are part of this 'leapfrog' of ideas. The impassioned Cecily of p. 77 of *Travesties* becomes the stripper of p. 78—and her argument becomes jargonized doctrine; the ludicrous Lenin of p. 80 becomes the terrifying Lenin of p. 85. Many others are the comic artist, recognizing possible deflation in stage overlap: more of this in my next chapter. Some are economical (the moves between pub and home in *Enter a Free Man*, the transition to Vienna in *On the Razzle*), or thrifty (the return of Easy, and of Dogg-language, in *Cahoot's Macbeth*). And some are poignant: the deaths of the tragedians dressed as Ros and Guil, while Ros and Guil are watching; the varied responses from George's Study to Dotty's cries of 'Help!' 'Murder!' and so on; the entrance of the Inspector in *Cahoot's Macbeth* on the line 'My countryman, but yet I know him not.'

A glance through the stage plays chronologically may help here.

Enter a Free Man alternates between the pub where Riley announces that he is 'free' but where no one really respects him, and his house where he is allowed to do just as he pleases and his wife is determined to cherish 'his belief in himself'. As the second set (the pub) first comes alive, Linda says 'There's two of everyone . . . and if the two of him's the same, I mean if he's the same in the pub as he is with us, then he's had it.'

Riley enters the pub with a flourish, *'but his entrance makes no impact'*. 'RILEY: Enter a free man!/LINDA: Poor old dad . . .'—Linda speaking, of course, from the other side of the stage.

In *Rosencrantz* Stoppard hit on an exceptionally fertile idea, founded in the very nature of theatre. The familiar action and dialogue of Shakespeare's *Hamlet*, and the transitory reality of the theatre audience, each have to contend with the offstage-*Hamlet*/onstage-Stoppard existence of two attendant lords who belong to Shakespeare but speak Stoppard's vernacular. In many ways they are more convincing and attractive than the quasi-realistic characters of *Enter a Free Man*, or than Hamlet himself is allowed by Stoppard to become; but they exist only for the action of a play, predetermined, in which we know they die (and, in Stoppard's title, 'are dead'). The poignant overlaps include the audience, whose own deaths are just as certain as those of Ros and Guil and more real; the 'what's it all for? what's it all about?' cries of Ros and Guil are those of many of Stoppard's audience considering their own lives. To Hamlet's bewilderment at human feigning Shakespeare added the travelling Players, to twist the knife further; Stoppard chooses to include them in Ros and Guil's offstage lives: they too are *used* by both Hamlet and the dramatist, and then dropped; and their whole profession is stage fantasy. The discussion above (pp. 22–3) of the Player's mock-death is a reminder of the richness of theatrical vibration in this inspired set-up.

Hound also offers a play within a play, but this time we watch a play *and* an audience, and the plot concerns the entanglement of the two. *After Magritte* starts and ends with moments of wholly misleading simultaneity. The sensational opening minutes of *Jumpers* are to some extent a riddle of the same kind (like George's appearance with tortoise, bow and arrow, and shaving foam 'expecting a psychiatrist'—p. 43); later the crazy fragments are, up to a point, pieced together. The intended mood of the play is, nevertheless, an agonized confusion, a seething relativity in which an apparently innocent don is killed by a never-certainly-identified hand, and a simple hare and tortoise are killed by tricks of chance; in which the cleverest and most articulate man on stage is clearly amoral, and in which, in the words of the poet, 'one is always nearer by not standing still'. The jumping is a stage vaudeville and also a potent symbol: Archie's troupe are ethically double-jointed, and not to be trusted as far as they can throw each other.

The staging of *Jumpers* is crucial. A fairly complicated layout defines three areas. Very roughly, the Study is George's realm, where he appears in command, or at least pursuit, of his ideas, his lecture, and his secretary (though we are to learn that he has no influence on her at all). The Bedroom is Dotty's area, taken over and possessed at the end of Act One (not for the first time, probably) by the demonic Archie; and the Hall is the area of Bones, the common man, the stage-door worshipper, the unsophisticated pursuer of wrongdoing. Each is the dominant figure in his or her own area, usually saying most and scoring most laughs: although George finds himself on p. 48 uneasily trying to expound 'mainstream' philosophy in the Hall, he does so under Bones's sceptical pressure; and although on pp. 64–5 Archie makes a spirited attempt to corrupt Bones in the Hall, he fails. It is when Bones is caught on Dotty's territory that he is done for (p. 71). The play is dark because we see the steady impinging of the alienated, disturbed personality of Dotty, and perhaps, behind that, the baleful influence of Archie, on George's desirable if naïve beliefs. Dotty's cries are those of all that is most savage and endangering: murder, horror, rape, wolves, fire. They anger George, and then (p. 28) they play havoc with his lecture: with a Stoppardian pivot on a word's two meanings, he fires his arrow on her cry of 'Fire!' At the time, it is funny. Late in the play (p. 81) we discover that the arrow killed the hare Thumper ('the late Herr Thumper, who was innocent as a rainbow'). The cry from the bedroom ruined the innocence of the study. And as George mourns this death, he steps on and kills the other innocent, Pat the tortoise—a grimly ironic realization, incidentally, of one of his own philosophical examples (p. 67). He puts up his head and cries, joining Dotty in her agony, 'Help! Murder!'—and falls to the floor.

The Coda, in dream form, and the prologue use a blank stage or at least a large empty area *away* from the three acting areas just described: I hope it is now clear why.

After the clever prologue of *Travesties* (see pp. 26–7 above), which shows us the three revolutionaries working independently in different areas of a large room—a visual message before anything verbal can be understood—the play then moves mainly between Carr's reminiscences (which can take place at one side, perhaps on a corner forestage) and the characters' erratic ride along the toy railway track (Stoppard's metaphor) of *The Importance of Being Earnest*. The interruptions of the timeslips do not necessarily lose touch with Wilde; the Leninist interruptions of the second do, and are meant to. Another simple visual message presents itself on p. 80, where the Leninist material and the *Earnest* material begin to share the stage uncomfortably: '(*The* LENINS *stop and stare at these events.*)'

The general effect of the play is of being passed from player to player, from conviction to opposite conviction, and from mode to mode, like a volley-ball that must be kept in the air and receives a new impetus from each punch in a new direction—except in the Lenin sections, where the ball grates unexpectedly heavily on a hard ground. As well as comic and ironic juxtaposition there is effective simultaneity, best illustrated perhaps by the Carr–Cecily scene, pp. 71–9.

The track along which this encounter is supposed to run is that of Algernon's visit to Cecily in Act Two of Wilde's play: he purports to be Ernest, Jack's younger brother; he flirts with Cecily, who is supposed to be studying but hates books. They are interrupted by Jack's return; when they resume their tête-à-tête the control of the scene passes swiftly to Cecily, who discloses that she has already been engaged to Ernest in fantasy for many months. In Act One of *Travesties* Carr has shown interest in Tzara's description of Cecily, and has acquired his library ticket (where Algernon had Jack's calling-card). Carr has also learned that when introduced to Cecily (by Lenin!) Tzara called himself Jack rather than Tristan because she showed such disapproval of Dadaism. Tristan, he explained, was his decadent younger brother.

So: on his arrival at Cecily's desk, Carr, a British Consul with an enthusiasm for Gilbert and Sullivan but strong reservations about the adulation of artists, is supposed to pass himself off as the Dada-ist Tzara, with whom he has violently disagreed in Act One. Cecily is a severe Marxist–Leninist librarian (at the opposite pole from Wilde's Cecily who thought Political Economy 'horrid'), and she repudiates fluently, sharply, and coldly, Carr's attempts to defend art. This is quite a derailment from Wilde. We are curious how Stoppard will get us back on the track; we are continuing, as earlier, to follow the debate about art; we enjoy the irony that Carr, who was attacking art earlier, is now (clumsily) defending it; and we are aware that the historical Carr actually played Algernon. The grating note of dogma becomes steadily stronger and it is less and less easy to laugh; yet surely *this* tangle of simultaneity has to be comically untied.

With the 'stripper' fantasy (p. 78) we seem to be going right over the top, losing all touch with Wilde and also with the art-debate: we are in a fantasy inside a fantastic reminiscence, Carr inside Carr inside Carr. It is very funny theatre, but the ball seems to have gone right out of play. Yet it is just this excess which makes the time-slip—back to 'I don't think you ought to talk to me like that'—acceptable: the travesty Wilde now seems positively sane and rational, and as soon as Carr/Algernon/Ernest/Tzara declares his love Cecily responds with the same enthusiastic efficiency of her political argument, dragging him down behind her desk—a send-up of the decorum of Wilde's characters, but also, we note with bewildered admiration, true to Wilde in that both Cecilys are attracted to the idea of *reforming* the decadent younger brother. . . . There is not time, in one's first viewing of the play, to sort out all this multiplicity in one's mind; but maybe, as with, say, musical counterpoint, one is not meant to sort it out, only to relish it.

New-Found-Land takes place, as it were, in the interval of *Dirty Linen* and when *Dirty Linen* resumes the two tangle for space. The nominal content is the naturalization of an American not altogether unlike Ed Berman, the dedicatee and original director of the plays (which were first performed on the day of his naturalization—a rather special piece of theatrical simultaneity). The Select Committee on Promiscuity in High Places meets in the *tower* of Big Ben; by a series of misfortunes its secretary, Maddie, is steadily stripped to her underwear during the scene and yet only the audience notices: a development to extremes of one of the most basic jokes of all theatre—the audience aware, the characters unaware. At each revealing moment in Maddie's involuntary striptease, the Committee is preoccupied with papers—not their work but newspaper pin-ups of scantily-clad secretaries. Meanwhile at each such moment the audience sees Maddie—in a brief freeze—as a live pin-up.

From André Previn came the original stage idea for *Every Good Boy*—a conundrum to which Stoppard's solution is abundantly theatrical. The orchestra plays a genuine accompaniment to the story; it also represents a real orchestra, in which the Doctor happens to play the violin—the State machine working in disciplined co-ordination—and an illusory orchestra heard in his head by the lunatic Ivanov. The acting moves among three other small areas (cell, office, school). Sacha and Alexander can cry to each other, loud and clear in the theatre, but not hear each other. Later Sacha travels freely, anywhere: he is not to be trapped in a single area. (Compare *Professional Foul*, p. 79: the child has a clearer perception of moral absolutes.) At the end of the play the Teacher, the Doctor and the lunatic all join the orchestra; but Sacha walks through the middle of the orchestra, leading his father and singing independent of the orchestra's music.

Dogg's Hamlet, Cahoot's Macbeth sustains this astonishing sequence (I deliberately omit *Night and Day* for a moment). In the first half we are in a bare school hall, on which a platform is gradually built up for a Speech Day presentation: we become the Speech Day audience, preparing to watch the shortened *Hamlet* with perhaps similar sense of duty and leaden heart displayed by the schoolboy actors. In the second half we are also watching a shortened Shakespeare tragedy, but this time in the living-room of a flat; this time we are an eager and illegal audience, ready to shy away from the Inspector's torch when he shines it on us. The State's invasion of privacy and mistrust of artistic freedom are strikingly symbolized in the Inspector's intrusion into *Macbeth* and his construction of a wall across the stage.

The genesis of this three-in-one evening illustrates again Stoppard's ability to respond to an opportunity. Thinking of Pavel Kohout's Prague *Macbeth* for living-rooms, Stoppard saw that it could be linked with his own nonsense fifteen-minute *Hamlet*; and then, in a real inspiration, linked that to another short piece written for Ed Berman, *Dogg's Our Pet*. The jokes and ironies made possible by Dogg-language could now reach out to the comedy of ideas. The subversiveness of Dogg enables *Macbeth* to be concluded in the face of police interfer-ence—good—but also destroys its poetry, turning it into gibberish which gives us belly-laughs but also adds desperation to the scene. Finally, the key figure of Easy, the Common Man, is the foil to both halves of the evening, the real voice of normality; and there is much poignancy in his final line: 'Well, it's been a funny sort of week. But I should be back by Tuesday.'

Back where? Did he drive his lorry to Prague? Is Britain now a police state? And will the *actors* be back by Tuesday?

As an adaptation of someone else's play, *On the Razzle* is more conventional in its use of theatre, but highly accomplished. Stoppard enjoys to the full the flapping open and shut of cupboard, trapdoors and bedroom windows which is the percussive music of this kind of farce—developed to splendid absurdity in the moment when Melchior, who has been hiding (in venerable stage tradition) behind a screen, is folded up and carried away inside it (pp. 45–6).

THE PROBLEMS

It *is* a prodigious sequence. Who else has sustained, in so many plays, such variety and virtuosity of theatrical juggling? This is not to say that it is a sequence of unqualified success. The juggling may work, but the play as a whole may not—or (the commonest complaint) may still dissatisfy even when it 'works' on its own terms. There can remain an itch of restlessness, or frustration. The expectations are raised very high . . . and then, to some extent, disappointed. Uneasiness can spring from a feeling that the *thinking* of a play, though superficially dazzling, has not been taken to its right conclusions: more of this in chapter 7. Others feel that such manic humour, or even such cleverness, may inhibit sympathy; I think this fear is mistaken, as I try to show in chapter 8—there, too, I discuss Stoppard's characterization, which in most plays is unashamedly of a strip-cartoon kind. All these tend to be the objections of those who have enjoyed the plays but are far from certain that they 'ought' to have done so; they become a little like Stoppard himself, in

Kenneth Tynan's anecdote, arguing 'that Wagner's music is not as good as it sounds'. But what of the moments, or longer periods, when even in the theatre a play seems not to work? These, especially if they recur in different productions, may well be problems of stagecraft.

The commonest fault in Stoppard is going on too long. To be brutal: one could get the point of *Enter a Free Man* in ten minutes, and of *Rosencrantz* in half an hour. *Rosencrantz* tends to keep us hanging on to see if there will be a breathtaking denouement (there isn't) and, if not, how Stoppard will manage to end (and he does it deftly enough). But it is a blown-up one-acter, which invites substantial cutting. Each particular page is, on its own, good fun, and sometimes poignant; but overall there is much duplication. Act Three in particular, in spite of some good jokes and a stylish ending, feels superfluous, perhaps because it no longer has the action of Shakespeare to lean on—and also because it was added later, to commission.

Even *Hound* has been criticized (by C. W. E. Bigsby) as 'not a wholly satisfactory play. It is more adroit than it is convincing.' Bigsby seems in part to be wanting a degree of intellectual commitment which a 'nuts-and-bolts' farce need not be expected to show, and when he says that 'the metaphysical dimension ... is too often sacrificed' he sounds uncommonly like Moon himself. But the truth is that the plot, and the stage trick, are put over on us by speed and bluster rather than by an adequate logic however crazy, and that this may give us some mild irritation on the journey home. Towards the end, the actors playing Simon and Hound are parked awkwardly in the critics' seats and there is no satisfactory explanation of what they are doing there: their presence can be a physical embarrassment in the final scene. There is every chance that an audience will be too busy laughing to worry, but it is, perhaps, a limitation to the 'brilliance' of the play.

The heaviness of *Jumpers* has already been suggested. It was a fearful risk to throw so many bits of sensational theatricality into the first few minutes, especially when such extended solo and

duet passages of talk had to follow. The idea of the jumpers is a
better idea than the limited use which is made of it. They are
used so little that the Coda, part of the purpose of which is to
give them something to do in the second half, can seem an
encumbrance. Perhaps also we do return rather too frequently
to George's lecture, and Stoppard shifts hazardously the degree
of attention we are to pay to its argument: on pp. 24–9 we are in a
comic send-up, on pp. 54–5 in a poised, coherent prose we
should respect. Like some other apparent wobblings of stagecraft, the real problem here may be a wobbling in Stoppard's
thinking.

The other fundamental danger in *Jumpers*, extending in some
respects still more considerably to *Travesties*, is Stoppard's tendency to write in sketches, 'moments', or—a favourite
word—'ambushes'. His remarks quoted above (p. 35) about
injecting 'some sort of interest and colour into every line' are to
some extent self-diagnostic. In the 1974 interview with Ronald
Hayman:

I really like theatrical *events*.
[In *Jumpers*] I was in a fairly good position to indulge myself with
playing around with quite complex—not to say expensive—theatrical
effects and *images*.
You've simply committed yourself to giving 900 people in a big room
which we call a theatre a sort of *moment*—yes?

The italics above are mine. Finally:

Jumpers and *Travesties* are very similar plays. No-one's said that, but
they're so similar that were I to do it a third time it would be a bore. You
start with a prologue which is slightly strange. Then you have an
interminable monologue which is rather funny. Then you have scenes.
Then you end up with another monologue. And you have unexpected
bits of music and dance, and at the same time people are playing
ping-pong with various intellectual arguments . . . there are senses in
which *Travesties* is a great advance on *Jumpers*, but it's the same kind of
pig's breakfast. . . .

There can be difficulties for an audience in feeling involved in
such *pointilliste* drama. The more rapid, varied and brilliant it is,
the more it resembles a circus act and the less we are gathered

together within it. Many very funny lines in Stoppard seem to pass by audiences: a sort of inflation sets in, or a sort of exhaustion, or quite simply the man has been too clever for most of us to grasp it at the time.

Finally, there may be a lack of organic development. The background schemes of *Hamlet* and *Earnest* give some direction to *Rosencrantz* and *Travesties*, but it is direction rather than development because the source-plays are known to us in advance in their entirety, cannot be affected by the Stoppard action, and are not even in contest with that action. (Always excepting the departure of Lenin's train.) Of the word-play in *Rosencrantz* an American critic said, with a slight crack of panic in his voice, 'Stoppard can keep this sort of thing up indefinitely'; in *Travesties* it is not this 'fatal consistency' which troubles critics, but the dislocations: the play 'jolts along' (Bigsby) or even (Kenneth Tynan) lacks 'the sine qua non of theatre; namely, a narrative thrust that impels the characters ... toward a credible state of crisis, anxiety, or desperation' (p. 109).

Travesties has also the special problem of Lenin. But there is a tendency here for critics to want a different play, one more comfortable and slighter. The complaint is that Lenin is not 'incorporated' into the comedy—right; that the second Act of *Travesties* is dark and uneasy and that the farce begins to seem in uncertain taste. All this seems to me intended ('the second act is Lenin's act really'—Stoppard) and I find the disconcerting effects to be much more fruitful than a mere continuation of 'ping-pong' could have been. Lenin and what he did to Russia is the running wound of the second Act, and the blood seeps hot and wet into the Wildean lace of the conclusion. Bennett, urbane to the last, is nevertheless a traitor: 'implacably' he informs us that 'all the Perrier-Jouet, Brut '89' is gone—a line from Wilde's play here made a succinct summary of the passing of the old elegance—and his exit line (p. 95) is savagely ironic: 'The Minister urges you to prevent Mr Ulyanov leaving Switzerland at all costs. (BENNETT *leaves*. PAUSE.)'

The tension between stylish farce and Lenin's purges is arguably stronger and more organic than the rather willed pain of *Jumpers*; and it becomes a creative criticism not only of Lenin but also, *pace* Tynan, of escapist comedy and of mere Style. There may still be miscalculation, in the dragging sequence of letters and diaries (pp. 86–9); but to feel that the whole structure of the play is an error is to miss the point—a bit like complaining that Tennyson's *Ulysses* is languid or that Shakespeare's Hal is rather foxy.

NIGHT AND DAY

By the time *Travesties* had been staged Stoppard was evidently conscious that the theatre of frenzied activity has its limitations. 'I'd like to write a quiet play,' he told Ronald Hayman in 1974, and again in 1976, after watching J. B. Priestley's *The Linden Tree* on television: 'It would be rather nice to write about a professor or a doctor with a grey-haired wife and a problem child, and the maid comes in with the muffin dish and they talk about the weather a bit.'

That sounds not only like quietness but also like realism, a mode hardly previously employed by Stoppard away from television, *Enter a Free Man* being a fairly half-hearted use of it. A quiet, realist play which would nevertheless use the full imagination of Stoppard is something to dream of: perhaps a true succession to Chekhov at last. Meanwhile, it looks as if *Night and Day* is the play that grew out of the yearnings expressed to Hayman. Quite apart from being fed up with the 'paintbox' of *Jumpers* and *Travesties*, Stoppard the professional, the craftsman, the writer 'for hire', probably wanted to show that he could do a realist play every bit as well as his more eccentric pieces.

In important respects the play departs from realism. First, though, we can recognize how accomplished the realist writing is. The characterization is nothing extraordinary, but it is clear and convincing; as with many masters of realism, it is most questionable when most interesting—here, in the character of Jacob Milne, the young and not yet hard-boiled journalist who has struck lucky. We are not quite sure what to make of Milne; but then neither are the other characters. (It is a constant problem for the realist dramatist, as for the novelist: anyone unusual enough to be worth writing about may risk not being immediately credible. Most of us, after all, have our doubts about Hedda Gabler.) After the many caricatures of earlier Stoppard plays we can appreciate his care *not* to caricature such an obvious potential target as Geoffroy Carson, who is 'placed' but still respected, or as Dick Wagner, who is certainly a hard-boiled journalist but very much a distinct individual too: try his hurt indignation, probably involving self-deception, to Guthrie at the bottom of p. 25, his urgent shutting-up of Guthrie on p. 33, his 'Please call me Dick' after Milne's eruption on p. 36, and of course his exchanges with Ruth, pp. 53–5, ending up 'As you'll remember, it wasn't that good. If it reminded you you are in love with your husband, that's good news for the world.'

The shock opening of very loud noise and apparent slaughter impresses on our minds and senses the violence which is not far away and which is discussed at intervals throughout the action. The jeep with three people in it anticipates what is to happen outside Malakuangazi. But what follows is, relatively, a quiet play; and its most imaginative scene is very quiet indeed.

It can be said, in fact, to move from one stillness to the next. Some early examples: Guthrie on p. 16, who 'doesn't move at all' as he lets the nightmare drain away from him; Ruth on p. 17, who 'remains perfectly still' after Guthrie mentions Wagner's name; Wagner and Guthrie on p. 30 watching Milne; Wagner holding Milne's gaze at the top of p. 33 and his further stricken pause at the bottom of the same page. This is the technique of psychological realism: puppets are not interesting in stillness, and—quite reasonably and satisfactorily—most of Stoppard's plays are peopled by puppets. George and Dotty, and up to a point Ros and Guil, are the only earlier Stoppard characters with the depth to live through stage pauses like these; the others have to talk to react.

Long before *Night and Day* was written, Clive James wrote that Stoppard leaves 'weighty' dramatists behind 'not because he can't do what they can do, but because he can do what they can do so easily'. Certainly the conventional realist writing in *Night and Day* is highly skilled. (*Professional Foul* the previous year had already demonstrated, of course, Stoppard's delicacy in television realism.) On the third page of dialogue Ruth is badly upset by the news that Wagner is coming. 'RUTH: He told you to meet him *at my house*?' The tone alerts Guthrie, and the audience; and the 'my' is a give-away, as Guthrie indicates ('Well, he didn't mention *you*')—prompting the first 'Help' from Ruth's thoughts. 'The boy,' Guthrie goes on, 'said to sit in the garden till Wagner comes.' Ruth is lost for words for a moment, then struggles to establish a conversation. After two pauses, her edginess, and Guthrie's pushiness (we remember that he was badly rattled by his nightmare and woke to find himself at a disadvantage in Ruth's presence, so he has plenty of self-esteem to regain) break out in this exchange:

RUTH: By the way, we don't call them boy any more. The idea is, if we don't call them boy they won't chop us with their machetes. (*Brief smile*.) Small point.
(GUTHRIE *holds his arm out, palm to the ground*.)
GUTHRIE: Boy about this high, fair hair, your mouth, knows about cameras, has a Kodak himself; said I could wait in the garden.
(RUTH *acknowledges her mistake, but* GUTHRIE *pushes it*.)
His name's Alastair.
(*He has pushed it too far and she snaps at him*.)
RUTH: I know his bloody name.

This is worlds away from the double-acts of *Jumpers* or the operatic duets of *Travesties*; but it is superbly done, creating that feeling of naturally-growing encounter, which realism achieves at its best. The play sustains this poise.

Its effectiveness is founded, as much as that of the earlier plays, in theatrical method. Take, for example, the basic element mentioned above, the audience tingling with special knowledge. We share throughout the play Wagner and Ruth's knowledge of their encounter in London; on p. 30 we share Wagner and Guthrie's knowledge of Milne's front-page success (and the stage-direction describes them as *'like people watching a play'*), and three pages later we enjoy Milne's unawareness that he is talking to the man he's talking about, and Milne's naïve association, a little later, of Guthrie with Alastair's camera. A version of this element is watching one character playing another like a hooked fish, while others (and the audience) are in the know: on p. 43 Wagner begins to play Ruth ('Do you know London, Ruth?'); she takes over and between them they are teasing first Carson, then Guthrie—who takes his big spill at 'When were you last there?/RUTH: Friday./GUTHRIE: (*Pause*). I think I'll just sit and drink my beer.' Mageeba's playing of Wagner is on a grander and fiercer scale: the climax is on p. 85 but already by p. 76 Ruth's thoughts are crying 'Run' to Wagner and on p. 77 telling us that Mageeba is going to have Wagner on a plate for his supper.

Again, in the traditional 'well-made play' it is an allowed convention that one or two characters may enter at peculiarly appropriate moments, and Stoppard employs this once for comic effect (Milne's first entry, p. 30) and once to sustain maximum theatrical urgency (Guthrie's return, p. 86, as Mageeba finishes his onslaught on Wagner).

On first view, the play seems to do what it sets out to do neatly and modestly—the faintest hint of Arthur Miller in Ruth's *arioso* (p. 91) is a warning of how the argument could go if pushed harder. If the play has disappointed Stoppard's admirers, it is because what it sets out to do still seems to them restricted. A critique of the Press, nicely balanced between affection, respect, and outrage, is offered, and our attention is mildly engaged by the abortive relationships of Wagner and Ruth and of Ruth and Milne. This is not enough to make us feel, for example, like recommending it to friends or going to see it again ourselves. The limitation seems partly traceable to the realist, single-view, fourth-wall method. 'You get into trouble with my plays,' Stoppard told Ronald Hayman in 1976, 'if you think that there's a static viewpoint on events. There is no observer. There is no safe point around which everything takes its proper place, so that you see things flat and see how they react to each other.'

Of the main action of *Night and Day* this seems untrue.

But the play is not so simple. Disconcertingly, but often funnily, Stoppard intrudes into the dialogue the private exclamations of one, but only one character. Why Ruth? Well, she is in the falsest position. 'I'm in the wrong movie, I think. I should be in *Ruth Carson, Speakeasy queen*.' This to her *husband*, whose response is 'I really don't know what you're talking about half the time./RUTH: And that's the half I do out loud./CARSON: (*Confirmation*) There you are.' (p. 51).

Her audible thoughts achieve different and equally useful effects at different times—Stoppard's thriftiness at work. By them Ruth can clearly communicate her own momentary panics; she can also voice, poignantly, to her husband the confession she is unlikely ever to make (pp. 51–2); and once Mageeba is on stage she can alert the audience, by her unspoken but audible warnings to Wagner.

All this gives piquancy to the realist action, but hardly affects it. Something more fundamental happens at the start of Act Two. The 'true' action of the Act begins on p. 70 when Ruth asks Carson for a cigarette. Pp. 64–70 are a sad fantasy by the lonely Ruth waiting for Milne's return—while he in fact lies dead in a jeep jolting its way back from Malakuangazi. This is why her understudy is asked to walk off naked into the darkness after Milne (p. 70); and in passing we should note a delicate touch which this enables for the actor playing Carson, who 'stands thoughtfully watching as "Ruth" moves into the dark'. The gentle implication is that Carson has at least some understanding of Ruth's fantasy life, and particularly perhaps of her feelings for Milne. It is a small touch, Stoppardian in its humane appreciation of an aspect of marriage.

The fantasy scene is perplexing for the audience, because as it occurs it is likely to be taken as 'real', in spite of the clues (p. 68: 'RUTH. No. Fresh start. Had a good trip?' ... p. 69: 'You say something.') Stoppard attempts to get away with two different layers of theatrical irony at the same time: a realistic Ruth–Milne conversation when the man is actually absent; and even within *this* conversation the former distinction between Ruth's words and 'Ruth''s thoughts. 'Ruth' is allowed to explain it later:

> I talk to myself in the middle of a conversation. In fact I talk to myself in the middle of an *imaginary* conversation, which is itself a refuge from some other conversation altogether, frequently imaginary. I hope you don't mind me telling you all this.
>
> (p. 80)

The 'you' is herself. . . .

It is risky; it is not entirely absorbed into the play as a whole; yet it is also the best of the play. Without it, the emphasis would be firmly and unambiguously on Wagner, the need for a scoop, and the ironies of his various professional fouls; a play about newspapermen, with a woman thrown in for diversity. Milne would not appear at all in Act Two, and his death, though still upsetting, would carry less pain, as would Ruth's feeling for him. *With* the fantasy scene, the play is at least as much about Ruth as it is about newspapermen (Bigsby sees this as a weakness, but many successful plays do handle multiple topics); and it takes a look at questions of private morality, to balance the debate about the morality of 'junk journalism'.

Let me develop this last point: we are still talking about 'staging', because it is the fantasy scene which really creates the inter-relationship of two moral areas in the play. The title *Night and Day* is loosely used to suggest similar dualism. Milne in Act One describes himself as a young reporter feeling 'part of a privileged group, inside society and yet outside it, with a licence to scourge it and a duty to defend it, night and day'. Guthrie's final speech sees information as 'light'. 'It's worse in places where everybody is kept in the dark.' In the fantasy scene Ruth presses Milne to describe his 'lewd thoughts' (her phrase) about her: 'Was it dark or daylight? . . . In the jeep? (*Pause*) It was in the jeep./MILNE: (*sharply*) No it wasn't.'

(We are to discover later that at this moment he is lying shot to pieces in the jeep.) He continues, after a pause: 'It was in a parallel world. No day or night, no responsibilities, no friction, almost no gravity./RUTH: I know it.'

Doesn't she just? A moment later she tries to take up Milne's 'parallel world' idea, but in a cheaper, less creditable way: 'hotel rooms shouldn't count as infidelity. They constitute a separate moral universe.'

The audience gets a laugh. But we know that this isn't true about hotel rooms. We also know—or rather, we are to discover—that we are in the 'parallel world' of fantasy throughout this scene. All the moral debate is Ruth's. Milne here is her imaginative extension of him, and one of his attractions is his honour. (It recalls momentarily Angelo lusting for Isabella.) Her fantasy makes him hard to get—though more likely to yield, by a shrewd psychological intricacy, when she admits that it would be *wrong*. ('Be a bastard. Behave badly./MILNE: That's better.') Ruth here almost acts as her own confessor, to whom the fleshly sin would be all too human, but the attempt to deny that it was wrong would be satanic.

What is heavily on Ruth's mind here and throughout the play, of course, is her 'slip' with Wagner a few days earlier in London. If we are to believe her—and it makes sense—this is the first time she has been unfaithful to Geoffrey Carson. The coincidence of Wagner's turning up at her house on another continent shakes her fundamentally: it reminds her that hotel rooms are *not* in a different universe; and she fears that Wagner 'thinks I hop into bed with strange men because I hopped into bed with a strange man'. (The real point is that she fears it may be true.) To Wagner himself she says:

I let you take me to dinner because there was no danger of going to bed with you. And then because there was no danger of going to bed with you a second time, I went to bed with you. A lady, if surprised by melancholy, might go to bed with a chap, once; or a thousand times if consumed by passion. But twice, Wagner, *twice* ... a lady might think she'd been taken for a tart.

(p. 53)

As it seems the priest of her conscience has told her, the adultery will be a great deal easier the second time, and the vehemence with which she resists the idea of being thought a tart, together with the slippery escape clause ('or a thousand times if ...') suggests that she is in fact well on the road downhill. As she herself says to herself in Milne's presence a few moments later, 'Watch yourself, Tallulah'.

Even a very sympathetic priest would suggest that it was experience with Wagner, unsatisfactory though that was, which has now opened to Ruth the fantasy of possibly sleeping with Milne. The fluttering uncertainty of her own sense of moral identity comes through in the fantasy scene, even to an audience not yet aware that it is fantasy. When we are fully aware—as in reading the text afterwards—the scene seems wonderfully subtle and regrettably short; perhaps its subtlest point—and a very Stoppardian one—is Ruth's consciousness of the meaning of her own name. That Jacob Milne, the young Grimsby reporter, should quote Milton is a shade unlikely, (but he is, as we have said, an unusual man, as Stoppard himself was an unusual cub reporter before him); but that Ruth should project the quotation on to him, in her fantasy, is entirely believable and very poignant. She knows, and is weighed down with the knowledge, that her name means 'that which is lacking in ruthlessness.... Compassion—contrition'. Terribly, she plays upon it a moment later: 'What's PCR?/Post-coital remorse. Post-coital ruth.'

This woman needs no priest to sharpen her moral sensibility; what she needs acutely is some firm but generous sustaining person, probably male, to help her through the next hours and days as the woman of honour she still wants to be. Her husband is cheerfully baffled by her and in any case preoccupied with matters of war and peace (it recalls George's trying to get Ber-

trand Russell 'away from the day-to-day parochialism of international politics'). With Wagner she ends the play: we know
that he will sleep with her this once more and then will ditch her,
and we recall 'but twice, Wagner, *twice* ... a lady might think
she'd been taken for a tart.'

Wagner, who doesn't miss much and has shreds of honour of
his own, is far from throwing himself at her at the end and
explicitly reminds her that she 'didn't want to be a tart'. But
Milne's death has demoralized her: the lady will be a tramp
(though *Wagner* doesn't hear her sing this) and perhaps the
kindest thing he can do as the play ends is exhaust her physically—'I want,' she tells him, 'to be hammered out, disjointed,
folded up and put away like linen in a drawer.'

I wrote of being fully aware when reading the text afterwards,
and the charge of 'literariness' in Stoppard may again be made,
this time where the characterization is realistic and moving. I
don't think the full subtlety of the fantasy scene, and its place in
the play, do come across on first seeing; but then the same is true
of some of the finest effects of major dramatists, and when we
return to the plays on stage they are *dramatic* effects. *Night and
Day* is about Ruth, and about 'ruth' or the lack of it: it is the play
in which Guthrie refers to the Vietnam war as having killed
forty-five 'people' (p. 24) (he means pressmen), in which Carson
can say 'We're Geoff and Ruth to everyone round here. Isn't that
right, Francis?' and *expect* the reply 'Yes sir, Mr Carson' (p. 42),
and in which Wagner can scheme relentlessly to get his story
with absolute indifference to Guthrie, Milne, or—it goes without saying—the people of Kambawe. Of course there is no
attempt at an over-neat parallel between the ruthlessness of
journalists or politicians and the moral lapses of Ruth; but they
fit well in the same play and it feels like the same universe. Two
scenes bring them most delicately together—the 'real' scene
between Milne and Ruth, late in Act One, at the end of which
'MILNE goes into the lighted house. RUTH stays in the dark', and
the fantasy scene at the start of Act Two, 'in a parallel world'.
Perhaps the shift between the two remains uneasy, and perhaps

indeed Stoppard may eventually be criticized for not carrying the moral issues further (a death is, in one sense, an easy solution); but this still seems to me one of his most thoughtful pieces of theatre yet.

RADIO

As well as occasional relatively major productions such as the MacNeice, Dylan Thomas or Beckett plays, BBC Radio has always offered a steady though not well-paid market for young playwrights learning professional competence (Stoppard himself wrote many episodes of a serial to be translated into Arabic, and also five episodes of *The Dales*) and at the same time flexing their muscles in experimental pieces. Stoppard appears just as much at ease with the radio medium as in the theatre, and at least one of his radio plays, *Artist Descending*, seems to me to stand among his best work. As in the theatre, the essential question for a playwright to ask himself is 'What special opportunities does this medium offer?' rather than 'How can I cram my concerns into this medium?'

Well, look at it this way, firstly it's an enormous audience—small compared with TV perhaps but bigger than anything else. Therefore it's to be taken seriously. Secondly, there are no limitations at all.
I'll give you an example: this new play has three people aged 20 to 80, and in the first scene they're walking through the woods when the First World War breaks out all around them. Try putting that on the stage of the Old Vic or the Shaw Theatre. The lovely thing about radio, you see, is that it's liberating.
(Stoppard to Barry Norman, *The Times*, 11 November 1972)

Radio happens inside the listener's head, whether he is sitting with headphones in his favourite chair, driving along a motorway, or painting the house, and it is the best medium of all—better than the novel—for interior monologue, stream of consciousness, fantasy, and recollection. An early Stoppard play, *M is for Moon Among Other Things*, presents a husband and wife making only token contact in conversation, each thoroughly alive in separate musings. A good deal of *If You're Glad I'll Be Frank* happens inside Gladys's head (she herself is, of course, a fantasy figure whom it would be a pity to present visually on stage: she *is* her voice). In *Albert's Bridge* we go inside Albert's thoughts.

And we do this hundreds of feet above the city. The most obviously 'liberating' opportunity of radio is to take us into unlikely places, and many of them, and very quickly. *Albert's Bridge* shifts from the bridge to the ground—we climb down with the characters—to a Committee Room, to Albert's bedroom, to the Committee Room again, and so on; and it spans more than two years in time. The fifteen-minute early play *The Dissolution of Dominic Boot* is all about being constantly on the move, as Dominic rushes round in a taxi trying to raise money to pay the fare. These plays could, with considerable expense, be adapted for film or television (*Albert's Bridge* and *If You're Glad* have actually been staged, and *The Dissolution* was blown up into a fifty-minute American television film called *The Engagement*) but the result would always be second-best, and perhaps irritating because so fundamentally missing the artistic point. Perhaps the best thing of all about Stoppard's radio plays is their use of radio.

Then again, radio is *sound*. A good dramatist will take the opportunity not afforded him elsewhere—the first two pages of *Albert's Bridge* are a joyful indulgence for the writer, who becomes rather like a hi-fi fiend, as we hear Albert's three fellow-painters calling to each other from their various distances up the bridge, followed by the voice of Albert himself 'very close, crooning softly'; and soon afterwards the descent of the bridge, the painters getting steadily closer together, makes a slow madrigal of credible cries:

Mind my head, Dad./Watch my feet, Charlie—comin' down—/I'll watch your feet—you mind my head. Watch your head, Bob—/Watch your feet, Charlie—/Mind my feet, Bob—watch my head, Dad . . ./I'm not your dad, and mind my feet—that's my head, Albert. . . .

Then there are the radio sound-effects. The trouble with these in the heyday of radio in the 1940s was that they tended easily to become clichés (presumably the same 'effects' recordings were frequently used), a point nicely made by Beckett in *All That Fall*:

MRS ROONEY: All is still. No living soul in sight. There is no one to ask. The world is feeding. The wind (*brief wind*)—scarcely stirs the leaves, and the birds—(*brief chirp*)—are tired singing. The cows—(*brief moo*)—and sheep—(*brief baa*)—ruminate in silence . . .

and comprehensively enjoyed for many years by the Goons—thus, for the *reader* of *Albert's Bridge*, the delicious Goons-joke direction on p. 37: '*He tails off as there is the faintest sound of 1,800 men marching . . .*'

The (literal) denouement which follows is conceivable only in radio, the progressive and total collapse of a huge bridge under the unbroken tramp of 3,600 feet: another feast for the hi-fi man.

Sound, clearly, is capable of some of theatre's rapid overlap of different modes. *Where are They Now?*, a piece written for Schools Radio for the princely sum of £75 when Stoppard was already a world-famous dramatist, is done with considerable care; and it makes effective use of the opportunity for rapid juxtaposition of utterly different scenes or times by inter-cutting past and present, the schoolboys and their adult selves at the Old Boys' Dinner. The cuts back and forward are always appropriate or ironically so, not least the first, when the polite rumble of Old Boys taking their seats for dinner is immediately followed by the schoolboys' 'Eurgh!' The uncertainty or ambiguity which radio makes possible is also delicately used here. Three Old Boys, Gale, Brindley and Marks, are the grown-up selves of three schoolboys, Chico, Groucho and Harpo; but not until late in the play do we learn who is who. Chico and Groucho are chattering ebullient kids; Harpo, appropriately to his name, speaks only two words, 'Yes, sir'. Brindley and Marks are talkative Old Boys; Gale is silent for a long time, then speaks bitterly and introspectively about the past. But Gale turns out to be not Harpo but Groucho, and this trick played on the audience's expectations goes to the heart of Stoppard's amused but sympathetic human study: Gale was a good deal happier at school than he now likes to believe, and his stereotype view of his schooldays is as unreliable as the rosy-tinted one of Marks and Brindley.

Artist Descending, Stoppard's last radio play to date, was written just after *Jumpers* and already anticipates some material of *Travesties*. It was commissioned jointly by six European radio companies. They can hardly have been disappointed. The structure is elaborate, best summarized in Stoppard's own note:

> There are eleven scenes. The play begins in the here-and-now; the next five scenes are each a flashback from the previous scene; the seventh, eighth, ninth, tenth and eleventh scenes are, respectively, continuations of the fifth, fourth, third, second and first. So the play is set temporally in six parts, in the sequence ABCDEFEDCBA ...

Here the ambiguity of radio is crucial. We begin (and end) with a tape-recording of Donner's death (actually an accident) which sounds like strong circumstantial evidence of murder. The dramatist plays fair by giving us many clear pointers to the true explanation of the sounds, but our assumption that when Donner said 'Ah! there you are' he must have been speaking to Martello or Beauchamp is hard to shake. This ambiguity is the trigger to the play. We become curious about the steady cuts back into the past, and then forward again, because we are trying to identify a motive for Donner's death; perhaps he wronged one of the other two. Ironically, what we find out is that, if anyone has been wronged in the past, it is Donner himself; and he discovered it only last week. On the way we come across joke sound-ambiguities practised by the artists themselves in their youth—all part of Stoppard's audience-teasing. The first we hear through the ears of a blind person: a time-honoured tradition of radio drama characteristically made by Stoppard absolutely essential to the plot (if Sophie's sight had not been failing there would be no doubt which was the artist she found attractive). As Sophie for the first time enters the artists' shared drawing-room in Lambeth in 1920 she (and we) hear the sounds of a game of ping-pong. More interest for the hi-fi man: we can deduce a winning shot *'by the hiatus where one has been led to expect, from the rhythm, contact with the other bat'*.

Martello introduces Sophie and to her dismay the ping-pong game resumes, as if she is being entirely ignored. In fact it is a recording and the artists are coming forward offering their hands. Here the ambiguity switches suddenly—we gather that Sophie's blindness is not immediately apparent, and indeed even when Martello tells them about it Beauchamp thinks he is making an outrageous sick joke.

We tend to follow the whole of this scene from inside Sophie's head, though we have not her expertise at recognizing a brewer's dray from the sound of the hooves in the street outside. This gives the cue for the final flashback, to the artists walking in France in 1914. Again Stoppard plays fair, including not only plenty of fly-swatting (the repetitive clue to how Donner actually died) but also emphasizing that this is a flashback to a *game* (see the last lines of p. 41) and that it is a *walking* holiday; yet the cue of 'Beauchamp's Tenth Horse' has led us through typical radio clip-clop sounds to assume that when Beauchamp says he is riding, he is. In fact he is walking and knocking coconut shells together (a cliché radio sound effect, whether true or not) and the others are humouring him: 'MARTELLO: Tell you what—give Mouse a go on the horse. BEAUCHAMP: No . . . This horse only believes in me' (p. 44).

As Beauchamp has said earlier in the play—that is, nearly sixty years later—'People have been taught to expect certain kinds of insight but not others.' He goes on, immediately, 'The first duty of the artist is to capture the radio station.' (p. 20). Normally, of course, this is one of the first aims of a political *coup*; and what the ping-pong and the clip-clop demonstrate to us is how trusting we tend to be of the dear BBC Sound Effects men and their tapes. We are too well trained in the convention, and our reasoning tends to suffer. We need a Magritte-like alertness, the sound-symbol for 'horse' labelled 'coconut'.

TELEVISION

Stoppard's vivid response to the opportunities of theatre and radio raises one's hopes for his use of television, by now the most familiar of all art-media. The medium offers a fair degree of *flexibility* of location, acting area, and cast, but usually within a distinctly limited budget; *speed* (a great deal of exposition can be achieved in ten minutes, for example, by neat cutting; even very young children are now adept at grasping the story-line from a rapid succession of indicators); *realism* (stage sets always look like stage sets; television *can* look like 'real life'); *drama without dialogue* (not, on the whole, something one would expect to appeal to Stoppard); and *intimacy*—the television set is in one's living-room; domestic scenes feel like a partial extension of one's own house, and close-ups of faces approach life-size (in the cinema, of course, they are gigantic). Stoppard's 1967 half-hour play *Teeth* (which I have not seen) sounds as if it made excellent use of the last three, presenting the close contact of a dentist and his patient. As Ronald Hayman puts it:

> The camera can move in close on eyes dilated with fear about what is happening inside the mouth; our own anxieties about teeth and sexual attractiveness make us more vulnerable in the privacy of our home than we would be in a cinema; sandwiched between newsreels and studio discussions, the fantasy takes on a dangerous aura of reality.
>
> (p. 79)

The vastness of the television audience may exhilarate a dramatist; but it also presents immense problems. Other 'play-ings' are consciously chosen; for large numbers of television viewers the choice is merely between channels. A major concern of those selecting plays is that they should be as accessible as possible to any section of the community. The dramatist too has probably no wish to disappoint or bewilder. Whatever the reason, Stoppard's television plays tend to be his most conventional.

They also include one great popular success: *Professional Foul*. This play manages to combine, without a hint of strain, Stoppardian intellectual and moral concerns (moral philosophy, linguistic ambiguity, ethical double standards in many fields, and the suppression of liberty) with humorous twists developed slowly enough to be grasped by an audience unaccustomed to the usual Stoppardian quick-fire or overlap (Anderson's confusions over girlie magazines, McKendrick's mistaking footballers for philosophers, the interpreters baffled by Stone's lecture) and a walking-bass of traditional story line of a kind familiar to modern television audiences (documents to be smuggled from behind the Iron Curtain). The television medium enables Stoppard to set the action pretty well anywhere—thus, starting and ending on board the aircraft. The developing climax of the play is pointed up by more frequent intercutting of scene (pp. 89–91) including that special simultaneity which film and television can offer: two scenes, one on sound, one visual (p. 90). The play starts in particularly televisual terms: the initial exposition is done without dialogue, using the Colloquium Philosophicum brochure and the girlie magazine neatly to give information, to attract amused interest, and to state at the outset both the 'story' theme of concealing a document and the intellectual theme of the double standard. Once the dialogue begins the play proceeds, quite acceptably, in more routine ways. There is one crisply-made point *about* television: McKendrick, having had his mistake explained to him, is still puzzled by the fact that 'I knew his face'. Anderson explains: 'Match of the Day'. Television brings faces so clearly and recognizably into our homes that when we meet a much-televized person in the flesh our reflexes treat him as a close acquaintance. The interchange between McKendrick and Anderson takes place during a lecture on ambiguity....

The problem of audience-span can be set against the chance to reach, instantly, enormous numbers. In three showings, *Professional Foul* has been seen by nearly six million people in the United Kingdom alone. For this reason it was also abundantly worth televizing *Every Good Boy*, as was done in autumn 1979, though there was considerable loss in the transference from live theatre, especially in the interaction of areas. This play—far too expensive to be often put on live—was seen in one showing by an estimated 900,000 people in the United Kingdom. That instant impact is particularly appropriate when a play makes a political statement: Alexander's monologue (p. 23) was immensely compelling, the close-up solo speaker reaching into the private home.

4 · LAUGHING

It is Sir Archibald Jumper who tells us, at the end of his play, that 'no laughter is sad'. He is not the most trustworthy of witnesses, and his remark seems to contradict the common observation that sadness and comedy are often inextricably involved. The subject matter is human failing; the clowns themselves are often depressives. Archie is not, however, talking of the trigger for laughter, but of the laughter itself. One hates to agree with him, but he may be right here. That we can laugh *together* is not sad: it places and accommodates our sadness.

We do also laugh in delight—in our ordinary lives, at intense happiness or unexpected success; and in the theatre, at astonishing technical dexterity or bewilderingly neat fits—the disparity between our normal expectation of loose ends and the actual spectacular design. Stoppard's plots and games often work like this: the revelation of Puckeridge at the end of *Hound*, the freeing of Alexander and Ivanov at the end of *Every Good Boy*, Wagner's discovery near the end of *Night and Day* that his scoop interview will not be printed because of industrial action that he has set in motion himself, or Anderson's disclosure to McKendrick once they are on board their aircraft returning home. The absurdly neat fit of names in Stoppard is discussed below, pp. 120–6.

The neat fits of irony are darker, moving us back towards sadness. That Dotty should cry 'Is there anybody there?' exactly on cue after George's climactic 'the how and why of the overwhelming question'; and that, two pages later, she should cry

'Fire!' when George has a tensed bowstring—the result of *this* neat fit is the death of Thumper (pp. 26 and 28). Or that the blind girl should fall among *painters*, with the several painful twists that Stoppard works on this basic irony, in *Artist Descending*. Frequently in Stoppard we both laugh and wince because the fit is too good.

Mostly, though, laughter is about what doesn't fit: failure, lapse, misunderstanding, inappropriateness. The notes which follow indicate some familiar kinds of comic disparity and examine how they appear in Stoppard's plays. They are in a sort of classification here, because that may be useful: but of course as they actually occur in the plays they constantly overlap.

THE INTOLERABLE

Laughter is one defence or stalling operation when we are confronted with something intolerable. Sexually inhibited people laugh or giggle as soon as conversation enters areas they can't easily contemplate. Another form of sexual unease takes the form of telling blue jokes, making, one might say, a kind of art in which to play at an envied confidence. Much the same goes for embarrassment about death. Children and adolescents may make appallingly sick jokes about hideous suffering, the skeleton figures of starvation, the severely crippled or the senile; this laughter can seem quite devilish, but it may often be a confused expression of outrage, rather than of primal evil: a plea for time to grow into a more adequate response.

From his writing Stoppard's personality comes through as fundamentally whole and calm, as well as acutely intelligent. He stands outside the nerviness, irascibility or obsession of his characters; as good a way as any to recognize this fact is to note his instinctive avoidance of the sick joke, the sexually abusive, the essentially mean-minded (for example the 1960s and 70s cliché of comic homosexuality). Such nerviness is isolated and placed in the characters of the Tragedians in *Rosencrantz* or the M.P.s in *Dirty Linen*. The Swiftian laugh—of agony, or at an obscene disparity between the tolerable and the real—comes only rarely in Stoppard: perhaps in Carr's reminiscences of the trenches, or in the laconic Wagner–Guthrie exchange ('Maybe it's the same kid./Later he stepped on a land mine./*(Pause)*. It probably isn't, then.'); most finely in the deadpan of Alexander's monologue (pp. 23 of *Every Good Boy*)—'You see all the trouble writers cause.... They spoil things for ordinary people.' It is also a grim underlay to the manic goings-on of *Cahoot's Macbeth*; and it is perhaps the intended effect of the Scott/Oates joke in *Jumpers*, though that can seem a rare case of stooping to cheapness.

ALTERNATIVE EXPLANATIONS

The hopping figure described in *After Magritte* is interpreted in at least seven different ways. Part of the joke is at the expense of our tendency to classify what we see as we are seeing it, according to unconscious preconceptions, and thus to delude ourselves. *Artist Descending* plays hard on the same tendency to make assumptions about what we hear: the droning on p. 13 is a fly not a snore; the 'Thump' is a swat at a fly not an attack on a man; the 'smack' on p. 22 is Donner hitting Beauchamp not Donner hitting a fly; the 'Paris music' on p. 29 takes us to Lambeth, not Paris; the ping-pong on p. 34 is a recording not a live game, which leads Sophie (and us) to distrust the genuine whistling of the kettle on p. 35; and Beauchamp's horse (p. 42) is a coconut shell. In *Jumpers* George quotes the following anecdote, which goes deep into Stoppard territory:

> Meeting a friend in a corridor, Wittgenstein said: 'Tell me, why do people always say it was *natural* for men to assume that the sun went round the earth rather than that the earth was rotating?' His friend said, 'Well, obviously, because it just *looks* as if the sun is going round the earth.' To which the philosopher replied, 'Well, what would it have looked like if it had looked as if the earth was rotating?'

The anecdote is turned against George a little later (Archie on p. 78) and indeed Stoppard has already been playing this game with us earlier, p. 60:

> (*These sounds are consistent with a proper doctor–patient relationship. If* DOTTY *has a tendency to gasp slightly it is probably because the stethoscope is cold.* ARCHIE *on the other hand might be getting rather overheated under the blaze of the dermatograph lights.*)

Usually in Stoppard the alternative explanation is more ordinary and more innocent than our first impression. We are to laugh at our fears and suspicions and be humbler in coming to conclusions. This is true also, of course, of the strangeness of Dogg-language to Easy and of Easy's English to Dogg and the boys. The first reaction is to assume that an insult is intended; gradually trust is established.

ALTERNATIVE MEANING

The conscious pun is not as important in Stoppard as some might think. There are a few laboriously set up to show the laborious humour of the *character*: Withenshaw in *Dirty Linen*: 'There's trouble in t'*Mail.* . . ./I'm the clerk, Miss Gotobed./ And I'm Malcolm Withyou. (*He laughs uproariously.*)' Sometimes Stoppard possesses characters and spins them on a whirlwind of punning; one feels almost sorry for them, twitching with an energy outside themselves:

> But the tape recorder speaks for itself. That is, of course, the point about tape recorders. In this case it is eloquent, grandiloquent, not to say Grundigloquent—Oh, God, if only I could turn it *off*!—no wonder I have achieved nothing with my life!—my brain is on a flying trapeze that outstrips all the possibilities of action.
>
> (*Artist Descending*, p. 16)

Ivanov starts in apparent control (*Every Good Boy*, p. 16) but the dramatist soon runs away with the character:

> Listen, I've had clarinet players eating *at my own table*. I've had French whores and gigolos speak to me in the *public street*, I mean

horns, I mean piccolos, so don't worry about *me*, maestro, I've sat down with them, *drummers* even, sharing a plate of tagliatelle Verdi and stuffed Puccini—why, I know people who make the orchestra eat in the kitchen, off scraps, the way you'd throw a trombone to a dog, I mean a second violinist, I mean to the lions. . . .

(Every Good Boy, pp. 17–18)

So it is with Carr:

and by the way you'd never believe a Swiss redlight district, por-nographic fretwork shops, vice dens, get a grip on yourself, sorry, sorry . . .

(Travesties, p. 24)

The Player in *Rosencrantz* may be expected to deal in blue innuendoes, and does, and we have seen Withenshaw's attempt in *Dirty Linen*. Stoppard is much more interested, however, in the innuendo that may not be intended—the many Freudian slips in *Dirty Linen*, or *On the Razzle*; the suggestiveness of the new random order of Shakespeare's sonnet 18 as Gwendolen draws it out of the hat (*Travesties*, p. 54); or, in the case of George and Archie, remarks which George, being George, would like to persuade himself are innocent:

GEORGE: Well, I don't know what's the matter with her. . . . All she says is, she's all right in bed.
ARCHIE: Yes, well there's something in that.
GEORGE: (*Restraining his going; edgily*) What exactly do you do in there?
ARCHIE: Therapy takes many forms.
GEORGE: I had no idea you were still practising.
ARCHIE: Oh yes . . . a bit of law, a bit of philosophy, a bit of medicine, a bit of gym. . . . A bit of one and then a bit of the other.
GEORGE: You examine her?
ARCHIE: Oh, yes, I like to keep my hand in. . . .

(Jumpers, p. 70)

MISUNDERSTANDING

Puns are intended; we control them; perhaps that is why we like to groan at them. Our mistakes produce fresher and keener laughter. Language offers itself as an aid to reason and communication, yet it repeatedly tips us in the mire. Such falls produce many of Stoppard's funniest—usually very rapidly passing—moments.

> CYNTHIA: Thank you so much for coming.
> HOUND: Not at all. You never know, there might have been a serious matter.
> CYNTHIA: Drink?
> HOUND: More serious than that, even ...
>
> (*Hound*, p. 31)

> CECILY: I am afraid that I disapprove of servants.
> CARR: You are quite right to do so. Most of them are without scruples.
> CECILY: In the socialist future, no one will have any.
> CARR: So I believe.
>
> (*Travesties*, p. 73)

Professional Foul, mostly restrained, begins with a little Stoppardian jig:

> McKENDRICK: I wasn't sure it was you. Not a very good likeness.
> ANDERSON: I assure you this is how I look.
> McKENDRICK: I mean your photograph.... The photograph is younger.
> ANDERSON: It must be an old photograph.
>
> (*Professional Foul*, p. 44)

Misunderstanding is gripping to theatre audiences because we can see the disaster or discomfiture brewing and developing, but have neither the responsibility nor the ability to intervene; and of course also because we watch playings-through of events analogous to our own past errors. Such misunderstandings, apparently minor and comic, can be profoundly resonant.

> ALEXANDER: I have a complaint.
> DOCTOR: Yes, I know—pathological development of the personality with paranoid delusions.

The Doctor chooses (or has been conditioned) to understand all complaints (protest, dissent) as complaints (medical conditions). As the Inspector in *Cahoot's Macbeth* says: 'Words can be your friend or your enemy, depending on who's throwing the book, so watch your language.'

The Guthrie and Carson slips instanced on p. 65 above illustrate similar callousing or conditioning; and the early brush between Guthrie and Ruth about the word 'boy' (*Night and Day* p. 18, discussed on p. 59 above is finely economical, saying a good deal about the British in Africa past and present as well as about these two speakers.

There are comic misunderstandings in Stoppard which are not merely verbal, though words sustain the error: it is reasonable for Carr to assume that Gwendolen's friend and chaperone is a woman, quite apart from 'her' name being Joyce; it is understandable that McKendrick, recognizing a face in a Prague hotel at which members of a philosophy congress are staying, should assume that it is a fellow-philosopher, and it is bad luck (and Stoppardian impishness) that makes words compound his mistake: 'He's what used to be called left wing. Broadbent's in the centre. He's an opportunist more than anything' (*Professional Foul*, p. 50).

SLIPS

Misunderstanding is only one kind of mistake. Sheer forgetfulness, following inappropriate logics, makes Carr call Joyce 'Doris', 'Janice', 'Phyllis', or 'Deirdre', or Beauchamp call Tzara 'Tarzan'. The farces *Dirty Linen* and *On the Razzle* clatter with linguistic slips, Freudian give-aways in the one and improper stumblings around innocent statement in the other. Freud and the satire of cliché combine in Withenshaw's 'Don't talk to me about voluptuous—mine was Titian like two Botticellis fighting their way out of a hammock.' (*Dirty Linen*, p. 50)—where both painters' names carry erotic suggestions, where meaning has entirely collapsed ('titian' should refer to *colour*, and Titian's paintings are not much like Botticelli's) and where the delicacy of the art contrasts with Withenshaw's own crudity.

The verbal give-away is not, of course, new with Freud: no one does it better than Shakespeare or Ben Jonson. How much the Inspector in *Cahoot's Macbeth* is conscious of all he is saying is debatable: it may be that—as certainly in 'Between you and me and these three walls and especially the ceiling' he doesn't mind giving anything away because his power will be absolute. More like a true give-away is his line 'I'm the cream in your coffee, the sugar in your tank' (p. 56); or, in *Every Good Boy*, the Doctor's 'Yes, he has an identity problem. I forget his name,' (p. 27).

DISINTEGRATION

In Beckett, Stoppard's early master, yearning is the root of most misery, and 'nothing is funnier than unhappiness'. The yearning is often for faculties and conditions now lost, in the steady process of breakdown. *Endgame* ironically reverses this, into a yearning for ultimate stasis. Stoppard's Dotty, drying after a big build-up at the start of *Jumpers*, is funnier at that moment than she is pathetic, because she has sufficient showbiz style to snap out a parody build-up before someone else can do so, because she returns a few moments later looking '*stunning*' and radiating apparent brash confidence, and because—a characteristically Stoppardian uplift—her confusion of moon songs begins to be in itself a comic creation, not just disintegration. At this point, the stage direction on p. 20 tells us, she may simply appear '*pleasantly drunk*'. In fact, however, she is '*breaking up mentally*', and our laughter at Dotty later in the play is accompanied by wincing. George is steadily dragged by her influence (see p. 49 above) towards a disintegration he is intellectually resisting with passion; meanwhile his own lecture shows early signs of erosion which could in the course of time become the chaotic landslip of Lucky's 'thinking' in *Waiting for Godot*. There is something of this also in Carr's reminiscences in *Travesties*, not least in the final line—'I forget the third thing'. And Archie's testimony at the Symposium (p. 83) is even further gone than Lucky. Our hope is in reason; our despair in the crumbling of the language of reasoning. 'All I know,' says George, 'is that I think that I know that I know that nothing can be created out of nothing.' It is a serious line, yet obliged to laugh at itself.

UPSET EXPECTATION

In Stoppard, the audience take more pratfalls than the characters. In *Artist Descending* (see p. 70 above) we are repeatedly duped: it is like the fun of a maze or a game of forfeits, and we can laugh at our own discomfiture. All Stoppard's theatrical surprises might be included here. To set up a structure with one expected outcome, and surprise us with another or opposite outcome, is a classic process (not necessarily comic, incidentally: consider Mageeba's sport with Wagner in *Night and Day*). The banana-skin gag, in which pomposity skids to a merited fall, is infrequent in Stoppard because his characters are generally ironically self-aware and often humble—we have seen Dotty soon joining in the laughter at herself, indeed, leading it. When it happens to Bones, in the same play (the elephant bray on p. 52) it is his *fantasy* which takes the fall, rather than he himself, and even his fantasy has recovered by the opening of Act Two—see p. 58. The first appearance of Foot, the Inspector in *After Magritte*, is a gigantic banana-skin slide: confident that he is bursting in on the extraordinary scene glimpsed through the window by Holmes at the start of the play, he hurls out the question: 'What is the meaning of this bizarre spectacle?' when for the first time in the play the scene does *not* look bizarre. Just as Stoppard enjoys demonstrating that the weirdest combinations of events can have logical causes, so he contrives to make a conventional living-room scene into an upset expectation. Foot blusters on through the play but has always the wrong end of the stick; at the end, like Oedipus, he reveals to us that he himself is the person he is seeking, but—unlike Oedipus—remains disconsolately unaware of it (and of the fact that there has been no crime at all).

There is a number of small-scale verbal gags of this kind consciously set up by characters: Joyce's 'The proudest boast of an Irishman is—I paid back my way', Ruth's 'Soho' (*Night and Day* p. 44), the Czech Inspector's 'And that's only the audience' (*Cahoot's Macbeth* p. 53), and French's 'I was sick on her shoes' (*Dirty Linen* p. 49). A truer banana-skin fall is Carr's exploded pomposity in *Travesties* (p. 50).

CARR: The Prime Minister—?
JOYCE: Mr Asquith.
CARR: I am perfectly well aware who the Prime Minister *is*—I am the representative of His Majesty's Government in Zurich.
JOYCE: The Prime Minister is Mr Lloyd George, but at that time it was Mr Asquith.
CARR: Oh yes.

A variety of this humour is that of unexpected appropriateness. When determined to get Albert away on holiday his wife resists his sly proposal of the Firth of Forth and triumphantly gets him to Paris, only to find that he becomes totally hooked on the Eiffel Tower. When George appears with bow, arrow and tortoise, and wearing shaving foam, and says he was expecting a psychiatrist, it is funny, as it was earlier when he first appeared with shaving foam on his face as Dotty referred to God 'not as a true invocation'. The appropriateness of Dotty's cries to moments in George's lecture is often rich with irony—and with pain; and there is also a dark appropriateness in Archie's appearing (p. 67) as a callous immoralist to contrast with St Francis.

Cahoot's Macbeth works sharply in ironic fits of Shakespeare to the Czech police State. When we expect the Porter to enter as comic though sinister relief, altering the tone of *Macbeth*, the Inspector enters—duly comic, duly sinister, and duly altering the tone. His exit on p. 63 ('Cloudy with a hint of rain') is answered defiantly by Cahoot 'Let it come down!' (the actual Shakespearean exchange takes place two pages later). Students of *Macbeth* will know that the Third Murderer is a disputed figure, variously interpreted by commentators and mistrusted by the first two Murderers themselves. Stoppard sports wickedly with this by allowing the lorry driver Easy to wander in at this point, wholly unexpected by everyone (the audience thought he belonged in a different play) and wholly bewildered by being addressed in blank verse (he has only just got used to Dogg). The mistrust of the first two Murderers, meanwhile, is personally felt. A third unexpected appearance in the original Shakespeare is that of Banquo's Ghost—and again Stoppard arranges for Easy unwittingly to fill this role ('MACBETH *does his best to ignore him*'). The final bitter appropriateness is the Inspector's return on p. 72 to the words 'My countryman, but yet I know him not.'

Towards the end of *Jumpers* we are rocked back on our heels by several upsets, comic but in each case also ironic or painful. That the porter Crouch should be able casually to demolish George's argument (top of p. 79) is wholly unexpected and very funny, but it saddens us for George; it is followed almost at once by Crouch's disclosure about McFee (his 'mentor', with whom he was on first-name terms)—that McFee was 'going through a crisis', losing faith in faithlessness. ('If altruism is a possibility, he said, my argument is up a gum tree.') This slightly disturbs the balance of our sympathies—for an amoral, faithless McFee to have been shot was less regrettable than had it been, say, George himself. The knife goes on twisting, however: we discover that McFee was 'secretly betrothed' to the secretary of his academic opponent, George. Our minds reel as it begins to appear that the secretary, previously out of consideration, is now the likeliest suspect for McFee's murder, since, although 'terrified to tell her' that he was already married, McFee had finally just done so. While we struggle to assimilate this information, a yet further twist may convulse us with laughter—Crouch's casual 'I mean, with him going into the monastery'. Suddenly McFee is known to have lurched into a religious position far more committed than George's: it appears that George has been preparing an attack on an opponent who might, if he had lived, have proved bewilderingly an ally, while within George's own study may be the murderess. Throughout the Crouch–Archie conversation the secretary, alone in the Study and unable to hear what they are saying, is '*the only person moving on stage*'; when Crouch says 'And now he's dead,' she '*snaps her handbag shut with a sharp sound and takes her coat out of the cupboard*'. She has never faltered ('*a grim, tense, unsmiling young woman*') but now the laugh turns against her, though she is never aware of it; as she leaves we see a bright splash of blood on the back of her coat. And it is the wrong revelation!—or possibly the right revelation though the wrong murder, for the blood is not McFee's, but Thumper's.

So to the last and bleakest of the upset expectations: the discovery that Thumper was killed not by a demented Dotty but by George himself in the course of an attempt to demonstrate the existence of God, though the shot itself was a result of a cry from Dotty. To sum up: the girl who so dutifully noted George's argument for absolute values may well have killed cold-bloodedly, like the sharp snap of her handbag; and the more innocent victims, the animals, are killed accidentally by George himself. A moment earlier we have seen a porter patronizingly dismantle the argument with which the play has invited us increasingly to sympathize. As Stoppard says, 'Firstly, A. Secondly, minus A.'

JUXTAPOSITION

Most of us live in several different modes. It is funny to see them mixed: Ruth's thoughts and unspoken confessions torpedoing her conventional social utterances; a Home Secretary encountering as secretary of a Parliamentary Committee the girl he took out, incognito, the other night; a lorry driver wandering through the action of *Macbeth*. There is, as with many kinds of laughter, potential pain (Ruth indeed is in a poor state), but the humour is warm, confirming that we are single beings who wear varied masks, not genuinely fragmented personalities. *Dirty Linen* is all about this kind of juxtaposition; and a touch of the same humour is put to more delicate use early in *Professional Foul*. On p. 47 McKendrick is being put down rather by Anderson's elegant indifference towards him and his university (indifference unconvincingly disguised as enthusiasm); as McKendrick ruefully acknowledges Anderson's Oxbridge wit, the air hostess reveals the girlie magazine which is on Anderson's lap. This allows McKendrick to move smoothly from 'A higher civilization alive and well in the older universities' to 'I see you like tits and bums, by the way.'

There is a special Stoppardian absurdity to the mismatches of Joyce's clothing, in *Travesties*—the pretence that each mode has its own independent programme: 'My wardrobe got out of step in Trieste, and its reciprocal members pass each other endlessly in the night.'

It's also funny to juxtapose the grouses of schoolboys and the comfortable reminiscences of their later selves, and to juxtapose their different linguistic codes or registers. The game of speech-registers is played like a sound-diagram on pp. 8–9 of *If You're Glad*; and like a banana-skin gag in the deflation of George Riley's 'And now you, whom destiny has cast in this shabby place at this golden moment—in you I see a fellow spirit.' by Florence's 'Well, that's nice' (*Enter a Free Man*, p. 33).

There is a more savage point to the shift of register in Carr's: 'And multi-coloured micturition is no trick to those boys, they'll have you pissing blood.'

George drinks from a tumbler full of pencils; and a *janitor* carrying *drinks on a tray* wanders about between the *swings* of a *secretary* behaving like a *circus* or *striptease* artiste—the juxtaposition or overlap of six roles. After the Philosophy Congress/girlie magazine juxtaposition early in *Professional Foul* we later see a Cambridge Professor of Ethics attempting to give two England footballers tactical advice (a pleasant allusion, perhaps, to the enthusiasm for football of the Oxford Professor A. J. Ayer)

—and he is right! We welcome both these juxtapositions: both make Anderson more 'human'; we don't really want people to live in one mode only, and the comedy that shows that they don't is heartening.

THE LUDICROUS

The grossly inappropriate carries in it a potential offence to reason, to hope, and to dignity. Most of the cruellest moments in drama are ludicrous; and the consciously Absurdist theatre is often enough grim: Ionesco spoke of wanting to remind each man that he would one day be 'un cadavre'. But it has also given ideas to less depressed writers, rather as Dada overlapped with the freakish humour of less angry artists. Stoppard's ludicrousness is not often bitter. But neither is it often merely frivolous: absurdity, in Stoppard, is part of the truth, and dealing with it is part of our response to life.

The wild implausibility of some of his theatrical events doesn't trouble us much, if they seem extensions along a convincing line. Nobody, surely, could be as dim as Riley over his envelope; but inventors do have to think unexpectedly, and little self-deluding men do exist. George's laborious arrangements to include in his lecture live hare and tortoise, real bow and arrow and target, and a recording of a trumpeting elephant, are only a development to absurdity of the earnestly playful examples of many dons, particularly philosophers; and the pain which ensues from their confusion is the absurdity gripping fiercely back at us when we might have thought it merely amusing.

Jumpers offers a succession of grotesquenesses: the chandelier-swinging secretary, the agnostic Archbishop of Canterbury, the acrobatic dons, the 'dermatograph', the policeman calling on his murder suspect with a bouquet, the story of McFee shooting himself inside a plastic bag; and the Coda. It comes closest of Stoppard's plays to the darkness of Absurd

Theatre: behind the play is a violently disturbed Britain; for every character, one way or another, things are falling apart. Whereas a number of odd events in Stoppard turn out to have reassuringly rational explanations, in *Jumpers* things really are adrift, and more specifically the moral sense is adrift. George's attempt to moor it to stable ground fails at home—in his failure of Dotty and (in the dream-Coda) in his failure to speak for Clegthorpe.

In *Every Good Boy* and *Cahoot's Macbeth* much of the ludicrousness is that of the State and its minions; they are Absurdist dramas which are also reportage.

But we shouldn't forget the nonsenses of sheer exuberance, or fail to be grateful for them. Many of these are linguistic and will be mentioned in the next chapter. But there are visual feasts as well—two on-stage and one off-stage in *After Magritte*, Joyce's conjuring and Cecily's 'stripper' act in *Travesties*, Maddie's continuing with her secretarial duties as she steadily loses items of clothing, and Inspector Hound, foghorn in hand, paddling on to the stage on his pontoon-swamp-boots.

RECURRENCE

Some things become funny in being repeated. I'm not thinking now of Absurdism, of a coin coming down heads ninety-two times, of an apparently sane and intelligent man saying 'Dada' ('articulately') thirty-four times; but of the humour of coincidental recurrence made plausible. The radio comedy of which Tom Stoppard probably heard a good deal while growing up specialized in the 'catchphrase', a not particularly interesting remark, made in lugubrious tones by the same character in episode after episode. The joke, mainly, was in how we got there, and whether—in spite of our expectations—it could take us by surprise. Beckett does the same with the many repetitions of 'Let's go./We can't./Why not?/We're waiting for Godot.' Classic farce such as *On the Razzle* delights in accumulations of interruptions and concealments as similar as possible: we laugh at the unlikeliness of the occurrence, and at the degree to which it is made plausible; and we laugh, perhaps, with the reassurance of familiarity.

Typically, Stoppard does it that bit more neatly, ingeniously, or ironically than the average comic scriptwriter. The twists are better and more pregnant. The 'Mind my head watch my feet' interchanges early in *Albert's Bridge* take on the rhythm of chant, without losing plausibility. The 'I'll kill you for this, Simon Gascoyne!' shouts in *Hound* send up real cliché, as do the 'cheerful redcaps' of *New-Found-Land*. The reason George cannot lay the ghost of Bertrand Russell is that he cannot find the right *linguistic* pattern in which to put him to rest, which is also his more general problem. The 'Strewths' in which the M.P.s always fail to notice Maggie's undress carry a moral point behind them. The time-slips in *Travesties* ('I have put the newspapers and telegrams on the sideboard, sir') have the dual function of indicating Carr's failing powers and of giving us neatly staggered newsreels of events during the First World War—a lot of sheer information is got across. Dotty's cries of 'Help!' 'Murder!' 'Rape!' and so on gradually come to be so familiar that George feels he can ignore them; but in this case something really is up and indeed the cries do eventually impinge, in mini-tragedy, on George's world. Finally, when Easy throws *himself* through the wall (*Dogg's Hamlet* p. 30) he is making a Pavlovian reaction to a repeated pattern—he has learnt *this* language of action just as, later on the same page, we discover that he has learnt Dogg.

A version of this comedy is that of *transmutation*. In the second Act of *Waiting for Godot* things are the same but different; lines are swopped from Vladimir to Estragon, Pozzo is blind, Lucky dumb, and the tree—against all other apparent drifts of the play—has leaves. The ending of Stoppard's *After Magritte* is a tableau just as ludicrous as the opening; and while the play has been *explaining* the second (offstage) irrationality (the hopping man with handbag) it has been setting up this third irrationality on stage. At the end of the early radio play *The Dissolution of*

Dominic Boot, Dominic is heading for a repetition of the opening situation, as a smooth talker riding round in a taxi having dropped off a girl, only this time penniless, minus girl-friend, and reduced to pyjamas and raincoat. The plunge into the past and back so skilfully made in *Artist Descending* alters our understanding of many things to which we return, notably the death with which the play opens. Near the end of *Hound* the critics become stage characters and the characters become critics, travestying the earlier travesty. The transmutation joke is at its crispest and most physical when Birdboot, now on stage in the role of Simon, attempts to use his previously acquired knowledge to avoid the careering wheelchair entrance of Magnus (whom he saw knock over the previous Simon). He '*prudently keeps out of the chair's former path but it enters from the next wing down and knocks him flying*'.

And the final trick of *Professional Foul*, where Anderson slips Hollar's manuscript into McKendrick's briefcase in order to get it on to the aircraft, is an echo and transmutation of several previous elements: Anderson's embarrassment at being found in possession of a girlie magazine which is not his but which he appears to be concealing (p. 48), the footballer's 'professional foul' (p. 71), the secret police's 'professional foul' in 'finding' contraband currency in Hollar's flat (p. 73) and McKendrick's own talk of 'reversing a principle' (p. 78).

Characteristically, Stoppard carries this transmutation joke into the detail of particular phrasing.

ROS: I wish I was dead. (*Considers the drop.*) I could jump over the side. That would put a spoke in their wheel.
GUIL: Unless they're counting on it.
ROS: I shall remain on board. That'll put a spoke in their wheel.
(*Rosencrantz*, p. 81)

(The joke is fully relevant to the question of predestination which hovers over the play.) Equally pointed is the light but ruthless exchange:

SOPHIE: But I am—blind as a bat, I'm afraid.
BEAUCHAMP: Oh. I'm sorry.

SOPHIE: Please don't mention it.
BEAUCHAMP: I will not, of course.
SOPHIE: Oh, mention it as much as you like.

(*Artist Descending*, p. 35)

Or consider this, from *Professional Foul* (p. 77):

McKENDRICK: He's being mysterious. I think it's a woman.
ANDERSON: (*To Chetwyn*) What were you doing?
CHETWYN: I was meeting some friends.
McKENDRICK: He's being mysterious. I don't think it's a woman.

—it is a gag, and yet it is briskly appropriate to McKendrick's hasty and fundamentally uninterested classification of people and actions.

In *Every Good Boy* Sacha's geometrical axioms become ironically distorted first by his own protests—'A plane area bordered by high walls is a prison not a hospital' (p. 26)—and later by the musical lunatic, Ivanov: 'A triangle with a bass is a combo. . . .' In the same play we see a reversed-transmutation joke, where the words change but the threat is the same and its manipulation of a human situation appears nakedly:

DOCTOR: Look, if you'll eat something I'll send for your son.
ALEXANDER: I don't want him to come here.
DOCTOR: If you don't eat something I'll send for your son.

(*Every Good Boy*, p. 31)

Finally one can note the joke of imminent catastrophe repeatedly avoided. This is stock material of farce (for example, in *On the Razzle*, Weinberl's and Christopher's near-encounters with Zangler in Vienna, and their many appearances and disappearances through doors, chimney, trapdoor, shute, or in tartan 'drag') and Stoppard uses it throughout *Dirty Linen* (Maddie's undress repeatedly unnoticed). In *Hound* it also mocks theatrical convention: everyone fails to notice the corpse on stage until Inspector Hound himself, about to abandon his murder enquiry because no one has actually been murdered, find himself standing on top of it. ('Is there anything you have forgotten to tell me?'—p. 33.) It is a corpse again in *Jumpers*, always appearing as soon as George leaves the bedroom and being obscured when he re-enters: this is a joke, but also a vivid visual symbol of the fact of evil which George is not able to notice; moreover, it has been anticipated dumb-show fashion in the prologue, when Crouch carrying drinks repeatedly strays in and out of the path of the swinging secretary. The simple farce joke becomes part of the interlocking ironic artifice of the play.

5 · TALKING

Perhaps it is the words one notices first, in Stoppard. Later the sense of theatre, the craftsmanship, the thinking and the caring may seem more important; but at first one is dazzled—the cliché seems accurate—by the brilliance of the verbal polish. Stoppard comes across as fluent to the point of facility, gifted with the gab of the Irish: Wilde, Shaw, Joyce, Beckett, and perhaps through these if not directly, Swift. The brilliance also seems to have an academic element: he might well be taken for a University Wit.

As in the plays themselves, things are not all they appear. Stoppard was born Czech; he was eventually brought up to speak English, but in India, moving to England only at the age of nine. His education was traditionally academic but he threw it up in boredom at seventeen. He has been self-taught since then and rather relishes the gaps in his literary education. He reads a great deal now, but, he says, 'very slowly'. Writing, he revises 'each page half a dozen times, four times or twenty times' as he goes (*Theatre Quarterly*, summer 1974); and actors speak of his almost brooding deliberation if a word is to be changed. His own speaking voice is rather meticulous, with time to savour a word.

Perhaps it is not facility we are talking about, so much as energy. The initial idea for a play comes, Stoppard has more than once said, very reluctantly, but once started, the writing is self-fertilizing. Whatever this energy is in Stoppard, it has little to do with creating relationships or with character development (except in *Night and Day*). It is partly theatrical and partly comic, as we have seen; and it is partly a lively delight in—and an alert suspicion of—language itself. Behind these lie a special ear for words, and particularly for the contradictions, ambiguities and double-truths always unstable within them.

It is playing; but it's also digging for truth. Stoppard began work as a journalist, and the critique of the Press in *Night and Day* is still offered almost from within the ranks, and not without relish. To Ronald Hayman in 1974 he spoke of spending an hour a day reading the national newspapers; on the other hand, 'My time for reading fiction had been spent. "Your time is up. Come in Number 7." Because the time I had left was only sufficient to read factual and expository, non-imaginative material.'

The drive is towards knowledge rather than intuitive insight; the separate enthusiasms for journalism and for philosophy are both rootings for truth. And they struggle alongside in the old trench warfare of language.

Mid-twentieth-century philosophy laid heavy emphasis on our dependence on language and on its inadequacy. Words enable us to form concepts, yet trip us up in the most elementary ways. George is hardly caricaturing when he tells us that 'the subject, "Man—good, bad, or indifferent", is in fact the same every year but there is enough disagreement about its meaning to ensure a regular change of topic.' His own difficulty in beginning—'Is God?' or later 'Are God?'—is a failure even to leave the runway, in spite of his engines of academic training.

To Stoppard language is an *aspect* of human life; it happens to be one he enjoys and in which he has flair, but he warns us against over-estimating its importance, and the games, mockery, relish and cherishing of it which he offers are only part of his general humane and comic statement. It is a *humorous* view, most of the time: man's self-importance is ill-founded, but there can be a solidarity in recognizing our inadequacy. It is *affectionate*: talking, however clumsy, is vitality; its mazes are interesting and often amusing, like people themselves, like living itself. It is *troubled*: if language, our closest ally, can so betray us, can be so easily distorted by commercial or totalitarian forces, what chances of survival exist for truth and value? And finally there is a faith beyond it; through language Stoppard argues that there is an abstract reality beyond language, which cannot be damaged because it 'precedes utterance' (*Professional Foul*), because 'it is knowable but not nameable' (*Jumpers*). Here, as it were, language bows the knee.

The humorous statement about language pervades Stoppard's work, and has been partly sketched above. This chapter begins with his affection for language and delight in it; and then looks at how he dissects its treachery. Finally we shall look at how Stoppard uses names.

It would be a mistake to think that Stoppard always presses his language to deviousness. In all the more serious plays there are sustained passages of coherent and felicitous argument in the Shavian tradition. Ros and Guil have few problems with language though they meet difficulty in almost everything else. They voice their perplexities fully, Guil with eloquence and traces of a philosophical training, Ros more colloquially but still with relative ease. Here Stoppard allows himself a neo-classic lyricism (briskly dismissed by John Weightman as 'kitsch') which is perhaps justifiable in the 'stagey' world of the play and is well done of its kind:

> It could have been—a bird out of season, dropping bright-feathered on my shoulder. . . . It could have been a tongueless dwarf standing by the road to point the way . . .
>
> (Guil, p. 20)

> A man standing in his saddle in the half-lit half-alive dawn banged on the shutters and called two names. He was just a hat and a cloak levitating in the grey plume of his own breath, but when he called we came. That much is certain—we came . . . we are comparatively fortunate; we might have been left to sift the whole field of human nomenclature, like two blind men looting a bazaar for their own portraits. . . .
>
> (Guil, p. 29)

The Player's set-piece on pp. 46–7 is particularly sonorous and indulgent and earns an ironic slow handclap from Guil when it is over (the dramatist getting it both ways). There are also some fairly cavalier shifts of linguistic mode; on p. 63 the Player can pass from 'but occasionally, from out of this matter, there escapes a thin beam of light that, seen at the right angle, can crack the shell of mortality' to 'had to change the plot a bit but I thought it would be effective, you know—and you wouldn't believe it, he just *wasn't* convincing!'

In *Jumpers* George, in spite of considerable problems along the way, is allowed to voice with some grandeur his beliefs (pp. 53–5, 71–2) and Stoppard clearly wants the audience to attend sympathetically. Dotty too has moments of eloquence, the voice admittedly tending to become Stoppard rather than Dotty: compare the Player in *Rosencrantz* (p. 63) 'They can die heroically, comically, ironically, slowly, suddenly, disgustingly, charmingly, or from a great height' with Dotty (p. 41):

Things ... can be green, or square, or Japanese, loud, fatal, waterproof or vanilla-flavoured; and the same for actions, which can be *disapproved of*, or comical, unexpected, saddening, or good television, variously, depending on who frowns, laughs, jumps, weeps or wouldn't have missed it for the world.

The arguments about art in *Travesties* are, again, articulate and 'straight'—the crookedness is in the way Stoppard thrusts one against another with apparently equal conviction and without resolving the conflict. Tzara on p. 39 is almost quoting from Shaw's *Major Barbara* (Undershaft: 'No, my friend; you will do what pays us. You will make war when it suits us, and keep peace when it doesn't. ...'). Shaw too shuffled puppet-characters around to develop arguments; and Shaw placed all his money on the efficacy of language. His plays do demonstrate the two-dimensional tendency of reliance on straight dialectic—which Stoppard avoids by his various comic and theatrical subversions. A Stoppard argument is not allowed to stay still for long. My point here, however, is that for substantial stretches of *Travesties* and other plays the subversion is *not* linguistic.

Similarly Stoppard often relishes rhetoric and expressive language. In *Rosencrantz* it tends to be histrionic and camped-up; in *Travesties* it borrows the fluent elegance of Wilde for many very unWildean statements. *Night and Day* is highly competent realist writing, with a number of 'big speeches'—try Wagner on pp. 53–4, Milne on p. 61, Mageeba on pp. 84–5, and Ruth on p. 91; there are also superb brief moments: 'The populace and the popular press. What a grubby symbiosis it is. Which came first? The rhinoceros or the rhinoceros bird?' (p. 48) and 'I lost my view of myself. I was unembarrassable.' (p. 69).

The eighteenth-century epigram or moral 'sentiment' appears a good deal. Sometimes it is shifty in the mode of Archie:

Religious faith and atheism differ mainly about God; about Man they are in accord.

(*Jumpers*, p. 68: this is Archie's 'careful phrasing').

Unlike mystery novels, life does not guarantee a denouement; and if it came, how would one know whether to believe it?

(*Jumpers*, p. 81)

I know that in this loop of tape there is some truth about how we live, Donner. These unheard sounds which are our silence stand as a metaphor—a correspondence between the limits of hearing and the limits of all knowledge: and whose silence is our hubbub?

(*Artist Descending*, p. 53: Beauchamp in fact *misinterprets* the tape)

Sometimes it is simply elegant:

Surely belief in man could find room for man's beliefs?

(*Jumpers*, p. 84)

Language is a finite instrument crudely applied to an infinity of ideas.

(*Jumpers*, p. 63)

An artist is the magician put among men to gratify capriciously their urge for immortality.

(*Travesties*, p. 62)

And sometimes it burns off all irony:

The easiest way of knowing whether good has triumphed over evil is to examine the freedom of the artist.

(*Travesties*, p. 39)

No, no, each one is vital and every moment counts—what other reason is there for trying to work well and live well and choose well?

(*Artist Descending*, p. 51)

There is a sense of right and wrong which precedes utterance.

(*Professional Foul*, p. 90)

They have forgotten their mortality. Losing might be their first touch of it for a long time.

(*Every Good Boy*, p. 29)

Considerable parts of Stoppard's plays, then, employ traditional strengths of rhetoric. But he is more interested than most dramatists in the fact of language itself. Often the codes confuse and break down, but Stoppard is also impressed by how well they stand up; and a good deal of comedy is made out of meanings which will not lie down, as in the vulgarity of much of Dogg-language to an English-speaking listener.

Stoppard's interest in Dogg-language goes beyond joking. In 1974, looking back to the 1971 play in which it originated, he said:

I was really excited by the idea of the language I was using having a double existence. One of the things I hope I'll do one day is really to make full use of that little idea....

(to Hayman, 1974)

In the preface to the later play, *Dogg's Hamlet, Cahoot's Macbeth*:

The appeal to me consisted in the possibility of writing a play which had to teach the audience the language the play was written in. The present text is a modest attempt to do this: I think one might have gone much further.

This makes it all sound like a serious linguistic experiment, especially when it originates in as distinguished a source as Wittgenstein. The broadness of the verbal humour ('LADY: (*Nicely*) Scabs, slobs, yobs, yids, spicks, wops ...') and Stoppard's readiness to bend the rules (the speech ends 'frankly can't stick kids. Mens sana in corpore sano') compromise it as an experiment; but to some extent the audience does learn the language, though not so suddenly as Easy (their link-man), who becomes proficient at a stroke on p. 30, anticipating the later remark that 'You don't learn it, you catch it.' Our main fun is in recognizing the familiar rhythms beneath unfamiliar and apparently subversive collections of words, as in the classified football results: 'RADIO: Oblong Sun, Dogtrot quite, Flange dock; Cabrank dock, Blanket Clock quite; Tube Clock dock, Handbag dock ...' (p. 25).

To me Dogg-language is most interesting once the Shakespeare is added. The moment (p. 18) in which, in the middle of their sandwiches the Dogg-speaking schoolboys suddenly mutter the opening scene of *Hamlet* makes me laugh aloud, especially since they hardly understand the words which to us are the first comprehensible ones in Stoppard's play. And the use of Dogg-language as a subversive medium to bewilder the Inspector is a splendid resolution of a situation otherwise difficult to resolve comically. It is arbitrary—it has nothing to do with Prague, and indeed Easy is still prattling about the A412 and Rickmansworth—but its zany independent logic also subverts the police State ('If it's not free expression I don't know what it is!'—p. 75). In spite of the symbolic wall shutting off the action at the end, the Dogg-language makes it feel like a victory. In passing we can note that the Inspector is allowed moments of his own private language, on p. 76 ('Wilco zebra over! . . . Green Charlie Angels 15 out') but it stands no chance against the power of Shakespearean rhythms and glorious ludicrousness:

MACBETH: Rafters Birnam cakehops hobble Dunsinane,
           fry counterpane nit crossly window-framed,
           fancifully oblong!

The Lady's Speech-Day address recalls other aspects of Stoppard's joy in language itself. First, it has its own grating sound-music—mostly monosyllabic, short-vowelled, and consonantal; though avoiding the notoriously obscene ones, it is made up largely of four-letter words. Stoppard is interested in the way such words (often described, more or less accurately, as 'Anglo-Saxon') tend to cluster together, and in their assonance. The fact that brats both 'pule' and 'puke' would have interested Shakespeare (his own phrase is 'mewling and puking'); that, a

little older, they tend to have 'rank socks' and 'dank snotrags'
would have pleased James Joyce. This is language hanging
together in ways that seem beyond coincidence. It is also brilliant as a compression of all that is nastiest about children,
advancing through adolescence and, in the final phrase 'bank
kickbacks', into adulthood. Within itself it contains at least one
brisk and subtle linguistic progress: 'catch pox, pick spots,
scabs, padlocks'.

The most extended use of this percussive music is in the
restaurant names of *Dirty Linen*. The obsessional chants of
Maddie's attempts to memorize what she must forget introduce
the music: 'To see the moon come up—forget Crockford's,
Claridges, Coq d'Or—remember the Crock of Gold, Box Hill,
the Crooked Clock and the Green Door—' (*Dirty Linen*, p. 24).

Later four M.P.s declaim their alibis. The restaurant-names
are 'Anglo-Saxon', with short vowels (mainly 'o') and recurrent
alliteration of the hard 'c'—they are streamers flying round the
phallic maypole-word 'Cock', which they are attempting to
deny. The names become—though anything is possible in
English pub-names—less and less likely: the Cross Cook, the
Crooked Grin, the Odd Sock . . . but the sound-pattern is main-
tained. Then:

WITHENSHAW: I didn't see you at the Cocked Hat—I went on to the
Cox and Box.

McTEAZLE: I was at the Cox and Box, and the Cooks Door, the Old
Chest, the Dorchester, the Chesty Cook and—er—Luigi's.

ALL: Luigi's?

McTEAZLE: At King's Cross.

CHAMBERLAIN: I was at King's Cross; in the Cross Keys and the Coal
Hole, the Golden Goose, the Coloured Coat and the Côte- d'Azur.

(*Dirty Linen*, pp. 49–50)

The solecism of 'Luigi's'—long-vowelled, Mediterranean
(McTeazle shows by his hesitation that he is upsetting the
music)—is redeemed by its setting, 'King's Cross', which
restores the sound-pattern. But it is the beginning of the end: a
moment later all four admit to having been at the Coq d'Or, the
tension relaxes, and soon Maddie herself extends the music into

such new sounds as 'Selfridges' and 'the Metropole'. In Maddie's final climactic chant assonance is generous but the obsession with the 'cock' sound is gone: the flow is open and easy, redolent (we may say, hurling ourselves into Pseuds' Corner) of promiscuity but not of concealment. The speech is worth studying as an example of Stoppard never giving up his attempts 'to inject some sort of interest and colour into every line', which may take the form of the realism and little verbal hop of 'Bob and the other Bob', or of the assonantal innuendo of 'Foo Luk Fok', or of the same name in four 'registers'—'With Mickey and Michael and Mike and Michelle', or of the alliterative rhyming sequence 'in the Westbury with Corkie and in the Churchill with Chalky. I was at the Duke of York, the Duke of Clarence ...', or, finally, of the hilarious grace-note—after all the commonplace names—of 'Plantagenet'.

Dirty Linen also makes fun of the now rather dated English intellectual tendency to use a Continental phrase instead of the straightforward native tongue. The first ten speeches of the play are entirely in Latin or French (with one Spanish exception); the affectation recurs in the repeatedly mentioned restaurant 'Le Coq d'Or' and in a broad caricature of the editorial style of *The Times* and the *Guardian* (pp. 52–3); and it is revived in the final pages (French's speeches pp. 71–2), with Maddie herself—the straightforward unpretentious one—rising to 'Finita la Commedia' for the last line of all. The first English words of the play are apologized for: 'Pardon my French.'

Travesties opens with a grander version of the same joke. The first words we hear are a 'cut-up' poem of Tzara's—English words assembled in a meaningless jumble, except that they just happen to make sense as rather clumsy *French*. Cecily shushes for silence; Joyce and Gwendolen chant Latin and early English and 'Uh-hum's' at each other, and the Lenins chatter animatedly in Russian. Here, in the medium of linguistic rather than visual absurdity, we have the familiar Stoppard pattern of a grotesque combination of circumstances for which there will prove to be logical reasons.

Minor byplay is made with other linguistic codes. The dissidents, in *Every Good Boy*, are represented as essentially ordinary people who have lost their individuality in their treatment by the State; this is done by simply calling them A,B,C,D etcetera (and by not omitting 'I' from the alphabetical sequence Stoppard adds another momentary *frisson* to Alexander's account—p. 23). Even the children's joke 'You see, I see: UC, IC' is worked for what it's worth in the committee in *Albert's Bridge*, as a snook cocked at the pompous algebra of Fitch ('The resultant equation determines the variable factor X—i.e. the number of painters required to paint surfaces A at speed B within time C.' (p. 12)). The lack of sympathetic interest in the countries visited by the hard-bitten reporter Wagner, in *Night and Day*, is effectively shown by his caricature of Kambawe place-names (p. 28). On pp. 73–5 of *Professional Foul* we listen at some length to the artificially slow and meticulous telephone dictation by journalists summarizing the England–Czechoslovakia match. The journalists' tone is expressionless (though we note the amusing contrast between two different newspaper styles) and their exaggerated articulation sounds mechanical—but Anderson is intently involved; through the strange medium he lives through the drama of the match, and his expression is that of a man watching a tragedy.

Within a single language there are different vocabularies, formal and vernacular, distant and intimate, called by the linguisticians 'registers'. Good realist dramatists take pains to get these right, and to differentiate characters by the words they use. To read, say, a Wesker speech aloud is to feel rapidly in the shoes of another personality; the same is true of Shakespeare's prose, for example of Falstaff, Hamlet, or Iago. In Shakespeare's verse, on the other hand, one is often more conscious of shared modes between characters within a particular play; and of the distinctiveness of one *play* from another. Claudius and Hamlet, ironically, often speak rather alike; so do Macbeth and his wife; so do Antony and Cleopatra. In Jonson's great comedies the images delineate character, but the images (and diction) are of the same *kind*. Wilde's characters seem to try to speak as much like each other as possible: the voice is Oscar's, there is one acceptable register and the rest of the world is cheerfully excluded.

These and other examples may be remembered in case there is a feeling that Stoppard's plays are unusual in the frequent tendency of their characters to be energetic marionettes speaking in a single, fluent, erudite, and witty voice. Generally, this presents no problems. One hostage may be granted readily—*Enter a Free Man*. This is the early work of a writer not yet bold enough to give his characters the elegant brilliance of his very special marionettes, and not sufficiently experienced or informed to give them the consistency of realism. In three pages Riley can shift from ''course I always go home late, I've got to, you see, because of my work' to 'indoor plants have withered and died on a million cream-painted window-sills, attended by haphazard housewives bearing arbitrary jugs of water'.

The former is closer to realism, the latter (distinctively in its adjectives) is Stoppard, and more entertaining. There are hints of similar blurring in the early radio character of Gladys (*If You're Glad*) but the stylization of verse and the fantasy nature of the whole piece excuse them. We are into the puppet world, and none the worse for that. Albert, in another radio play, is allowed, by virtue of his philosophy degree, unashamed linguistic sport:

I'll have to get myself articled to a philosopher.... Start at the bottom. Of course, a philosopher's clerk wouldn't get the really interesting work straight off. I know that. It'd be a matter of filing the generalizations, tidying up the paradoxes, laying out the premises before the boss gets in—that kind of thing; but after I've learned the ropes I might get a half-share in a dialectic, perhaps, and work up towards a treatise....

(pp. 14–15)

There is perhaps an echo of Hamlet at the graveside ('is this the fine of his fines, and the recovery of his recoveries'); the joke anyway is a linguistic one particularly popular in English: the application of the vocabulary of one activity to another.

The plays which might have been handicapped by implausible Stoppardian elegance and lack of characterization by register are, of course, the realist successes, *Professional Foul* and *Night and Day*. But here, where it matters, the craftsmanship of register is assured. Even when Anderson is speaking about football to football players, and at his most colloquial, he is—without a trace of caricature—distinctively himself:

> I realize it's none of my business—I mean you may think I'm an absolute ass, but—(*Pause*) Look, if Halas takes a corner he's going to make it short—almost certainly—push it back to Deml or Kautsky....
>
> (p. 59)

Not only the 'absolute ass' but also, more subtly, the 'almost certainly' are what the football coach *wouldn't* say and the professor would. A moment later McKendrick joins him and makes his massive *gaffe* (which has originated on p. 50):

> McKENDRICK: Good morning! You've got together then?
> ANDERSON: A colleague. Mr McKendrick...
> McKENDRICK: You're Crisp. (*He takes Crisp's hand and shakes it.*) Bill McKendrick. I hear you're doing some very interesting work in Newcastle. Great stuff. I still like to think of myself as a bit of a left-winger at Stoke. Of course, my stuff is largely empirical—I leave epistemological questions to the scholastics—eh, Anderson? ...
>
> (pp. 59–60)

Visually, in their suits, football players might pass for academics, and academics as football fans (after all, Anderson *is* a fan). For a moment, to our amusement and vicarious embarrassment, the diction overlaps—'a bit of a left-winger at Stoke'—before flying wildly apart; but the manner and register *don't* overlap, and we realize, interestingly, that Anderson would probably not have introduced McKendrick to a fellow *philosopher* as 'Mr', and that a young philosopher might permit himself to be patronized like this ('Great stuff') by another philosopher but that the *footballer* may reasonably feel insulted. We can also notice how McKendrick's bluff, crashing idiom is distinguishable from the rapid, nervy, darting style—always aware of his interlocutor's possible reaction—of Anderson. Then, with 'empirical', 'epistemological' and 'scholastics', and still more a moment later with 'neo-Hegelians or Quinian neo-Positivists', we are into a different Stoppard game, the language which though English is so specialized and unfamiliar that it appears foreign. The whole brief scene is both *echt* Stoppard and also realistic; it is finely characterized—McKendrick's unawareness is what the play's partly about, and culminates in his being picked as the unwitting carrier of Hollar's manuscript. And at the same time a further point is made about *visual* confusion: footballers for academics, television faces for personal acquaintances.

Test the linguistic registers of the characters in *Night and Day*, and they stand up surely. Geoffrey Carson is allowed the telling phrase 'rotter' but is not caricatured. Wagner, Milne and Ruth each have fluent tongues and ironic perceptions, but none is singly the Stoppard voice and they are not alike, even when their perceptions are about *words*. Listen: 'I've given up on place names here—they all sound like games you play on board ship. If a place isn't called Tombola it's called Housey-housey.' The deliberate insensitivity of this—and its datedness—are Wagner, hard-bitten, Australian, in his forties. Now:

> I'm sorry—I was just taken aback. I never got used to the way the house Trots fell into the jargon back in Grimsby—I mean, on any other subject, like the death of the novel, or the sex life of the editor's secretary, they spoke ordinary English, but as soon as they started trying to get me to join the strike it was as if their brains had been taken out and replaced by one of those little golf-ball things you get in electric typewriters.... 'Betrayal' ... 'Confrontation' ... 'Management' ... My God, you'd need a more supple language than that to describe an argument between two amoebas.
>
> (p. 37)

'House Trots' is right for Milne's age, 'taken aback' and 'little golf-ball things' for his middle-class background, and the

'electric typewriters' for the inexperienced journalist still notic-
ing the equipment of the office. Most convincing here—and
always the hardest thing to get right—is the rhythm, which is
very much that of the chattering youngster. Now Ruth:

> ... no, no it isn't that. It isn't even—or anyway not entirely—the
> way it was written up, or rather snapped together in that Lego-set
> language they have, so that poor Geoffrey's wife, a notably hard-boiled
> zoologist who happens to breed rare parakeets, and who incautiously
> admitted to a reporter that, yes she would like to give me up, and yes,
> she would have him back, was instantly dubbed Heartbreak Parrot
> Woman In Plea for Earl's Brother.
>
> (p. 48)

The rhythm is premeditated here—Ruth is creating a rhetorical period, and loving it; it is colloquial but stylish, and the
upper-crust drawl is particularly clear in the adverbs—'notably', 'incautiously', and 'instantly'. Upper-crust or not, as
mother of an eight-year-old she is quite likely to know about
Lego. . . .

Still on the subject of the Press, the slightly prissy and
academic language of the English-public-school-educated
African leader is again finely caught:

> I did not believe a newspaper should be part of the apparatus of the
> state; we are not a totalitarian society. But neither could I afford a
> return to the whims of private enterprise.
>
> (p. 85)

These few examples, which are representative, indicate how
subtly Stoppard can handle idiom and usage when he wishes. He
also takes a lively interest in the difference of register within one
speaker, especially when, as is the case with Mageeba here, this
has been artificially extended by education. The climax of *Night
and Day* is in part a linguistic event: a moment after the lines just
quoted, the deceptive heavy elegance of Mageeba's prose steps,
almost gravely, into a pun which is at best unfunny and at worst
sinister ('relatively free press . . . a free press which is edited by
one of my relatives'); and then erupts:

(*Shouting*) So it doesn't go crawling to uppity niggers!—so it doesn't let traitors shit on the front page!—so it doesn't go sucking up to liars and criminals! . . .

(p. 85)

If You're Glad demonstrates linguistic registers in almost textbook precision near its opening, when five characters enter on the first, third, fifth, seventh, and ninth strokes of Big Ben respectively, and each exchanges greetings with the Porter and later with the First Lord. The social nuances of 'Tommy', 'Tom', 'Mr Thompson', 'Thompson' and of 'my lord', 'Your Lordship', 'Lord Coot' and 'Cooty' are calculated to make Americans crow with incredulous delight. I suppose it is conceivable, on the other hand, that Geoffrey Carson wouldn't notice anything funny about them. ('We're Geoff and Ruth to everyone round here. . . . Isn't that right, Francis?/Yes, sir, Mr Carson.')

Mageeba's deliberate linguistic nose-dive, just quoted, has a number of antecedents in Stoppard. Birdboot, answering the phone on stage, and flannelling his wife with his prattle about 'keeping *au fait* with the world of the paint and the motley', is suddenly reduced to 'I love your little pink ears and you are my own fluffy bunny-boo' (*Hound*, p. 36). Joyce, left alone onstage after the baffling and almost portentous opening of *Travesties*, suddenly declaims a limerick. Two pages later Carr's sketch of Joyce passes through convolutions of prissiness into the sudden 'in short a liar and a hypocrite, a tight-fisted, sponging, fornicating drunk not worth the paper, that's that bit done' (p. 23) and there are several similar collapses before the monologue is over. Towards the end of the limerick sequence (pp. 33–5) Gwendolen's attempts to preserve decorum in fact lead her into the biggest lapse herself: 'I thought he was going to say "Shit on it". (*Her hand flies, too late, to her mouth.*)' (p. 35).

The limerick sequence itself, led as it is by Joyce, is characteristic of Joyce's own enjoyment of words as playthings, which Stoppard to some extent shares. Examples have been given earlier (the 'Anglo-Saxon' sound-patterns of *Dirty Linen* or

Dogg's Hamlet, or the use of pun); here we can note the creative transmutation of a word: to Joyce Tzara speaks of 'the right to urinate in different colours'; when Cecily speaks to Carr (posing as Tristan), it has become 'ruminate in different colours'—a play on words, a suggestion of bowdlerization for the feminine speaker, and—mainly—a new joke which is more genuinely surrealistic than the Dadaism it sprang from. When Joyce uses the phrase 'to conjure with' he immediately starts a conjuring act. A more serious point is made by Dotty in *Jumpers*:

> He'd stolen a march while you were still comparing knowledge in the sense of having-experience-of, with knowledge in the sense of being-acquainted-with, and knowledge in the sense of inferring facts with knowledge in the sense of comprehending truths, and all the time as you got more and more acquainted with, though no more comprehending of, the symbolic patterns on my Persian carpet, it was knowing in the biblical sense of screwing you were learning about....
>
> (p. 36)

To summarize so far: Stoppard's respect or enjoyment of language appear in traditional rhetoric, in languages as codes to be learnt, in sound-music, in 'foreign' patterns within a single language, in the variety of linguistic register, and in the creative suggestion of words. We now go on to language as the source of error, an even richer field.

The philosophical orthodoxy of the mid-twentieth century both attached great importance to language and also analysed fairly devastatingly its inefficiency. The combined effect tends to be reductive; and George in *Jumpers* and Anderson in *Professional Foul*, Stoppard's two supposed experts, are both determined to break out of the circle, for which they show a certain contempt. To George, McFee's reductive analysis of 'good' 'combines simplicity with futility'. To Anderson, 'a lot of chaps pointing out that we don't always mean what we say, even when we manage to say what we mean' are largely irrelevant; it costs him nothing to grant them their case ('Personally I'm quite prepared to believe it') or even collect 'little curiosities' for them ('it's like handing round a bag of liquorice allsorts. They're terribly grateful.'). George and Anderson clearly have Stoppard's sympathy; on the other hand, he is much more interested than they are in the treacheries of language, for laughter and for the reasons behind laughter. The comic recognition is a step of humility, on the road to self-knowledge: we are not as logical as we would like to be, nor as lucid, nor as accurate.

Anderson's 'little curiosity' for the linguistic philosophers at the opening of *Professional Foul* is the realization that an *old* photograph makes him *young*. Words turn on their heel like this frequently in Stoppard, as indeed in the immediately preceding exchange ('I wasn't sure it was you. Not a very good likeness./I assure you this is how I look.').

Later a linguistic philosopher explains how 'Mary says to John, "Well, you didn't eat very well, but at least you ate well."' This throws the Prague interpreters into bewilderment: the point Stone is so learnedly labouring is in fact merely a trick of idiom in one language only, not a profound insight. The trick itself occurs twice in *Night and Day*: 'How did you find him?/A bit excitable but quite—/How did you *find him*?' (p. 31) and 'How can you get back into that place?/... There's no way you can get me back ... Oh ... How can *you* ...' (p. 41).

Neatly, a rather similar flick is made by Anderson himself as Stone is speaking:

McKENDRICK: Do you ever wonder whether all this is worth while?
ANDERSON: No.
McKENDRICK: I see what you mean.

(p. 62)

—the cautious questioning of a normally accepted *positive* is turned into an unquestionable negative.

The Freudian slip is what happens when we say what we mean (unconsciously), instead of what we mean to say. A crisp little variant on it is when Moon (the *Hound* one) takes a Birdboot cliché which was probably *not* a Freudian slip and turns it into one which does in fact indicate Birdboot's concealed intention:

BIRDBOOT: She's new, from the provinces, going straight to the top. I don't want to put words into your mouth but a word from us and we could make her.

MOON: I suppose you've made dozens of them, like that.

(p. 12)

Cliché is always fair game for Stoppard. The whole of p. 15 of *Enter a Free Man* is an anthem of clichés, ending 'Gurkhas are short./But exceedingly brave for their size./Fearless.' Martello in *Artist Descending* is making a statue in cliché: hair of ripe corn, teeth of pearls, ripe pears for breasts, swan-feathers for the swan-like neck. Sometimes the clichés are so time-honoured and gathered with such affection that they take on the air of noble tradition, like robins or snow-covered stage-coaches on Christmas cards, or a sort of pop art. Thus, a few moments after the lines quoted above, Moon says in all seriousness to Birdboot: 'Who was that lady I saw you with last night?'

The whole of the play-within-the-play in *Hound* is pop art of this kind.

Stoppard's satire of cliché often has more bite to it than this, however: the bite of George Orwell in his essay *Politics and the English Language*. If the limits of our language mark the limits of our thought, then cliché is pseudo-thought, an opting-out, sometimes at the moment when honest thinking is most needed. The idealistic Jacob Milne has evidently read Orwell at school (see the quotation above, p. 105).

Like many subsequent writers Orwell also had amusement out of the tendency of stale clichés to breed surreal mixtures of metaphor. There are many examples in Stoppard, such as:

You wouldn't take standing room only in your sitting-room lying down.

(*Cahoot's Macbeth*, pp. 53–4)

a vast flat plain stretches like an ocean, waiting to receive my footprints

(*Enter a Free Man*, p. 32)

when the smoke has cleared from the Augean stables, the little flame of our love will still be something no one else can hold a candle to

(*Dirty Linen*, p. 23)

At one point in *Cahoot's Macbeth* the satire develops into a relatively bitter and serious indictment. The speaker is the Inspector.

> The way I see it, life is lived off the record. It's altogether too human for the written word, it happens in pictures ... metaphors. ... A few years ago you suddenly had it on toast, but when they gave you an inch you overplayed your hand and rocked the boat so they pulled the rug from under you, and now you're in the doghouse. ... I mean, that is pure fact. Metaphorically speaking.
>
> (p. 61)

Words here are respected as little as individuals. 'It's altogether too human', coming from the Inspector, must be one of the most cynical lines in drama. We are alerted to the pictorial quality of metaphor so that we shall notice the more the Inspector's absolute insensitivity to it; and 'pure fact' to him is a débris of metaphor. In spite of its laughs, this is a tough moment in Stoppard. Cahoot is given a brilliant satirical response to one of the stale metaphors—'Now you're in the doghouse.' For the next couple of pages dogs run in and out of the Inspector's rhetoric, while Cahoot *'howls like a dog, barks, falls silent on his hands and knees'*. As 'Macbeth' says, 'He's been made a non-person.'

'Pure fact. Metaphorically speaking,' is an extreme example of the tendency of cliché to destroy meaning (as the word 'literally' is often used to mean its exact opposite). *Albert's Bridge* gives us several laughs of this kind, each of which betrays a loss of meaning which is mildly disturbing and could if extended be really dangerous:

> Clufton Bay Bridge is the fourth biggest single-span double-track shore-to-shore railway bridge in the world bar none
>
> (p. 10)

> If you fell I'd die, Albert./So would I.
>
> (p. 20)

> Mr Chairman, gentlemen, I have served Clufton man and boy for five years.
>
> (p. 33)

This last speech, of Fitch, is worth continuing, since it offers a kind of poetic subversion not common in Stoppard. The italics are mine:

Clufton is the repository of my dreams and boyhood memories, the temple of my hopes to *transform* the running of *a living community to a thing of* precision and efficiency, a cybernetic poem—a programmed *machine* as perfect as a *rose*—

More glancingly, but still with point, we have in *Rosencrantz* the casual remark that 'you can't treat royalty like people with normal perverted desires' (p. 48); and the absurdity—and poignancy, coming from this character in this play—of Ros's

we've been spinning coins for as long as I can remember.
GUIL: How long is that?
ROS: I forget.

(p. 10)

—a joke which Stoppard, perhaps because of its relevance to their situation, thinks worth reviving almost immediately:

GUIL: What's the first thing you remember?
ROS: Oh, let's see . . . The first thing that comes into my head, you mean?
GUIL: No, the first thing you remember.
ROS: Ah. (*Pause*). No, it's no good, it's gone. It was a long time ago.

(p. 11)

Much the same gag comes in *Hound*, when Moon, referring to the failure of his own reviews to be posted on billboards outside theatres, says 'All I ever got was "Unforgettable" on the posters for . . . What was it?' (p. 15).

—where, again, there is a real criticism of cliché's destruction of meaning.

Related to these is the verbal automatism which substitutes for true response. Again, *Albert's Bridge* has an almost Freudian example:

MOTHER: Do you love me, Albert?
ALBERT: Yes.

MOTHER: Yes—what?
ALBERT: Yes please.

(p. 16)

Compare the automatic response of both Archie and George to Dotty's offstage cry of 'Darling!' (*Jumpers*, p. 69). Characteristically Stoppard turns this excellent stage moment to extra point by following it with the simultaneous question 'How is she?' from each man to the other.

Anderson is so accustomed to stalling when asked if he knows philosophers, in whom he has tended to lose interest, that he presents the same automatic defence to the name of the city he is to visit: 'Do you know Prague?/(*Warily*) Not personally. I know the name' (p. 45).

His vagueness at this early stage of the play is hardly less than a general reduction of interest in life, people, and values: he shows alertness only at the idea of football, until the situation of Hollar gradually impinges on him and reawakens the best of him (which Hollar saw as his student years before). He goes, one might say, through layers of cliché, jargon, and forms of words and returns to 'a sense of right and wrong which precedes utterance'.

The dark grimaces of *Jumpers* perhaps sum up this area of Stoppard's humour.

DOTTY (*off*): Help!
(BONES *reacts.* ARCHIE *restrains him.*)
ARCHIE: It's all right—just exhibitionism: what we psychiatrists call 'a cry for help'.

(p. 66)

If cliché gradually and unconsciously destroys meaning, as in this last alarming example, euphemism is a conscious attempt to hide from meaning. Stoppard sends up both in his description of Jane, in the novel *Lord Malquist and Mr Moon* (pp. 15–17), 'at her toilette' (which turns out, by a nice linguistic reversal, to mean sitting on the lavatory):

It was the height of the Season in London, and an onlooker might have been forgiven for wondering why it was that this mere slip of a girl with hair like spun gold, with exquisite features that proclaimed a noble breeding, should sit alone with sadness in her heart . . .

In the best Edwardian gentlemanly style, but with comically misplaced ingenuity, Carr attempts to shield Gwendolen from offence by referring to Oscar Wilde as a 'Gomorrahist'. Her comment on this, after his exit, is pure Stoppard: '(*Absently*): Gomorrahist . . . Silly bugger.'

And four related bits of naughtiness in quick succession slip from the probably innocent lips of Cecily:

It is a play written by an Irish coxcomb and bugbear of the Home Rule sodality, so I hear.
CARR: Your ears deceive you.

(p. 74)

A similar joke, which one can only call euphemism reversed, is Mother's first audible word after having her foot burned (*After Magritte*, p. 15):

MOTHER: *Butter!*
THELMA: (*Primly*) Now there's no need to use language. . . .

And in the midst of the fun of *On the Razzle* there is a gag worth noting here. Melchior's single approval-word is 'classic'.

ZANGLER: Why do you keep using that word? It's stupid.
MELCHIOR: There's nothing stupid about the word, it's just the way some people use it without discrimination.

(p. 15)

This is rich, of course, coming from Melchior himself. But that line 'There's nothing stupid about the word' is a sharp Stoppardian note. Throughout his work the laughter—and the occasional anger—is not at words but at what we do to them.

That language is exploitable as well as innocently misleading is abundantly demonstrated in the vehement exchanges of *Travesties*. In *Jumpers* the exploiter is the smooth-talking Archie (echoed sometimes by Dotty). To Archie is given the almost ultimate challenge of arguing 'that belief in God and the conviction that God doesn't exist amounts to much the same thing' (p. 68).

George, a moment earlier, has touched the heart of his faith; we warm to him and respect him for it, but his very integrity shows itself in a near-breakdown of language: 'All I know is that I think that I know that I know that nothing can be created out of nothing.'

George's relationship with his wife is shown by various verbal oddities. His first words, appearing at the party, are 'For God's sake'. Dotty, ignoring him, refers to her 'unshakeable belief'—merely a sarcasm aimed at the 'incredible' jumpers (she is picking up the tendency of cliché to destroy meaning) yet we are soon to see that she is unbalanced because all her beliefs *have* been shaken. To the musicians she continues: 'I'll do the one about the moon. I'm sure you know it.'—but *she* no longer does, her whole spiritual equilibrium having been damaged by the moon-landings. Everything is now relative: 'to somebody *on* it, the moon is always full, so the local idea of a sane action may well differ from ours' (p. 38). As she shuffles the words and tunes of moon-songs—a vivid image of instability—she blames not herself but the musicians. The only time the words and music fit is when the words have particular relevance to her own condition: 'You saw me standing alone/Without a dream in my heart'.

In the following scene, Dotty's wild cries of 'Help!' 'Murder!' and 'Rape!' interrupt George's rambling dissertation, and are then ignored. We gather that she has literally cried wolf too often, and that George has ceased to attend to her. The result is that not only Dotty's cries but also George's philosophy have lost their force, and the point is made in the linguistic disjunction of their separate modes (as well as in stage-spatial terms—see p. 48 above).

Looking for Thumper, George glances into Dotty's bedroom but ignores her nude body 'sprawled face down and apparently lifeless on the bed'. After searching the bathroom he reappears and without hesitation guesses the book-title she is miming—*The Naked and the Dead*—even though he is unaware that there is a real corpse in the room (the *audience* is to enjoy the extra significance of the title). The book-title game is played by George without interest, automatically. When it recurs—*The Moon and Sixpence*—it again has ironic appropriateness, and this time has involved Dotty in a piece of bland cruelty (leaving the goldfish stranded in the bath) characteristic of a mind at the end of its tether. Archie the goldfish is in fact the second innocent creature to die as a result of Dotty's demented whimsies, though the audience do not learn of either till much later in the play (the first, of course, is the hare Thumper, killed when her cry makes George fire his arrow).

George and Dotty do later communicate with vigour and some coherence; but between them all the time is not only their long-term estrangement (her refusal to sleep with him) but also the body of McFee, of which George is unaware. At several points Stoppard has two characters talking at cross purposes—another aspect of the general vulnerability of language, and more particularly an aspect of George's old-fashioned idealistic isolation: it is always George who suffers even when the misunderstanding (a failure to listen properly) is by Bones:

> BONES: A consummate artist, sir. I felt it deeply when she retired.
> GEORGE: Unfortunately she retired from consummation about the same time as she retired from artistry.
> BONES: It was a personal loss, really.
> GEORGE: Quite. She just went off it. I don't know why.
> BONES: You don't have to explain it to me, sir. You can't keep much from her hard-core fans....
>
> (p. 58)

When George and Dotty discuss 'the crime' (p. 50) George is referring merely to his anonymous phone call to the police. 'One can easily get things out of proportion.' Dotty responds with delighted surprise: 'That's just what Archie said about it,' and George, who has been explaining with distaste to Bones McFee's theory that killing people isn't 'inherently wrong in itself', is now inadvertently allied with Archie's similar remark about the murder of McFee himself. It is comic, but it has also a sadness underlying much of the play—the steady impinging of the amorality of the philosophical jumpers on George's attempt to stand by 'the irreducible fact of goodness'.

Similar misunderstanding is drawn out to still more ludicrous and more painful comedy towards the end of the play, in George's conversation with Crouch (p. 77). Crouch is referring to the killing of McFee and George to that of Thumper; which means that Crouch has to contemplate the idea of Dotty eating McFee's body:

CROUCH: (*Pause*) You mean—raw?
GEORGE: (*Crossly*) No, of course not!—*cooked*—with gravy and mashed potatoes.
CROUCH: (*Pause*) I thought she was on the mend, sir.
GEORGE: Do you think I'm being too sentimental about the whole thing?
CROUCH: (*Firmly*) I do not, sir....

—before George is stunned by Crouch's revelation:

GEORGE: ... Lot of fuss about nothing. I know things got a bit out of hand but ... I'm surprised at your puritanism, Mr Crouch.... A little wine, women, and song....
CROUCH: Yes, sir. Of course, it was the murder of Professor McFee that was the main thing.
(*Long pause.* GEORGE *sits perfectly still, and continues to do so, sightless, deaf, while* CROUCH *speaks.*)

Such misunderstandings, springing from self-absorption and unawareness of others, lie at the heart of *Professional Foul*. In the first conversation, on the aircraft, McKendrick persuades himself that Anderson is up to something politically, and attempts to involve himself. 'I have an open mind about it.' Anderson, still embarrassed about the girlie magazine, assumes that McKendrick is talking about erotica. Realizing this, McKendrick says: 'Perhaps you've come across some of my articles' (p. 48).

ANDERSON: (*Amazed and fascinated*) You mean you write for—? (*He pulls himself up and together.*) Oh—your—er articles—I'm afraid as I explained I'm not very good at keeping up with the philosophical ...

But McKendrick *does* in fact mean a girlie magazine, and he is able to complete his early rout of Anderson by offering him evidence.

Little else in the play goes right for McKendrick, however. With Anderson and Chetwyn he discusses Crisp and Broadbent under the impression that they are philosophers and, as we have seen, actually greets them as such. Later he joins the footballers' bottle party, harangues them—crudely and insensitively—about footballing ethics, and earns a smash in the face. Finally his own dictum of 'reversing a principle' is applied to him by Anderson.

Anderson's self-absorption is expressed in two more crucial examples of parallel conversation. Hollar's phrase 'not a safe conclusion' (p. 55) is taken by Anderson to refer merely to suspect logic. Hollar tries to clear this up, with the simple line, which ought really to shame Anderson, 'I mean, it is not safe for me.' But Anderson still doesn't grasp the brute truth of this. Rather as Hollar and Chetwyn each say that their young sons have a clearer sense of moral justice than clever philosophers do, so here it is Hollar, speaking in a foreign language, who uses the words in their fundamental meaning; Anderson's academic fluency has hidden their meaning from him.

The further parallel conversation is brief but just as telling. Stoppard, who is honourable about giving his audience fair clues before misleading them, has warned us about Chetwyn at the outset: 'Letters to *The Times* about persecuted professors with unpronounceable names. I'm surprised the Czechs gave him a visa' (McKendrick, p. 46). A further clue to the possibility that it is Chetwyn who will be stopped at the airport before departure is the parallel conversation on p. 77.

ANDERSON: Weren't you there for it?
McKENDRICK: No, he sloped off for the afternoon.
ANDERSON: Well, you sly devil, Chetwyn. I bet you had a depressing afternoon. It makes the heart sick, doesn't it.
CHETWYN: Yes, it does rather. We don't know we've been born.

As with 'safe conclusion', as with the clichés quoted earlier from other plays, Anderson can take 'We don't know we've been born' as a conventional whine at the poverty of English football. For Chetwyn, of course, it refers to the very unawareness which Anderson and Stone and McKendrick manifest.

The parallelisms of the 'professional foul' on which the play's title and plot are based are appropriate to the main point: that Anderson and McKendrick are inclined to talk about ethical judgements and philosophical 'rules' as if they *were* merely games; that their habitual language fails to recognize true need and true moral outrage; and indeed that Anderson, the highest man in his field in his country, has for years been more excited by football than by his subject or its human significance. All the misunderstandings of the play thread humorously and also disturbingly in and out of these concerns.

More lightly, but still pointedly, self-absorption is revealed by overlapping independent monologues, like those of very small children playing together. Just before the last example quoted, we observe the conversation of six philosophers at dinner. Two of them, Stone and a Frenchman, are engaged in energetic if fruitless discussion about 'saying' and 'meaning'; McKendrick is asking, without apparently receiving or expecting an answer, whether he is likely to pick up 'a free and easy woman' and whether it would be 'safe' (that word again); Chetwyn is talking about the menu in a desultory fashion to Anderson (they are both upset by their meetings with victims of State oppression during the afternoon—but neither knows of the other's involvement). The resulting montage is funny and ironic and never strays far from the subject of meaning—even McKendrick has to explain what he *means* by the word 'safe'.

CHETWYN: You don't often see goose on an English menu.
STONE: The French have no verb meaning 'I mean'.
CHETWYN: Why's that, I wonder.
STONE: They just don't.
CHETWYN: People are always eating goose in Dickens.

McKENDRICK: Do you think it will be safe?

FRENCHMAN: Par exemple. Je vous dis, 'Qu'cest-ce que vous voulez dire?'

McKENDRICK: I mean one wouldn't want to be photographed through a two-way mirror.

STONE: I don't want to ask you what you would wish to say. I want to ask you what you *mean*. Let's assume there is a difference.

(p. 76)

In *Albert's Bridge* a conversation between Albert and his mother starts in unity and then forks into independent monologue; Albert is talking of his bridge, his mother of Kate. It is in fact to be Kate who brings Albert briefly down to earth (immediately after this conversation)—pp. 15–16.

Finally, names. These are perhaps, psychologically, the most important words of all. Tragic and heroic stories make much of name = identity (Emmanuel, Paul, Siegmund, Stalin; compare also the new name taken on joining a religious community) and of name = reputation (the deaths of Hotspur, Hamlet, Othello and the neo-classical protagonists of Arthur Miller's plays). In the comedy of humours, and in Dickens, names define characters; in much slapstick comedy, children's comics or *Carry On* films, the names are ludicrous or suggestive enough to extract a few laughs in themselves. *The Importance of Being Earnest* turns, lightly enough, on a name and on Victorian themes of the double life, the second identity; somewhere behind its laughter are Dr Jekyll and Mr Hyde, or Oscar Wilde's own clandestine affairs.

Novelists often choose names for characters with great care, and many would endorse Stoppard's comment (to *Theatre Quarterly*, May–June 1974): 'the name itself must be right. All I know is that if you're writing a play and somebody ought to be called Boot and is called Murgatroyd, it's impossible to continue.'

In most of Stoppard's work, though, the names show not the subtle suggestion of those chosen so carefully by Henry James or Iris Murdoch, but the fixed outline of strip-cartoons, through which the head of Thomas Stoppard himself pokes with passages of unlikely verbal fluency. The early Stoppard returns frequently to the same few cartoon outlines. Evelyn Waugh's novel *Scoop* turns on the confusion of two journalists both called Boot; and Stoppard took this name as his pseudonym when reviewing for *Scene* magazine in 1963. Dominic Boot, in the 1964 radio play, was joined in the same year by Jonathan and Samuel Boot of the never-performed television play *This Way Out with Samuel Boot*. Birdboot, the butler in *Lord Malquist and Mr Moon*, lends his name to the reviewer in *Hound*; and the other reviewer is called Moon, taking us again back to the novel and perhaps to the other 1964 radio play *M is for Moon among Other Things*, which in turn was followed in 1967 by a television play (an early version of *Jumpers*) called *Another Moon Called Earth*. (It is almost as if we move in a caricature Islam where there are really very few names to choose from.) *Enter a Free Man* is clearly derivative from Arthur Miller's *Death of a Salesman* and Miller's only significant female character, Linda, lends her name to one of Stoppard's two female characters; the other, Persephone, seems echoed by Penelope in *Another Moon Called Earth*, while George Riley gives his Christian name to George Moore in *Jumpers*, whose *whole* name is cribbed from a real English twentieth-century philosopher (whose wife was also called Dorothy). Bone, Penelope's husband, has his name shifted to the policeman Bones in *Jumpers*. The moon itself is of course an important topic in both plays; the idea of moon-*songs*, however, and of muddling them up, had already been used in the opening of *Albert's Bridge*. Maggie in *A Separate Peace* is a kindred spirit to Maddie in *Dirty Linen*. Coot in *If You're Glad* and Foot in *After Magritte* clearly come from the tribe of Boot and Moon. Even in the realist play *Where are They Now?* (1970) the central character, Gale, got his name from the real journalist John Gale (though the school and the story are fictional), Anderson will clearly grow up to be J. S. Mill Professor of Ethics at Cambridge, and Geoffrey Carson, the manager of the mines in *Night and Day*, is already winning the O.B.E. for services to national industry—as Lady Bracknell says, 'it is obviously the same person'.

One can hardly call this economy: it seems more like a kind of reductive obsession. What I take to be going on in the early Stoppard nomenclature (leaving out *Rosencrantz* where Shakespeare provided all the names except Alfred's) is a determined disclaimer of psychological realism and of 'straight' seriousness. The recycling of the boot and moon names seems like the dramatist's reminder to himself to stay in the cartoon world, which increasingly marked out its own territory. (It may be worth noting that the novels of Samuel Beckett show a similar tendency to revert to 'M' names.) Stoppard told Ronald Hayman:

> In some limited sense I write about the same character a lot, and I think I've got a small, unimportant neatness complex. Occam's razor. Keep the names down. Don't proliferate nomenclature unnecessarily. So I use them whenever they might help.

To other interviewers he has agreed that 'Moon is a person to whom things happen. Boot is rather more aggressive.' Lord Malquist, of course, is associated for us from the novel's second page with a kind of *boot*. 'I'm a Moon myself', Stoppard told Robert Cushman; this is worth insisting on in the face of Kenneth Tynan's attempt to associate Stoppard with Malquistian attitudes.

Jumpers marks the end of this kind of cartoon-naming (the seaside-postcard-suggestiveness of the names in *Dirty Linen* being another sort of stylization)—and takes the opportunity to luxuriate in it. We may be embarrassed by, and try not to notice, the appropriateness of Dotty's name, but we are bound to relish Inspector Bones investigating murder (his brother, we are told, was an osteopath; he changed his name to Foot and became a chiropodist); and, as Sir Archibald Jumper remarks, the Cognomen Syndrome is not only something he studies, it's something he's got. George Moore has similar views to his real antecedent, but Scott and Oates are in sadly reversed relationship. Perhaps the most interesting naming in *Jumpers* is that the goldfish is called Archie—on the one hand, a constant reminder to George, within Dotty's stage-area, of the athletic Vice-

Chancellor; on the other, an unlucky victim of Dotty's craziness (the death of the goldfish Archie is perhaps the only setback which the satanic Sir Archibald receives during the play). The tortoise, Pat, is so called for the sake of two jokes—one about the difficulty of discovering a tortoise's sex, and the other (p. 43) a splendidly awful pun-allusion to *Hamlet*: George thinks he is going to let in Archie; he carries a weapon and it occurs to him facetiously that he *might* use it to kill Archie—a similar thought to that of Hamlet when coming across Claudius praying—'Now I might do it pat.' The hare, Thumper, seems first a victim of Cognomen Syndrome, second a rhyme to Jumper, and third the excuse for a glancing pun at a sad moment—the last page of the play: 'the late Herr Thumper who was innocent as a rainbow'. Each is an example of Stoppard's thriftiness, not missing opportunities.

In *Artist Descending*, later the same year, this particular stylization is avoided, though the play is far-fetched enough in other ways. The three artists have very Continental and arty-sounding names—Martello, Beauchamp, and Donner, the first of which may have come to Stoppard's mind from his reading about James Joyce (*Ulysses* opens in a martello tower overlooking Dublin Bay, in which three students live together). In the earlier radio play, *Where are They Now?*, printed in the same volume, not only is the confusion between two people called Jenkins important, but there are various puns on Marks and the tendency for schoolboys at that time to use nicknames is put to really imaginative use: Marks and his two friends are the three Marx brothers, Groucho, Chico and Harpo, and the best twist in the play concerns our relating these to the three Old Boys, Marks, Brindley and Gale (see pp. 68–9 above).

In *Travesties* Stoppard had no need to invent new names: it was simply a matter of shuffling round those provided. With unusual restraint he avoids re-using the very funny error by which Beauchamp, in the dummy run for *Travesties* which occurs on p. 23 of *Artist Descending*, refers to Tzara as 'Tarzan'; but he makes much of the apparent femininity of the name

Joyce, inverts the real-life status of Bennett and Carr, and enjoys some of the odder real names of Dada-ist artists ('Good old Arp' ... 'Describe Ball by epithet./Unspherical ...'). The neatest twists behind *Travesties*, though, are not Stoppard's at all, but the 'little signs from God' (see p. 238 below).

The non-Shakespearean characters in *Dogg's Hamlet* have alphabetical code-names (Abel, Baker, Charlie, Dogg, Easy, and Fox)—again a disclaimer of psychological characterization. The only named characters in *Every Good Boy* all have the same name, Alexander Ivanov—more or less a Russian John Smith—and the play turns on the State's denial of their individuality.

The early play *Enter a Free Man* is never quite sure whether to be realist or cartoon. Riley's otherwise only-too-normal upper-working-class wife is saddled with the name of Persephone, which he promptly reduces to Percy. Part of Riley's bluster is to invent funny names for the barman (Carmen) and the sailor (Able); part of his lack of real grip on life is his failure even to discover Harry's surname: 'We'll be big business one day ... our name will mean something ... *Riley and* ... (*Pause*) ... Hey, what's Harry's other name?' (p. 73).

In the wholly realist plays, *Professional Foul* and *Night and Day*, the clowning has almost ended: the humour made out of Dick Wagner's name seems that of plausible chance, and the weak gag on Crisp's name is the weary wit of a hardened sports reporter. Ruth's name, on the other hand, is used *seriously* (see p. 64 above). It may just be worth noting the pleasant touch by which the young philosopher Chetwyn, who represents the clearest conviction of moral absolutes in any of the plays, bears the name of an early producer of Stoppard's plays of whom he has spoken warmly, Robert Chetwyn: it is a small nod, but highly characteristic.

The play I have deliberately omitted, of course, is *Rosencrantz*.

Shakespeare's Rosencrantz and Guildenstern are introduced and treated as a pair. The syllables and rhythm of one name can be substituted for the other without affecting the verse, and to prove it we have, very early in their first Shakespearean scene:

KING: Thanks, Rosencrantz and gentle Guildenstern.
QUEEN: Thanks, Guildenstern and gentle Rosencrantz.

(II.ii. 33–4)

Various grotesque options of stage business seem suggested by this odd reversal, and the one Stoppard chooses, reproducing the lines in his own play, is suitably farcical (bottom of p. 27). The main point is, as Kenneth Grose remarks, that 'they are mere ciphers in the royal calculations'. Their own first speeches are of identical length (two half-lines and two full lines each) and each begins by filling up the syllables of a verse line left unfinished by the previous speaker. They are fluent, obsequious, and confederate—and interchangeable; one doubts whether many people, without looking it up, could say whether, for example, it is Rosencrantz or Guildenstern whom Hamlet embarrasses with a recorder.

In Stoppard's play Ros and Guil have a good deal in common with stranded actors. For a long time they are unnamed and never address each other by name; when they need to introduce themselves to the Tragedians, they get their names the wrong way round, and—interestingly—are not *embarrassed* by the error; rather as two actors playing Rosencrantz and Guildenstern might claim it was an understandable slip. But they are not actors. As characters, called into existence for the play only, they are much more like men suffering from amnesia; and their difficulty in being certain of their names is appropriately made symbolic of their general uncertainty of identity, not only of where they came from but of where they are going. Ros throughout the play responds to either name, and although Guil generally seems to have more of a grip of his name, even he is in doubt at the end:

(*He looks round and sees he is alone.*)
Rosen—?
Guil—?'

(p. 95)

Amnesiacs, however, are usually recognized by *other* people: in Stoppard, Ros and Guil are constantly confused by King, Queen and Hamlet as well. It is a source of humour, moment by moment; it suggests problems of identity, of course; finally, like several other aspects of the play, it is a not-too-serious criticism of Shakespeare himself, who appears to have *used* these two characters as shamelessly as Claudius himself; as Clive James has said: 'The mainspring of *Rosencrantz and Guildenstern are Dead* is the perception—surely a compassionate one—that the fact of their deaths mattering so little to Hamlet was something which ought to have mattered to Shakespeare.'

6 · TRAVESTYING

The title of *Travesties* could have been used for several other Stoppard plays. There is probably no precedent for so lively and original an artist choosing so regularly to work in and out of classics, clichés, and popular culture: the nearest parallels are in the twentieth-century visual arts. Even when Stoppard moves closest to the realist well-made play—in *Night and Day*—much of the zip comes from allusion. Dick Wagner ('is he a composer?', 'Wagnerian', 'Compose yourself, Wagner', 'Mr ... Strauss ... I knew it was Richard'); the Beatles ('Help'); 'April in Paris'; *Pygmalion*; Liz Taylor in *Elephant Walk*, *The Winslow Boy*. Tallulah Bankhead, the *Titanic* disaster, Clarissa Harlowe, *Paradise Lost*, Deborah Kerr in *King Solomon's Mines*, 'The Lady is a Tramp', *Othello* and *The Tempest*—all figure, together with abundant reference to and pastiche of British newspaper styles. Each separate allusion is plausible; together they possibly make just too synthetic a hinterland of reference—Stoppard's Africa having the authenticity of the London theatre rather than of the real place. To which Stoppard might however retort that the British in Africa have lived on just this artificial imported and rather dated culture, and that he has got the faded-pop allusions exactly right.

Allusion at times seems to be the petrol that drives the machine, and in *Rosencrantz* and *Travesties* it is virtually the road system. And the normal mode of allusion appears to be that of travesty. A hasty glance may suggest that Stoppard is cutting Shakespeare (Joyce, Lenin, and so on) down to half-size. Moustaches on the Mona Lisa. Is nothing sacred?

Well, no; the first thing to say is that nothing *is* sacred. The artist is free, the art is vulnerable, and it is very important to Stoppard not to get trapped. Much of his artistic instinct seems a distillation of the painting of the 1910s and 1920s. Cubist, he wants to 'dislocate the audience's assumptions'.

There's a Beckett joke which is the funniest joke in the world to me. It appears in various forms but it consists of confident statement followed by immediate refutation by the same voice. It's a constant process of elaborate structure and sudden—and total—dismantlement.

(to Hayman, 1974)

There is no safe point around which everything takes its proper place, so that you see things flat and see how they relate to each other.

(to Hayman, 1976)

We are to see round a point of view, see its backside. A fine, sad example of the Beckett joke is Ruth's comment on her feeling for Milne, at the end of *Night and Day*: 'Well, it was a very elevated, intellectual sort of thing. I wanted to undress him with my teeth.' (p. 94).

Carr's monologue about Joyce and, later, about the trenches presents comically a Cubist restlessness of viewpoint. In *Jumpers* values are in a state of whirling disintegration, like the more extreme of Picasso's or Braque's experiments, culminating in Archie's solo at the beginning of the Coda, with its echoes of Joyce and even more of Beckett's Lucky.

Surrealist pastiche in Stoppard is explicit in the titles and implicit in the content of *After Magritte* and *Artist Descending*, and, filtered through Absurdist drama and popular comedy such as the 1950s Goon Shows, colours most of the plays to some degree. There is however in Stoppard relatively little in the way of actually moustaching the Mona Lisa; a conservative with a high regard for traditional culture, he is not consumed with Dada-ist anger and is rarely satisfied with mere crudity, though there are such moments in *Dogg's Hamlet, Cahoot's Macbeth*, particularly when he slaps a very

large moustache across the tremulous lips of the sleepwalking
Lady Macbeth:

LADY MACBETH: Hat, daisy puck! Hat, so fie! Sun, dock: hoops
malign my cattlegrid! Smallish peacocks! Flaming scots git,
flaming! . . .

(p. 75)

What the eruptions of the early twentieth century did for the
great art of the past was to shake away the ivy of establishment
approval and the wrong kind of reverence. Picasso's drawings
after classical masters respect and develop their originals: he is
not scrawling moustaches but energetically and successfully
thumping the heart of a moribund tradition. Stoppard's dance
in the great cathedral of *Hamlet* is a devout dance; but to dance
in a cathedral you first have to get into the place, clear room, and
tune up the band, probably offending a number of whispering
doorkeepers, vergers and flower-arrangers on the way. If art is
alive for us, then it is in the open, unsheltered from irreverent
winds: vulnerable, mockable, travestiable. This is the feeling in
early twentieth-century art, and by the second half of the century it had tended to permeate popular Western culture as well
as that of the avant-garde.

The error commonly (and understandably) made is to find in
irreverence only cynicism and despair: to see the danger as
necessarily disaster. No doubt some Dada-ists, like some of
their popular successors the 1950s beatniks, the 1970s punks,
shouted not only of the break-up of society and the need to break
up art, but also of their own moral and spiritual break-up. (Nor
should we be patronizing towards that despair.) Iconoclastic
movements will tend to attract vandals. But wherever there is a
preoccupation with the possibility of *art*, cynicism can be only
partial. The modern cathedral (mausoleum?) in which Stoppard
dances is the art of Samuel Beckett, in which the compulsion to
create, and to create stylishly—in proportion and pattern, with
what we tend to call artistic integrity—catches up, includes, and
digests a stark nihilism. Beckett is an extreme, and manifests
exceptionally the tension between nihilism and art. Stoppard

can enjoy Beckett without at all sharing his vision; and Stoppard's plays about Communist states voice a commitment which Beckett would reserve strictly for his private life (notably, in the French Resistance), not his art.

We shall come back to Beckett. The point of mentioning him here is to dismiss the fallacy of nihilist subversion. Tearing the pages out of a Bible and scattering them on the wind does not make its words less valid, any more than kissing it makes them more so. God can stand being mocked, and so can the Mona Lisa and the Prince of Denmark. If they can't—if, as might be true of phoney gurus or cult salon poets, they totter as soon as anyone dares to rock the pedestal—then the sooner they are brought down the better.

Nor is it that *doubt* has emerged in this century: doubt, disbelief, and despair are not new. What has seemed more and more important, as the century has aged, is freedom. The more we have learned of relativity, the more skilled have become the totalitarian persuaders of absolutes; the more eccentric and experimental our art, the more academics, critics, and commentators try to classify it (this book may not escape being one more example). 'Stoppard's hard to write about', the degree-course drama students say; I imagine the dramatist grinning with delight. Central European by birth and a refugee twice in infancy, Stoppard more than most of us needs to feel slippery, able to wriggle.

Nor is it only a negative impulse to freedom, a fear of being caught. What Stoppard and many others feel today is the excellence of pluralism: that it is right to move *among* the philosophers and dance in different grandeurs. 'Not knowing' is not a negative loss of confidence but an alertness, an openness, perhaps a greater trust in life.

Stoppard's dance among the philosophers, his travestying of their intellectual and moral acrobatics, is an exercise of this kind of freedom.

And his travesties have to do with honouring. He speaks of Eliot's *Prufrock* as the insulin to his literary diabetes; and in the matters of travesty and allusion Stoppard and the early Eliot have a good deal in common. For Stoppard's generation as for the previous one, Eliot's was a key twentieth-century voice. For all its irreverences and shaking-free, twentieth-century art looks just as much to the past as did its forerunners; and in *Prufrock* or *The Waste Land* the allusions are intended to work largely like the kick of a gun, throwing a bruised gunner flat on his back while the target stands inviolate and if anything a little grander.

> In the room the women come and go
> Talking of Michelangelo.

From these lines of *Prufrock* Michelangelo looms up large. Whether the name calls up for us first a sensational cloister, an apocalyptic wall, a majestically implausible adolescent, a languorous *Pietà*, or athletes like boa-constrictors, it conjures perhaps the most obviously stupendous genius Eliot could have chosen. The kick back is mainly at Prufrock himself, at his total incapacity for heroism: it would be bad enough if they were talking about Asquith or Elgar or Emerson, but *Michelangelo* ... the butterfly is broken on the wheel. But the kick is also at the drawing-room and the drawling ladies, at the attempt to soften and package up such strenuous art into tea-time small talk. The comedy of allusion does perhaps also touch Michelangelo himself a little: one may smile at the 'placing' of his heavy misogyny and guess that he might have been almost as uneasy as Prufrock at the 'taking of a toast and tea'. This is the irreverent fun which one can enjoy towards those one most admires. Michelangelo, Hamlet, John the Baptist, and, less explicitly, Andrew Marvell: their seriousness, their extremity, are not mocked but wistfully celebrated by Prufrock/Eliot.

So it is with Stoppard, who borrows from, alludes to, and travesties the artists he likes. His main use of Prufrock, in his novel, characteristically turns the anti-hero back on himself. Moon, the protagonist, seems to be to Stoppard very much what Prufrock is to Eliot; but Moon and Stoppard will have the nerve to be, if not heroic, at least outrageous.

(But what can I do?—write a letter to The Times?) *Well, why not?*
Your words would be read by people of influence. You might well start a
correspondence, leading to an editorial, questions in the House and the
eventual return to a system of barter, if that's what you want.

(That is not it at all,
   that is not what I meant at all.

But when I've got it in a formulated phrase, when I've got it formulated, sprawling on a pin, when it is pinned and wriggling on the wall,
then how should I begin . . .?)
And how should you presume?
(He's got me there, cold. How should I presume?)

All the same Moon knew there was something rotten. He held the
vapours in his cupped hands but they would not crystallize. He did not
have the words. But whatever it was, it was real, and even if it was in
him, he had a bomb and the bomb promised purgation. He would be
presumptuous.

(Lord Malquist and Mr Moon, pp. 23–4)

The 'something rotten', of course, both glances at Prufrock's
'No, I am not Prince Hamlet, nor was meant to be' and makes its
own allusion directly back to *Hamlet* itself.

Allusion and travesty are at the heart of Stoppard's work.
They assert irreverence for sacred cows, the artist displaying his
freedom; they work by rebounds, one off another; and they are
forms of homage.

They are also fun. The glee of recognizing a sidelong allusion
is a pretty innocent pleasure. Like being good at crossword
puzzles, it's nothing to be proud of, but certainly nothing to be
ashamed of either. And if the allusion is to something classically
cultural, and we pick it up, it may cheer up a little the J. Alfred
Prufrock in each of us: ah, I am not wholly excluded, I have
shared *that* experience, perhaps after all I am in touch. Mostly
in Stoppard the allusions have no cultural hauteur; they are
more like instinctive casual gags between friends with a
common background. Many are references to pop songs or
the movies, and many are theatre-people's jokes. Many, too,
are the comprehensive sendings-up of clichés familiar to all
of us. As with most of Stoppard's effects, a prime aim is
entertainment.

To look more closely at the use Stoppard makes of his sources, I shall go by way of four other masters—Shakespeare, Wilde, Joyce and Beckett—to see what in them may have particularly interested him, and what he does with them.

HAMLET

Stoppard nowhere makes a direct appraisal of *Hamlet*. Yet his work suggests that it has been a key text for him, and that he chooses it to travesty because of his affection and regard for it. No doubt it helps that it is the most famous and best-known play ever written. More important, it deals with subjects, and deals in ways, some of which are also Stoppard's. Perhaps all this means is that like most English dramatists Stoppard derives a lot from Shakespeare, but let us for our present purpose deliberately look at it the other way on.

Hamlet is a serious play afflicted by hiccups of bitter laughter (Dr Johnson spoke of its 'merriment' and of the 'mirth' caused by Hamlet's feigned madness)—mainly because its hero is an anti-hero. Hamlet is an intellectual, brooding travesty of the traditional Revenger. He thinks when he ought to take action; he speaks subtleties when he should be yelling terrifying threats; his love, self-confidence, and sense of values decay into irony at the very times when they should, according to the theatrical and human traditions, be growing stronger, fiercer and simpler. The lion takes on the ways of the fox.

The foxiest things of all, though, are the play's *words*. Word-play is vital in all Shakespeare's writing, but never more than here, where words repeatedly turn on themselves. Hamlet's first two lines—'A little more than kin, and less than kind' and 'Not so, my lord; I am too much i' the sun' (son)—are those of a man aware that language is two-faced and can be ironically turned against two-faced people. The linguistic sport is at times exactly Stoppardian, in the deliberate misinterpretation of an idiom: 'What do you read, my lord?/Words, words, words./What is the matter, my lord?/Between who?/I mean, the matter that you read, my lord'. . . . 'Upon what ground?/Why, here in Denmark . . .' 'The king is a thing—/A thing, my lord?/Of nothing . . .' More seriously: 'Hamlet, thou hast thy father much offended./ Mother, you have my father much offended.'

The turning of words goes near the play's heart:

> That we would do,
> We should do when we would, for this 'would' changes,
> . . . . And then this 'should' is like a spendthrift sigh
> That hurts by easing

The words of a Revenger are travestied—mostly, by not appearing when expected, but also in the long soliloquy at the end of Act Two: 'Remorseless, treacherous, lecherous, kindless villain! Oh, vengeance!' where Hamlet as it were tries on the Revenger mask to see how it fits, and it feels false: it is insufficient to 'unpack my heart with words'. Insufficient, too, the words of stock drama: Shakespeare offers us first a travesty of the heroic, in the long speech of the First Player (started by Hamlet himself) and later a travesty of melodrama, in the clumsy play of The Murder of Gonzago. What Shakespeare does is, on both occasions, theatrically and psychologically complex, and of course on both occasions he is travestying an art-form which appeals to Hamlet himself and is blood-brother to the whole play we are watching.

The first really disconcerting stroke in these travesties, and it is not unlike a Stoppardian upset, is when the play Hamlet professes to admire so much, for its straightforwardness and simplicity, turns out to be a caricature of theatrical bombast—rather splendid of its kind, actually, with strongly Shakespearean verse-movement, but a caricature none the less. We aren't sure what to think of the bombast, and we are still more unsure what to think of Hamlet's praise of it. Meanwhile the Player (as in his 'death' at the end of Stoppard's play) is acting disconcertingly well, and when all but Hamlet have left the stage it is this verisimilitude which bewilders him most. The debate about illusion and reality is on, and is only a small remove from a debate about art and morality. 'Is it not monstrous?'—'monstrous', in Shakespeare, having to do with unnaturalness, the deep disruption of natural order. The Player has power which he may use irresponsibly. Hamlet has responsibility but cannot find the moral power, and has already himself resorted to feigning as an evasive device.

This discussion of theatrical effect, at a central moment in the play, is both realistic and 'alienating': it is both directly appropriate to the plot (which really is about false faces, and in which The Murder of Gonzago has a specific job to do) and yet undermining and questioning what we are doing in a playhouse at all. The soliloquy is itself a supreme test-piece for the actor, covering a large emotional range, a good deal of self-parody and a hint of Revenger-travesty, and likely to be as full of shivers and shakes—even more convincing, because subtler—as the speech of the Player. Is nothing to be trusted? Is nothing 'real'?

One answer Shakespeare and Stoppard can see is that art is real—is one of the ways of living 'real life' most fully—and that art in general and theatre in particular are not so much about breaking down, stripping the onion, as about building up. The 'play-scene' which follows a little later is a mountain peak of such art. As 'real' people, ourselves capable of adultery and jealousy if not usually of incest and murder, we watch actors acting people (Hamlet, Horatio)

watching actors acting people (Claudius, Gertrude)

watching actors acting actors (the Players)

acting people (Play King and Queen, Lucianus)

travestying people who are watching (Claudius, Gertrude, Hamlet).

I have to set it out in a sequential sentence; but the event is simultaneous, a unity, enriched still further, incidentally, by the byplay between Hamlet and Ophelia. This is the sort of thing which most clearly shows Shakespeare to be the supreme dramatist.

What Stoppard may have learnt, here or elsewhere in

Shakespeare, is the ability to be doing three or four things at once in virtually unparaphrasable ways: that one level of dramatic event can be piled on another, and a joke or two thrown in as well, and that plays within plays, including travesty of other art, can be particularly effective bases for such structures.

Stoppard's Ros and Guil are trapped inside the above discussion. Whereas players and spectators shift their identities, feign emotions, and exercise choice, *characters* are fixed in art and can never alter. This is the cry of the Father in Pirandello's *Six Characters in Search of an Author* (a play which Stoppard claims not to have known at the time, however):

> No, our reality doesn't change! You see: that's the difference between us! Our reality doesn't change, it can't change—it can never be in any way different from what it is. Because it is already fixed, just as it is, for ever. For ever it is *this* reality. . . . It's terrible, this immutable reality. It should make you shudder to come near us!

Like the jazz song in Sartre's *Nausea*, the play *Hamlet*

> stays the same, young and firm, like a pitiless witness . . . Nothing can interrupt it, nothing which comes from this time in which the world is slumped; it will stop of its own accord, on order.

The sonneteer's dream of art as frozen beauty becomes for Sartre's Antoine Roquentin attractive, not for its victory over death but for its victory over life, over the mess of contingency and change. Roquentin is an odd chap, and his dream seems close to a nightmare for us—'hard as steel, making people ashamed of their existence'. Ros and Guil are in that nightmare, trapped: when they discover that Hamlet has rewritten the letter to England (p. 92) they have no freedom to destroy it or again rewrite it. They have read their destiny.

For substantial sections of the play they are simply twentieth-century agnostics, uncommitted and frightened: little men being used by those in power, and cipher characters being used by the dramatist. There is a paradoxical inconsistency here between the rootless twentieth-century man and the defined

character imprisoned in his play. Pirandello put them at
opposite extremes:

> A character, sir, may always ask a man who he is. Because a character
> has a life which is truly his, marked with his own special characteristics,
> and as a result he is always somebody! Whilst a man ... and I'm not
> speaking of you personally at the moment—man in general—can quite
> well be nobody.

One of the points of art is to make a fixity against flux; and on
the whole Ros and Guil's uncertainty of identity is less frightening than their fixed identity, locked in the action of *Hamlet*. The
title of Stoppard's play is important. A single dismissive line
from the end of *Hamlet*, it hangs over the modern play like a
memento mori, inconsistent both with the squeaky vitality of
the two lords on stage and with the Flying Dutchman-like
immortality of Pirandello's Characters. One fundamental
difference between *Rosencrantz* and Beckett's *Waiting for Godot*
is indicated by their titles: in one play, the protagonists dead
from the start, in the other, always waiting.

The Tragedians are another matter, in many ways more like
Vladimir and Estragon, who 'got rid of' their rights and now
exist in the thin hope that there is a Godot and that he has not
forgotten them, that someone somewhere is watching. The
Tragedians sold their identities to become actors:

> You don't understand the humiliation of it—to be tricked out of the
> single assumption which makes our existence viable—that somebody is
> *watching*. . . . We ransomed our dignity to the clouds, and the uncom-
> prehending birds listened. Don't you see? We're *actors*—we're the
> opposite of people!

> (p. 47)

As so often in Stoppard, this is both a theatre joke, since the
play is played by actors, and a poignancy.

Stoppard's travesty includes some affectionate satire on
Shakespeare's play, not least on the basic point that Rosencrantz
and Guildenstern are so blatantly *used*, by the dramatist as well
as by Claudius, and also on Hamlet's point-scoring off everybody ('He murdered us'), Hamlet's gloomy introspection, and

Shakespeare's shameless plot-fiddling of the pirate attack. Stoppard adds borrowings from Beckett, from revue and farce, and from his reading of philosophy. His most significant additions are quite a turnabout of Shakespeare, and they say a good deal about Stoppard.

First, Stoppard's play is compassionate where Shakespeare's is surprisingly harsh. Few writers so consistently make us sympathize with their villains as Shakespeare, and Claudius in *Hamlet* itself has a scene of profound inwardness; perhaps the problem with Rosencrantz and Guildenstern was that they are not important enough. There is no denying, either, that we are invited to accept Hamlet's viewpoint on events almost uncritically—a fact which may both account for everyone's tendency to identify with Hamlet and also indicate a weakness which has caused some critics to be deeply dissatisfied with the play—and that Hamlet himself does not find their death near his conscience at all. Before, however, we rush to praise Stoppard for improving on Shakespeare we should consider not only that Shakespeare is busy with many other characters and events, but also that Stoppard is simply not so serious, and can afford to make Ros and Guil, in Robert Brustein's damaging phrase, 'charming'. Stoppard's characters haven't a clue what Claudius is really up to: Shakespeare's are knowing and corrupt.

This change is the second of Stoppard's adaptations: Ros and Guil are not at all like 'adders fang'd' and Stoppard's play is in no sense a *serious* gloss on Shakespeare's. On the other hand the innocence of Ros and Guil, though it may be censured as too easily 'winning' (Brustein again), is part of their Moon-iness, part of their position in the line of Stoppard protagonists who wish the world only well.

The first stage directions leave us in no doubt: 'ROS . . . *is nice enough to feel a little embarrassed at taking so much money off his friend. Let that be his character note.*'

The way Ros falls comprehensively for the Player's trick on p. 47 ('think of the most . . . *private* . . . *secret* . . . *intimate* thing you have ever done') confirms his 'niceness'; and much later in the play (p. 77) he is caught out letting Guil win every time, because 'I wanted to make you happy'. (Poor Ros! What he was actually doing was making Guil more 'desperate', because throughout the play he longs to believe in chance and freedom, rather than in his predetermined predicament; but Ros isn't bright enough to have realized this.)

Guil too shows no malice or slyness. He is gently wry in trying to sort Ros out ('Don't you discriminate at all?'); where Ros has a nervous curiosity about the tragedians' performances, Guil is genuinely shocked; and by far the most dramatic thing either of them does in the play is when Guil smashes the Player across the mouth for trying to excite him to indecency. The speech which follows is important in other ways.

GUIL: (*Shaking with rage and fright*) It could have been—it didn't have to be *obscene*.... It could have been—a bird out of season, dropping bright-feathered on my shoulder.... It could have been a tongueless dwarf standing by the road to point the way ... I was *prepared*. But it's this, is it? No enigma, no dignity, nothing classical, portentous, only this—a comic pornographer and a rabble of prostitutes....

(p. 20)

'It' is the confirmation, which Guil has hoped never to receive, but which if inevitable might at least carry some grandeur, that he and Ros are locked in a destiny. He has hoped for evidence of the opposite—of randomness and chance; but all the coins have fallen heads, and the Player has already tended to discourage the idea that his arrival is due to chance. ('GUIL: Fate, then./PLAYER: Oh yes. We have no control....')

What Guil displays in the speech is what we might least expect in routine travesty or routine Absurdism: a sense of values. There is an echo, of course, of the arrival of Pozzo and Lucky (much more obscene, really) in the first Act of *Waiting for Godot*; and in Guil's gentleness to Alfred a little later (quoted below, p. 149) an echo of Vladimir to the Boy; but the indignation and concern of Stoppard's character are much more deeply felt. As well as sympathy for Ros and Guil in their innocence surrounded by seediness, we may also feel a degree of moral respect.

A note on Dogg's Hamlet, Cahoot's Macbeth

Stoppard's fifteen-minute *Hamlet* was written for Ed Berman and Inter-Action 'for performance on a double-decker bus'. It appears in the later play as the school play performed after a memorable Dogg speech-day ceremony. The jokes are several: to see how such a long play can be made very short—perhaps an ironic sop thrown to Philistines who think Shakespeare over-performed (it is important, of course, that the original play should be very well-known—a fifteen-minute version of, say, *All's Well That Ends Well* would merely baffle); to show by this how much of the masterpiece is 'padding', repetition, poetic development—an affectionate dig at Shakespeare's profligate fluency, never richer than in *Hamlet*; to parody the cuts and compromises of amateur productions in general and school plays in particular; to parody schoolboy incomprehension of Shakespeare—to the Dogg-speaking actors the play is literally in a different language. Rosencrantz and Guildenstern, incidentally, do not appear: they are clearly dispensable.

The whole thing is a skit, and a funny one. In two respects, though, it suggests darker thoughts. First, the process of reduction would, one feels, delight Samuel Beckett; what is happening is a fanatic reduction of whatever might be regarded as gratuitous, consolatory, or self-indulgent in a work of art. In this case it amounts, of course, to a destruction of the work of art, and whether he intends to or not Stoppard may be dissociating himself from this tendency in Beckett. Secondly, our laughter at the compressed *Hamlet* becomes with hindsight uneasy, as in the second half of the evening we watch a *Macbeth* shortened to squeeze into a private flat to evade police repression, and then ludicrously interrupted by the police themselves. The joke turns a little sour.

The abbreviation of *Macbeth* is an attempt to thwart the ultimate Philistinism of the totalitarian State, not to make a ritual speech-day offering. Our sympathies are with the players and at first Shakespeare does not seem to be suffering very much. But the Inspector's intrusion is, disconcertingly, very funny; he is a comic, and we are in the field of the broadest possible travesty. Such wild farce, with such bitter if blurred political ironies thrown in, may seem to have little really to do with Shakespeare. But for Kohout and Landovsky, staging their real and serious truncated *Macbeth* in Prague flats, the choice of a great political tragedy was fully in earnest, and Stoppard's introduction to his published text alerts us to this by quoting Kohout in a letter of June 1978: 'I think, he [Shakespeare] wouldn't be worried about it.... I am sure it is nevertheless Macbeth.'

And Stoppard has the Inspector himself thumpingly sum up the danger intrinsic in the great master:

> If I may make one tiny criticism.... Shakespeare—or the Old Bill, as we call him in the force—is not a popular choice with my chief, owing to his popularity with the public, or, as we call it in the force, the filth. The fact is, when you get a universal and timeless writer like Shakespeare, there's a strong feeling that he could be spitting in the eyes of the beholder when he should be keeping his mind on Verona—hanging around the 'gents'. You know what I mean? Unwittingly, of course. He didn't know he was doing it, at least you couldn't prove he did, which is what makes the chief so prejudiced against him. The chief says he'd rather you stood up and said, 'There is no freedom in this country', then there's nothing underhand and we all know where we stand. You get your lads together and we get our lads together and when it's all over, one of us is in power and you're in gaol. That's freedom in action. But what we don't like is a lot of people being cheeky and saying they are only Julius Caesar or Coriolanus or Macbeth....
>
> (p. 60)

OSCAR WILDE

Any man able to write a play as funny as *The Importance of Being Earnest* might well earn Stoppard's interest and respect; but there is more than this in Wilde's appeal. Well before the stage success of *Earnest* and the legal melodrama which led to his public disgrace, Wilde and his 'aesthetic' followers had been travestied by Gilbert and Sullivan in the operetta *Patience*. Gilbert and the middlebrow British public were exasperated by the dubious aesthetic theories (derived loosely from Walter Pater) of Wilde and his group; and still more by their 'camp' style. Stoppard's sympathies are closer to 'art for art's sake' than to doctrines of commitment; and the 'style' which so irritated some Victorians appeals to him. Wilde's whole public life was, in a way, showbiz, imitated in later generations by many film and rock stars (such as Mick Jagger of the Rolling Stones, to whom the young Stoppard may have cultivated a physical resemblance). In Wilde's case the style evolved from a fluent Irish tongue, a classical education, a histrionic gift, and an impatience with slower wits and 'earnestness'—together, no doubt, with ordinary mischief. Much of it was deliberate over-reaction: to utilitarianism, to the social concern of Ruskin or Morris, to the growing study of psychology, and to the stiff bewhiskered masculinity of the Victorian middle class. Wilde preached the pursuit of Beauty, of style not sincerity, of the utterly gratuitous and the potentially outrageous. This tended to mean being extremely silly, which he if not his followers could carry off with panache.

Lord Malquist, in Stoppard's novel, is partly travesty Oscar. ' "Style, dear boy," said the ninth earl. "Style. There is nothing else." ' The great statesman's death

might well mark a change in the heroic posture—to that of the Stylist, the spectator as hero, the man of inaction who would not dare roll up his sleeves for fear of creasing the cuffs.

A minor Stoppardian flick is that Moon, who has cast himself as Boswell to Malquist's Johnson, is then affectionately addressed by Lady Malquist as 'Bosie' (the pet-name of Lord Alfred Douglas, whose relationship with Wilde caused Wilde's downfall).

In many respects Stoppard's writing 'places' Wilde's aestheticism. Our sympathies are with Moon not Malquist, Moon whose problem is that he is *too* 'wide open' to suffering, need, and instability. But the elegance and cleverness of Malquist are attractive, as are those of Archie in *Jumpers*, who descends in part from him; and it is part of Stoppard's 'not knowing' to be reluctant to reject a brilliant artistic witness.

The tantalizing sense, in Wilde's farces or in the melodrama of his more serious pieces, that some important ideas are lurking there makes it the more appropriate to use the scheme of his most popular play as the basis for *Travesties*, especially since it is hardly less familiar to audiences than *Hamlet* and likely to be known almost by heart by theatre people. A travesty is usually a trivialization and making-ridiculous of something relatively grand. Stoppard's play does caricature famous and serious people; but it also reverses the familiar process, using the trivial, flippant conversation of Wilde's characters as a basis for Joyce's passionate defence of his 'useless' art (p. 62); for Tzara's preaching of Dada-ism (pp. 38–9); and for a crisp introduction to and critique of Lenin's thinking and the story of the Russian Revolution. The issues debated matter not only to the twentieth century in general but to Stoppard in particular. The use of *The Importance of Being Earnest* as the initial float for such a major enterprise is as far as I know unique. It is very funny, provided one knows Wilde's play; and it sets a standard of theatrical elegance, partly in the Wildean patter itself (very few of the lines, incidentally, are *actually* those of Wilde, but vast numbers sound as if they might be), and partly in enabling the dramatist to drop abruptly and arbitrarily from high seriousness to familiar travesty, rather as two ad-libbing comics may return with relief to a traditional music-hall sequence.

On pp. 76–7 of *Travesties* Carr, suddenly possessed implausibly of a historian's confidence, dismisses Marx as having 'got it all wrong'. His deadpan, compelling speech ends:

The tide must have turned at about the time when *Das Kapital* after eighteen years of hard labour was finally coming off the press, a moving reminder, Cecily, of the folly of authorship. How sweet you look suddenly—pink as a rose.

The sudden return to Wilde inclines us to relax momentarily. The bait of continuing Wildean banter is, however, firmly rejected for the present as Cecily, in her furthest remove from the elegant girlishness of Wilde's character, erupts into passionate 'commitment' quite as compelling as Carr's. This in turn changes abruptly into authentic Stoppard:

CECILY: So don't talk to me about superior morality, you patronizing Kant-struck prig, all the time you're talking about the classes you're just trying to imagine how I'd look stripped off to my knickers—

CARR: That's a lie!

(*But apparently it isn't. As* CECILY *continues to speak we get a partial Carr's-mind view of her. Coloured lights begin to play over her body, and most of the other light goes out except for a bright spot on Carr. Faintly from 1974 comes the sound of the big band playing 'the Stripper'.* CARR *is in a trance. The music builds.* CECILY *might perhaps climb on her desk. The desk may have 'cabaret lights' built into it for use at this point.*)

CECILY: In England the rich own the poor and the men own the women. Five per cent of the people own eighty per cent of all the property. The only way is the way of Marx, and of Lenin, the enemy of all revisionism—of economism—opportunism—liberalism—of bourgeois anarchist individualism—of quasi-socialist ad-hoc-ism, of syndicalist quasi-Marxist populism—liberal quasi-communist opportunism, economist quasi-internationalist imperialism, social chauvinist quasi-Zimmervaldist Menshevism, self-determinist quasi-socialist annexationism, Kautskyism, Bundism, Kantism—

CARR: Get 'em off!

(*The light snaps back to normal.*)

CECILY: I don't think you ought to talk to me like that during library hours. . . .

There is a reminiscence here of Polonius introducing the tragedians at Elsinore. In both cases the credibility of the subject—the tragedians' repertory, Lenin's creed—suffers and so does the speaker regaling us with the absurd list. In *Hamlet* the laugh is on Polonius, more than on the tragedians, and here Cecily's commitment, persuasive and sympathetic a moment earlier, has become ludicrous fanaticism. Within seconds Stoppard suggests how enlightened radicalism can become totalitarian. It is done as a travesty of a striptease act (totalitarianism underneath radical clothing?) in a sensual fantasy of Carr's. Theatrically this is refreshing and funny; humanly it restores Carr to plausibility; as literary travesty it debunks the unfaltering panache of Wilde's Algernon, never disturbed by anything so crude as sexual lust; and intellectually it 'places' Cecily's enthusiasm. The erotic climax—Carr's shout of *'Get 'em off!'*—is also the moment at which the list of 'isms' becomes insupportably absurd. The lights snap back to normal, and we resume the close travesty of *Earnest*. Marvellous.

JOYCE

The Waste Land, T. S. Eliot's complex of travesties, and *Ulysses* were published within a year, and both had been a decade brewing, the decade also of the First World War, Dada, *The Rite of Spring*, the later Cubism, and the poetry of Apollinaire. Joyce's own view of *Ulysses* and of art is reasonably sketched (given the cartoon terms of the play) in his long speech to Tzara towards the end of Act One of *Travesties* (p. 62): 'An artist is the magician put among men to gratify—capriciously—their urge for immortality.'

Like *The Waste Land*, *Ulysses* is made up considerably of travesty and allusion. The Bloom/Ulysses parallel is perhaps the greatest, most creative artistic travesty ever perpetrated; and not only Leopold Bloom but the novel of which he is the central figure is systematically related, in travesty, or serious parallel, to episodes in the *Odyssey*. The effect is different from Eliot's, because of the different temperaments and convictions of the two writers. Joyce is *enhancing* his sympathetic study of Bloom, Molly and Stephen by the Homeric parallels. Bloom is (Joyce's phrase in a letter) 'a good man'; he is a modern hero. Stoppard may have learned from Joyce that it is possible to make a travesty which does not diminish either the original or the contemporary. He may also have learned that allusion can cheerfully include both the grandest and the most trivial material: *Hamlet* (again!) repeatedly crops up in *Ulysses*, but so do pop tunes from Italian opera, erotic novelettes, trash journalism and pornographic postcards.

Like most of Joyce's work, *Ulysses* works in many linguistic registers. It seems to attempt a comprehensive, or at least multiple, approach to humanity, and to one ordinary day. Pun, word-play, assonance and vivid rhythm enrich the more sustained descriptive sections; a scrupulous ear for speech guides dialogues and streams-of-consciousness. Giving Stoppard an idea for part of his novel, Joyce writes several pages in magazine-story cliché. There is a celebrated section, the opening of which is quoted in the opening section of *Travesties*, offering pastiche of English prose from its earliest origins to contemporary slang. There is crudity and buffoonery in plenty: the limerick sequence in *Travesties* marking Joyce's entry is highly appropriate, and Joyce would have loved *Dogg's Hamlet, Cahoot's Macbeth*. There is considerable attempt to explore the interplay of language and thought. There is vigour and warmth, and there is what Clive James calls in Stoppard the chill arriving from infinity, Joyce being one of the few writers to attempt to place his fiction in the context of our larger environment:

> of the parallax or parallactic drift of socalled fixed stars, in reality ever-moving from immeasurably remote eons to infinitely remote futures in comparison with which the years, threescore and ten, of allotted human life formed a parenthesis of infinitesimal brevity.

Stoppard does not refer closely to Joyce's book (though there is a nice touch on the last page of *Travesties* when he echoes the last page of *Ulysses*—'yes I said yes when you asked me') but it is one of the landmarks in the hinterland of his writing, a landmark of comedy, verbal ingenuity, and travesty, but above all of aesthetic commitment of the kind Stoppard is fifty-one per cent against but also (see p. 15 above) forty-nine per cent in favour of.

BECKETT

Samuel Beckett was a friend and admirer of Joyce when they were fellow-Irishmen in Paris in the 1930s, and Beckett's earlier, more comic work, where he is most under Joyce's influence and is still writing in English, have perhaps most appeal for Stoppard, though clearly the (French) play *Waiting for Godot* is a central text for both writers. Beckett's early novels *Murphy* and *Watt* have perhaps a little influence on Stoppard's novel, as well as on his nomenclature in general. The later writings, after *Godot* (which was written in 1948), take an increasingly bleak and reductive course along which Stoppard's exuberance could not temperamentally follow nor his philosophy approve. All Beckett's plays, however, use their theatrical or radio or television genres with remarkable imagination, and we can be sure that Stoppard has enjoyed, for example, the send-up sound-effects in *All That Fall* (quoted above, p. 68) or the mimed frustrations of the *Acts Without Words*, or the moment in *Play* when the single spotlight goes *'from W1 to M. He opens his mouth to speak. Spot from M to W2.'*

Beckett was trained as a philosopher and his writing alludes to and travesties academic philosophy at times, though more tersely and obscurely than Stoppard's, who is a layman. Beckett's subject-matter is human aspiration in a universe which gives it no encouragement: the tenacity, the pathos, and the absurdity of such aspiration. It is as impossible for man to rest without yearning, as for the artist not to create, however futile that seems. ('There is nothing to express, no power to express, no desire to express, together with the obligation to express.') It is also very difficult to be sure of anything. Watt, in Mr Knott's house (the names suggest the driest of philosopher's examples) cannot pin down his experience.

> Not that he was always unsuccessful either, for he was not. For if he had been always unsuccessful, how would it have been possible for him to speak of the Galls father and son, and of the piano they had come all the way from town to tune, and of their tuning it, and of their passing

the remarks they had passed, the one to the other, in the way he did? No, he could never have spoken at all of these things, if all had continued to mean nothing, as some continued to mean nothing, that is to say, right up to the end. For the only way one can speak of nothing is to speak of it as though it were something, just as the only way one can speak of God is to speak of him as though he were a man, which to be sure he was, in a sense, for a time, and as the only way one can speak of man, even our anthropologists have realized that, is to speak of him as though he were a termite. . . .

Hamm and Clov, in *Endgame*, aspire paradoxically to an ultimate ending and an ultimate absence of meaning, and are appalled by the discovery of a flea ('But humanity might start from there all over again! Catch him, for the love of God!') or by the thought—a jest at audience and critics as well, of course—that 'We're not beginning to . . . to . . . mean something?'

Exactly what happened on the train (in *All That Fall*) is never clear, particularly since Beckett plays a wicked joke on us by having, at the end of this radio play, a crucially important object handed over which the characters can see but which we shall never identify.

Much of Beckett's humour depends on this sort of uncertainty, sometimes ironically intensified by a dry meticulous tone as of a philosopher determined *not* to be distracted into uncertainty by emotion or poetry. The penultimate section of *Ulysses*, mentioned above, is the source of this tone. The funniest and broadest travesty of the philosopher's manner is Lucky's speech in *Waiting for Godot*, in which Lucky 'thinks. Aloud' in the tones of a distressingly senile academic, on the theme that man is doomed to die. Scholastic credits and passing references become an incoherent repetition, the scholars' names themselves become childish crudities ('Fartov', 'Belcher', 'the Acacacademy of Anthropopopometry'), 'Possy and Essy' (*posse* and *esse*) sound like French place-names, and academic pedantry becomes ludicrously bogged down in an elaborate list of health-giving sports, into which with Swiftian irony Beckett throws the words 'dying' and 'conating' (which my dictionary defines as 'the exertion of willing that desire or aversion shall issue in action'). Through the laughable gibberish the message of man's inevitable end thuds dully and more and more oppressively, until the onlookers physically silence the unlucky Lucky. 'There's an end to his thinking!' cries Pozzo, trampling on Lucky's hat. But not, of course, an end to the characters' living and suffering, to Pozzo and Lucky's travelling, or to Vladimir and Estragon's waiting.

Stoppard both celebrated *Waiting for Godot*, and largely got it out of his system, in *Rosencrantz*. His play is based on the scheme of *Godot* as much as on *Hamlet*, and *Godot* is the more travestied. There are simple affectionate jokes towards Beckett, such as the taking-off of belts to catch Hamlet (p. 67) at which Ros's trousers slide slowly down (a reminiscence of the end of *Godot*, which itself is using the most basic slapstick comedy routine) or the appearance of heads from barrels in Act Three, which recalls *Endgame* or *Play*. The jokes about being in a theatre and attempting to entertain an audience are taken straight from the spirit of *Waiting for Godot*, as is the general rhythmic patter of Ros and Guil's exchanges. Stoppard is of course able to make his own additions, such as the 'Fire!' shout to the audience (a cliché example of the misuse of free speech. The trouble is that Stoppard's audience don't react, which confirms Ros and Guil's fears that everything is predestined for them.) And Ros and Guil are more consciously inside *a play*—not only *Hamlet*, but also *Rosencrantz*, than Beckett's characters. There is a fine moment early on, which is both a reminiscence of Vladimir to the Boy in *Godot* and a sad new theatre joke:

GUIL: Come here, Alfred.
   (ALFRED *moves down and stands, frightened and small.*)
(*Gently*) Do you lose often?
ALFRED: Yes, sir.
GUIL: Then what could you have left to lose?
ALFRED: Nothing, sir.
   (*Pause.* GUIL *regards him.*)
GUIL: Do you like being ... an actor?

ALFRED: No, sir.
  (GUIL *looks around, at the audience.*)
GUIL: You and I, Alfred, we could create a dramatic precedent here.

Presumably what Guil is thinking of is that he and Alfred could simply walk out, now. *Rosencrantz* would grind to a halt, and so would *Hamlet* and *The Murder of Gonzago*: a 'dramatic precedent', indeed! It is a dream: Alfred after all has nothing to lose, and Guil is appalled at the predetermined existence he seems to be caught in. But the word 'could' means they won't, and the reason, ironically, is that Guil feels they *couldn't*. In any case, Alfred takes Guil's remark as another ominous physical threat to him, and begins to sniffle, so that Guil has to resort to conventional bracing manliness—with another *Godot*-like laugh for the audience, of course—'Come, come, Alfred, this is no way to fill the theatres of Europe.'

Ros and Guil's predicament, clearly, parallels that of Vladimir and Estragon. They can't remember much, including their own names; they don't know where they are; they have to wait around. The difference is that Ros and Guil are fixed in a play.

GUIL: Who decides?
PLAYER (*switching off his smile*): Decides? It is *written*.

                                                  (p. 60)

ROS: We're his *friends*.
GUIL: How do you know?
ROS: From our young days brought up with him.
GUIL: You've only got their word for it.
ROS: But that's what we depend on. . . .

                                                  (p. 83)

GUIL: They won't notice the broken seal, providing you were in character.

                                                  (p. 83)

Their function is everything (whereas Vladimir and Estragon find compulsion without freedom. What could they possibly do for Godot?) and their deaths are predetermined. They are trapped in a defined dramatic action towards the end of which the story lays down that they die. Vladimir and Estragon are at risk of waiting throughout eternity.

The nod to *Waiting for Godot* at the end of *Jumpers* is more in the nature of an isolated allusion than a travesty. *Jumpers* is not written to anyone else's scheme. Lucky's speech does, however, hover behind George's dictated paper on the existence of God, as a warning of what George's digressions and facetiousness might eventually degenerate into. But again it is worth noting the difference: Lucky is struggling to describe man's decline into death, George to justify his recognition of goodness.

Shakespeare, Wilde, Joyce, Beckett, and all those philosophers ... This chapter must end by emphasizing that there is nothing exclusively literary or academic about Stoppard's allusiveness. His comic rebounds are not only from cathedral walls but from advertisements, pop fiction, pop songs. Perhaps the commonest of all rebounds is from a stale pattern of language. *Hound* travesties Agatha Christie and village-hall amateur dramatics (and provincial reviewing), and *Where are They Now?* travesties (with distinct restraint, as if aware that attacks on public school sentimentality are themselves something of a literary cliché) an Old Boys' Reunion Dinner. No less than allusions to *Hamlet* or A. J. Ayer, such send-ups fill in our cultural framework. The rebounds from the clichés which surround us are part of the design.

7 · THINKING

A caricature image of Tom Stoppard, around in the minds of some who don't know his work well, is of a man all head and no heart. A dabbler in philosophy, conundrum and word-play, with little penetration into areas of feeling and value. Stoppard's avoidance of the socialist orthodoxy of intellectual theatre, and his readiness to talk cheerfully of himself as 'bourgeois', have exasperated many (one recalls Milne's diagnosis, in *Night and Day*, that to Wagner a 'right-thinking press' is 'one that thinks like him'). And this sin is compounded by financial success in show business. Kenneth Tynan makes much of a public stance of withdrawal which has served Stoppard conveniently in many interviews: a mixture of Oscar Wilde, Mick Jagger and Stoppard's own Lord Malquist. This image of 'withdrawing with style' is dented only slightly by Stoppard's concern for oppressed artists in Russia and Czechoslovakia.

Another view, not entirely contradictory, is of a writer whose thinking, though superficially agile, soon runs out of stamina and gives way to comfortable 'not knowing' and a sentimental heart. Far from being cold, Stoppard—on this view—is not cold enough: his dislike of logical-positivist philosophy is not an intellectual doubt but a gut reaction, a refusal to accept what offends his sense of how things ought to be. (A similar refusal is made explicitly by a respectable academic, Iris Murdoch, who rejects the 'behaviourist, existentialist, and utilitarian' modern image of man partly because 'I do not think people *ought* to picture themselves in this way.' Iris Murdoch's essays *The*

Sovereignty of Good seem to offer, lucidly for the layman, the professional philosopher's version of Stoppard's intuitionism. She too, incidentally, was much impressed by Beckett's early novels.) Stoppard, the second dismissal continues, ducks the nastiness of Ros and Guil because it will be easier and pleasanter to make them charming. He raises disturbing questions and turns them aside in a consolatory laughter; he dissipates grand conceptions in mere showbiz; his thinking is soft-centred and lazy.

The first, and commoner, caricature seems to me false, though it may have suited Stoppard to encourage it. My next chapter, *Caring*, will show his ability to present pain and recognize value; given that he is an entertainer, perhaps the surprising thing about Stoppard is how insistently he returns to earnest subject-matter. Clive James has suggested that 'the supposedly passionless intricacies of Stoppard's plays have all unfolded from a preliminary intuition of extreme intensity'; and here the events of Stoppard's early years are likely to have been important. His happiness in India, and later at prep school in England, were bright against a background of earlier fear and insecurity which the psychologists tell us is likely to have been formative even if later unremembered. ('My memory,' Stoppard agreed to *Theatre Quarterly*, '*is* very good at erasing things I'd rather not remember.') His appreciation of England, and of Western democracy, is sharper than in those of us who have taken them for granted. The stylishness, the exuberance, and the conservatism of Stoppard's public *persona* may add up to an implicit message to us (and particularly for those able to afford to patronize West End theatre) that 'you don't know how lucky you are'. Another aspect of conservatism, and of being uncommitted politically, is suggested by Mr Moon's anxious integrity:

I can't just align myself with whatever view has the approved moral tone to it. I'm not against black people really, I only recoil from the simplicity of taking up a virtuous position in support of them regardless of the issues.

(*Lord Malquist and Mr Moon*, p. 53)

The alternative caricature of the comfortable sentimentalist seems to me a shade closer to the mark, though still very far off. Stoppard's playing is about thinking; but his claim on our attention is not as a thinker but as a player. His equations and solutions are theatrical and often involve some corner-cutting; the playing does not present us with judgements, but offers us what Lawrence called 'the trembling instability of the balance' or what Stoppard calls 'the moral sensibility from which we make our judgements'. This is not to deny that some corners in the plays may be too easily cut, or that some solutions may be, even as playing, too convenient.

This chapter will examine first Stoppard's treatment of philosophy, since this (unnecessarily) unnerves some spectators. Next we will trace through the plays a distinctively Stoppardian pattern: the comic or tragicomic pursuit of a single logic, or rigid view of life at the expense of the flux of reality. Thirdly we shall look at the strategy of 'Tom Stoppard Doesn't Know', or its alternative 'Firstly, A; secondly, minus A' by which so much of Stoppard's thinking is presented, and go on to consider the charge of laziness. Finally it will be suggested that what Stoppard ultimately celebrates is not rationality but irrationality; not proof but failure to prove.

STOPPARD AND PHILOSOPHY

The plays make no pretensions to original philosophy and there is no need of a philosophical background to follow their arguments. 'I had a huge reading programme to get through,' Stoppard told Barry Norman about the preparation for *Jumpers*, 'to make sure that what I thought were my penetrating insights weren't simply the average conclusions of a first-year philosophy student'; but he then added 'which they invariably turned out to be.' A. J. Ayer was enthusiastic about *Jumpers*, but not about its philosophy; and a Canadian professor, Jonathan Bennett (writing in *Philosophy* 50, 1975) found it 'a poor effort'; 'there is nothing here that deserves the attention of philosophers'. The play has a 'musty, out-of-date quality, as though for Stoppard philosophy had died in about 1935'; and there are some errors, which Bennett is probably right in attributing to Stoppard rather than to George. The climax of George's lecture (pp. 53–5), to which a good deal of care seems to have been given, is dismissed as 'tedious disquisitions about ethical objectivity/subjectivity'. On the other hand, for Bennett *Rosencrantz* has 'that structuredness and that intellectual seriousness which *Jumpers* so lamentably lacks'; and this seems to be because, for Bennett, its situation, its games, its action are full of philosophical *suggestion*, in the way of Lewis Carroll's *Through the Looking-Glass*. In effect, on this view, Stoppard is more profound when playing than when trying to be profound. That sounds convincing.

Of course spectators may go off after seeing a play and read philosophy for themselves; but they will not *need* to do so to understand what they have seen. On the other hand it would be misleading to suggest that Stoppard is interested only in the *product* of philosophy: the offered interpretations. The pursuit itself fascinated him, as Malquistian withdrawal fascinated him: he could relish its appeal—'I think I enjoyed the rules that philosophers play by. It's an extremely formal discipline' (to Ronald Hayman, 1974)—yet ultimately reject it. A few days before the Hayman interview he told Mark Amory that as well as enjoyable, philosophy was also 'absurd. I have got very little desire to read any more of it now because the entire operation seems to be taking place in a large plastic bubble.'

The urgencies, and the comic extensions to absurdity, of Stoppard's early writing do point towards philosophy. The horror of Mr Moon is on behalf of mankind, whirled in vast, ever-expanding, fragile systems of economic or social contracts, or, in the Third World, simply starving; the lost faith is in an ultimate controlling agency, and the lament is for 'no one being *good* any more'. Ros and Guil complement his agony by constantly trying by reasoning to get a grip on where they are. By *Albert's Bridge* the protagonist is actually a philosophy graduate·

and in *Jumpers* and *Professional Foul* the dramas turn round academic philosophers expounding at some length their elegant diagrams about the undiagrammatic flux. Philosophy, in the eyes of its practitioners and enthusiasts, is the withdrawal to the heart of things. George speaks of trying to bring Russell's mind 'back to matters of universal import, and away from the day-to-day parochialism of international politics'. As such it is immensely attractive to the lover of logic who is also acutely responsive to suffering and need, as well as (no doubt) being attractive to the cold-blooded.

A key twentieth-century book is Jean-Paul Sartre's novel *Nausea* (1938). The narrator, Antoine Roquentin, is 'nauseated' by the physical flux of existence, by contingency, by being alive without meaning or purpose. He is puzzled that other people don't realize how 'hemmed in' and possessed they are by Nature—which 'has nothing but habits and may change those tomorrow'. 'What if something were to happen? What if all of a sudden it started palpitating?'

Looking down at the town of Bouville from a hill, Roquentin enjoys a brief respite from the Nausea. 'Is this what freedom is?' In the sun the town looks 'like heaps of shells, of splinters of bone, of gravel', and the people are 'little black dots'. Later, as the lights come on, he is aware, like Albert from his bridge, of the town's 'geometric patterns', but even then it looks '*natural* ... crushed by the evening'.

As the Nausea takes over Roquentin's life, his work as a biographical historian collapses. It was a soothing, enclosed logic, but now he knows that 'the past does not exist', and he is trapped in existence. His only reliable relief from the Nausea is a jazz song, a 'band of steel, the narrow duration of the music,' 'an unchanging order'. And his final hope is to write some sort of story, 'above existence ... the sort of story which could never happen ... beautiful and hard as steel'.

Stoppard's comic characters Mr Moon and Fraser (*Albert's Bridge*) are distant, travesty-style relations of Roquentin. See the discussion below, pp. 167–8. Against them are set Lord Malquist—'Nothing is the history of the world, viewed from a suitable distance'—and Archie: not characters with whom we are invited to sympathize, but characters whose view cannot be ignored, may even contain a truth. Remembering the reality of Stoppard's very early years, one may sense a faint similarity to Conrad—not insensitivity to human suffering, but an absolute refusal to tint, diminish, or sentimentalize it. The ironic harshness of Malquist or Archie may come to Stoppard from Swift (who cared very much indeed) via Samuel Beckett. In Beckett existence is never delighting: Roquentin's nausea is translated into more obvious physical oppressions—incessant or repetitive pain, stench, senile decay, the lust of dry loins. To exist is hell.

And is also, in Beckett, inherently comic—in its gratuitousness, its useless yearnings, the schemings of its tiny lusts and jealousies. Then, weirdly, but impressively, there is a value in form, in shape, in pattern: the logic of art 'above existence', like Roquentin's jazz song. Sheer counting, for Beckett, is one of 'the less intolerable activities'. And philosophical reasoning, even in travesty form, is preferable to the 'grotesque fallacy' of realist art.

Stoppard's art and temperament have, of course, very little really in common with either Sartre or Beckett. Good intent, innocence, the 'sincere flattery' of parody and irreverence, a joy in being alive and a healthy avoidance of death: these are the fuel of Stoppard's plays, quite apart from their explicit tributes to an external absolute good. But the recognitions of Roquentin and of Beckett are part of the background of Stoppard's thinking, especially in so far as they confront the general condition of mankind. Most people live—most people have always lived—pretty awful lives; and we do not *know* a purpose or a remedy. (It is the Marxist materialist *knowing* which particularly exasperates Stoppard, and he allows himself to refer straightforwardly to 'God', but he shows little likelihood of enthusiasm for the *religious* knowers either.) In the face of a human predicament which might well make us panic, there is the consolation of laughter—and the delicious temptation of arbitrary logics 'above existence', of which theatre is itself one kind. As we shall see, Stoppard returns repeatedly to various such logics and to characters who yearn for them. It seems to me that his own feet never cease to be firmly and gladly on the real earth. But he is ready enough to see the attractions of withdrawal, especially of withdrawal into the 'respectable' logics of philosophy.

In the novel, Mr Moon never discovers this possible withdrawal, which might make him calm. Malquist has a philosophy of sorts, stated unequivocally in the first pages of the book: an absolute cynicism (except in the matter of aesthetics, and that may well be merely a social affectation). Moon has all the raw material for philosophical enquiry—a hypersensitive awareness of existence, an ethical concern, a sense of 'real time' as opposed to 'time in his head'; but he is a sort of essential adolescent, eager but not yet able, too much caught up in the Nausea of contingency to be capable of withdrawal into logic; and his only transcendence of the world is archetypally adolescent, in sexual experience:

> the last shaking purgation . . . left him *solved* [my italics: a marvellous word]
> Moon lay still, trying to resist his return to the world.
>
> (pp. 144, 145)

Ros and Guil, of course, are trapped *out of* the world—in a fiction where coins always fall heads and their destiny is scripted, but without having had an existence within the world. Sartre's Roquentin would envy them. There is little doubt what Guil studied at college, and throughout the play he attempts to return to reasoning as their only defence.

> GUIL: The scientific approach to the examination of phenomena is a defence against the pure emotion of fear. Keep tight hold and continue while there's time. Now—counter to the previous syllogism: tricky one, follow me carefully, it may prove a comfort.
>
> (*Rosencrantz*, p. 12)

Ros at this early stage doesn't yet need comfort. Always the slower to catch on, he is untroubled by their situation, indeed rather tickled by it, until after the first scene with the Tragedians; and when he cracks he panics and grumbles instead of reasoning. In the second half of the play, however, both he and Guil try for all they're worth to keep a grip on what has happened or is happening.

A better intellectual match for Guil is the Player. Once he even turns their situation face about to make an ironic contrast with the normal world of flux: 'You know why you're here at least' (p. 49). This is the main line of Pirandello's *Six Characters*: the contrast between characters and people. But Pirandello's is a rather pretentious play, and Stoppard's—in spite of the manoeuvres round it made by some academics—is not. There is no philosophy in the play; but there are gestures *towards* philosophy, momentary poetic parallelisms between the human condition and the predicaments of Ros and Guil, and indeed of the Tragedians, and indeed of Hamlet. Perhaps the most poignant passage is the Guil–Player exchange:

> PLAYER: Uncertainty is the normal state. You're nobody special.
> (*He makes to leave again.* GUIL *loses his cool.*)
> GUIL: But for God's sake what are we supposed to *do*?
> PLAYER: Relax. Respond. That's what people do. You can't go through life questioning your situation at every turn.
> GUIL: But we don't know what's going on, or what to do with ourselves. We don't know how to *act*.
> PLAYER: Act natural. You know why you're here at least.
> GUIL: We only know what we're told, and that's little enough. And for all we know it isn't even true.
> PLAYER: For all anyone knows, nothing is. Everything has to be taken on trust; truth is only that which is taken to be true. It's the currency of living. There may be nothing behind it, but it doesn't make any difference so long as it is honoured. One acts on assumptions.
> (p. 49)

It isn't so far from these words to Sir Archibald Jumper. So many early audiences and readers of *Rosencrantz* attempted to trace a message in it, or at least a coherent study of the human condition, that Stoppard became aware of a possibility for the future: 'to end up by contriving the perfect marriage between the play of ideas and farce or perhaps even high comedy'. *Jumpers* was deliberately written as such, and the off-the-cuff interview phrase undercuts itself: *perfect marriages* are perhaps unlikely to be *contrived*. There is a ponderousness at the heart of *Jumpers*: the play is like a jumbo jet, powered by enormously capable engines of theatricality, humour and intelligence which make it arrive impressively, but one can still yearn for the acrobatic biplane which didn't know it had to be important.

Jumpers is actually about a philosopher, but (Stoppard says) 'could have been about a playwright or vicar'. Its thinking is 'just the thought process of any intelligent person' (to Amory, June 1974). In it Stoppard parodies some central philosophical debate of the mid-twentieth century. The play is harsh because, like Aldous Huxley's *Brave New World*, it sets the debate in a fictional context where it has already been fought and concluded, where George is out of touch with the times. The Rad-Lib millennium has arrived; whatever the original Oates did in Antarctica, altruism is now certainly dead, and Astronaut Oates will wave 'forlornly from the featureless wastes of the lunar landscape' to remind us of the fact. The new Archbishop of Canterbury is an agnostic vet.; the broadcasting services have been taken over, the Church will be 'rationalized', and the Association of National Newspaper Proprietors are 'sitting in the back of a police car with a raincoat over their heads' (a glancing bitter joke, but behind it is the sentiment—from a later play, *Night and Day*—that 'Junk journalism is the evidence of a society that has got at least one thing right, that there should be nobody with the power to dictate where responsible journalism begins.')

The harshness infects the audience's own blood: we probably laugh as McFee is blown out of the pyramid; we certainly laugh at his dangling body intermittently revealed in Act One, and at its disposal; and the audience is convulsed at the deaths of Thumper and Pat. We are like Swift's audience in *A Modest Proposal*: part of the inhuman cynicism is attached to us. George on stage is very lonely; he looks not at us but at a mirror; and if we find him sympathetic, we may yet find Archie scoring all the points, dazzling us.

This fictional context is Stoppard's extension of the ethical relativism which he and George see as 'mainstream' in our day—summed up both effectively and humorously by Dotty's 'Archie says' speech on p. 41: 'good and bad, better and worse, these are not real properties of things, they are just expressions of our feelings about them'.

The fact that society has not actually reduced itself to the heartless state of Rad-Lib Britain is itself some evidence, Stoppard would say, for the existence of the values the relativists deny; and what George and Stoppard try to bring out is the conviction that there is some fundamental flaw in the ethical relativist approach.

George's attempts to show the flaw by proving the existence of God are, of course, up the wrong street. The 'first-term' debate has been endlessly worked over; few of us have not to some extent puzzled it out for ourselves, like Molly Bloom, Joyce's non-intellectual earth-mother:

> as for them saying there's no God I wouldn't give a snap of my two fingers for all their learning why don't they go and create something I often asked him atheists or whatever they call themselves ... who was the first person in the universe before there was anybody that made it all who ah that they don't know neither do I so there you are
>
> (*Ulysses*, p. 931)

and the disciples of Russell or Ayer are not likely to be unaware of Zeno or in need of demonstration by hare and tortoise (a nice twist, this, of Zeno's original tortoise and *Achilles*—and ludicrous as a potential lecture demonstration!) This part of George's lecture is Stoppard caricaturing: a professor of Moral Philosophy gets muddled with material which might come in his first lecture for freshmen. And even if God's existence were proved by such logic, it wouldn't thereby become, for most of us, a matter of *belief*.

Where George's lecture is more disconcerting, is where it

takes the argument into the enemy's territory and fights on the enemy's terms, notably in the climax to Act One (pp. 54–5). A professional philosopher may find this 'jejune' (Bennett), but Stoppard is no longer caricaturing and the prose has, and is obviously meant to have, dignity and cogency. George has noted that the reductive analyses of many relativist philosophers are associated with reductive *linguistic* analysis—the demonstration that words are relative and shifty is taken to prove that the concepts behind them are equally unstable, are indeed not consistently *there* at all. George reveals in his opponents the concealed assumption that there is a direct relationship between a concept's existence and its name. His technique is to agree entirely with the reductive linguistic analysis and then express puzzlement that it can ever have been thought relevant. That 'good' has meant different things to different people at different times 'is not a statement which anyone would dispute' and 'nothing useful can be inferred from it. It is not in fact a statement about value at all; it is a statement about language and how it is used in a particular society.'

Much the same dismissal of hours of tedious linguistic philosophy is offered, more urbanely, by Anderson in *Professional Foul* (p. 63):

> The importance of language is overrated. . . . it is very useful for communicating detail—but the important truths are simple and monolithic. The essentials of a given situation speak for themselves, and language is as capable of obscuring the truth as of revealing it.

George now attacks with his opponent's material. Certainly different cultures 'honour' their elders in different and apparently contradictory ways; but it is (George manages to imply) naïve not to *expect* such differences. The remarkable thing is the sameness of intention—the idea of honouring elders at all, recurring in two cultures different in most respects.

> For what *is* honour? What are pride, shame, fellow-feeling, generosity and love? If they are instincts, what are instincts? The prevailing temper of modern philosophy is to treat the instinct as a sort of terminus for any train of thought that seeks to trace our impulses to their origins.

But what can be said to be the impulse of a genuinely altruistic act? Hobbes might have answered self-esteem, but what is the attraction or the point in thinking better of oneself? What is *better*? ... Professor McFee succeeds only in showing us that in different situations different actions will be deemed, rightly or wrongly, to be conducive to that good which is independent of time and place and which is knowable but not nameable.

(*Jumpers*, p. 55)

To crow over the fact that different codes of good conduct exist is to highlight yet signally fail to explore the impulse to behave well. There might be some respectability, George seems to be saying, in an absolute rejection of such concepts; but the relativists want it both ways. The blasphemy of the blasphemer proves him not to be an atheist. In his passionate final words, in the play's Coda, George again throws back the contradiction in his opponents' own beliefs:

And yet these same apparently intelligent people, who in extreme cases will not even admit that the Bristol train left from Paddington yesterday—.... will nevertheless and without any sense of inconsistency claim to *know* that life is better than death, that love is better than hate, and that the light shining through the east window of their bloody gymnasium is more beautiful than a rotting corpse!

(*Jumpers*, p. 87).

But immediately before this George has himself failed, seriously and unequivocally; Clegthorpe cried to him for help when about to be shot, and George attempted a 'professional foul':

GEORGE: Well, this seems to be a political quarrel. ... Surely only a proper respect for absolute values ... universal truths—*philosophy*— (*A gunshot.*)

Sir Alfred Ayer's own review of the play (*Sunday Times*, 9.4.72) offers the following philosophical comments:

George needs not one but two Gods, one to create the world and another to support his moral values, and is unsuccessful in obtaining either of them. For the creator he relies on the first-cause argument, which is notoriously fallacious, since it starts from the assumption that everything must have a cause and ends with something that lacks one.

As for the view that morals can be founded on divine authority, the decisive objection was beautifully put by Bertrand Russell, 'Theologians have always taught that God's decrees are good, and that this is not a mere tautology; it follows that goodness is independent of God's decrees'. This argument also shows that even if George had been able to discover his second God it would not have been of any service to him. It would provide a utilitarian motive for good behaviour, but that was not what he wanted. It could, more respectably, provide an object for emulation, but for that imaginary or even actual human beings could serve as well. . . .

The moral of the play, is so far as it has one, seemed to be that George was humane, and therefore human, in a way the others were not. This could have been due to his beliefs, but it did not have to be. Whatever Kant may have said, morality is very largely founded on sympathy and affection, and for these one does not require religious sanctions. Even logical positivists are capable of love.

Anderson in *Professional Foul* is in no sense a caricature, and it is therefore more difficult for Stoppard to bridge plausibly the gap between the lay audience and the Cambridge professor talking to fellow-philosophers. The main force of the play, though, doesn't depend on such bridging: a child can see that it shows a slightly complacent, cloistered academic, accustomed to *talking* about right and wrong, being shocked into *action*—into risking not only his comfort but also his ethical fastidiousness (smuggling the manuscript out is the sort of 'reversal of a principle' which McKendrick has unpersuasively recommended but which Anderson himself distrusts). Human need—and the child-like perception of what is fair—override the subtleties of academic ethics.

But this is a realist play and Stoppard is not tempted to parody, or camouflage in gobbledegook, Anderson's formal philosophy: it is worth attending to. His original paper to the Colloquium was to have been entitled 'Ethical Fictions as Ethical Foundations' and some gesture towards the original text seems to be made in the first page of this substituted paper (p. 87): even if a system of rights is only a man-invented system, it should be treated as if it was truth (presumably because otherwise it will not work as a system). On p. 88 there is a different nod, or rather a wave of dismissal, in the direction of Rousseau's Social Contract:

> that humanity is a rather large club with club rules, but it is not what is generally meant by human rights. It is not what Locke meant, and it is not what the American Founding Fathers meant when, taking the hint from Locke, they held certain rights to be unalienable—among them, life, liberty, and the pursuit of happiness.

A third nod follows, to the religious view that rights are 'the endowment of God', which view 'I do not hold myself'.

Anderson then points out, a little like George pointing out the prevalence of ideas of honour in different cultures, how much agreement there is on what human rights should be, whatever the beliefs from which they are promulgated. He is being as embarrassing as possible to his Czech hosts by quoting, in an apparent tribute, articles of Czech Constitution which he and everyone present knows are every day violated by the State itself. The irony is still apparent in the tone of the next paragraph (top of p. 89), but so is the urgency, shared with George in *Jumpers* ('What, in short, is so good about good?'):

> Is such a consensus remarkable? Not at all. If there is a God, we his creations would doubtless subscribe to his values. And if there is not a God, he, our creation, would undoubtedly be credited with values which we think to be fair and sensible. But what is fairness? What is sense? What are these values which we take to be self-evident? And why are they values?

(The last four rhetorical questions—the most reminiscent of *Jumpers*—were cut from the BBC production.)

Again at the top of p. 90 we are moving parallel to *Jumpers*, with the linguistic philosophers' reductive assumption, this time about the word 'justice'. Against this reduction Anderson puts a sort of reduction of his own (taking a cue from Chetwyn on p. 79, and perhaps from his meeting with Hollar's son, Sacha):

> A small child who cries 'That's not fair' when punished for some-thing done by his brother or sister is apparently appealing to an idea of justice which is, for want of a better word, natural.... Now a

philosopher exploring the difficult terrain of right and wrong should not be over-impressed by the argument 'a child would know the difference'. But when, let us say, we are being persuaded that it is ethical to put someone in prison for reading or writing the wrong books, it is well to be reminded that you can persuade a man to believe almost anything provided he is clever enough, but it is much more difficult to persuade someone less clever.

As Iris Murdoch says:

> The ordinary person does not, unless corrupted by philosophy, believe that he creates values by his choices. He thinks that some things really are better than others and that he is capable of getting it wrong. We are not usually in doubt about the direction in which Good lies.
> (*The Sovereignty of Good*, p. 97)

'There is,' Anderson goes on to say, 'a sense of right and wrong which precedes utterance.' At an earlier session of the Colloquium he has already said 'the important truths are simple and monolithic. The essentials of a given situation speak for themselves.' George's phrase was 'knowable but not nameable'.

This is as far as explicit philosophy in Stoppard goes. It is not all that far, and here it is confined to a test case—State oppression of individual freedom of speech and thought—on which the issues are indeed fairly clear-cut. What the small child would say at Ruth's yearning for Jacob Milne (*Night and Day*), or whether we would trust a small child's sense of fairness on such a matter, is more questionable. For a writer of his intellectual grasp, and one who uses the word 'moral' so relatively easily, Stoppard has in fact as yet dealt little with ethical predicaments. We may look almost impatiently to the play suggested by this remark (to the editors of *Theatre Quarterly*, 1974): 'all political acts have a moral basis to them and are meaningless without it'. They 'must be judged in moral terms, in terms of their consequences'.

What raises our expectations so high, here and elsewhere in Stoppard, is his sheer sharp-mindedness. His writing approaches its subject-matter with ears pricked and whiskers twitching, interested both in the main movement of an idea and also in its side-effects which less alert minds ignore—a twig of language crackling underfoot, a fascinating but irrelevant scent drifting across and distracting the subject, a stream of possible puns crossing the path. Both major and minor elements in Stoppard's work originate in readiness to tease out an apparently trivial notion to see what happens to it: painting the Forth Bridge, the girl's voice on the speaking clock, what happens *out* of *Hamlet*, Wittgenstein's cube and brick, A. J. Ayer's interest in football. What might have been only glancing jokes are worked out and develop their own considerable architecture of zany rationality.

RIGIDITY AND FLUX

Much comedy depends on the collision of differing logics—two confident and conflicting assumptions clashing; talk at cross purposes; the need for Tom to prey and Jerry to tease; the 'straight man's' exaggerated straightness and the comic's mania. In Stoppard a pattern appears, as one looks through the plays, which indicates his own special version of this comic collision. It is the contrast between a particularly neat and self-contained logic, often entirely arbitrary or fictional, but very attractive, and the mess, contingency, and awkwardness of the real world. It is the contrast between Yeats's extreme phases of the moon, which 'disdain All that man is', and the 'mere complexities of mire and blood'. *Albert's Bridge* will illustrate it well.

Albert is a well-meaning young man, but his study of philosophy has in some respects disabled him for ordinary life, and particularly for relationships. Painting the high bridge is for him 'Simplicity—so ... contained; neat ... there are no consequences to a coat of paint.' (p. 9).

The contingency of life at ground level distresses him (as a philosophy student he may well have read *Nausea*) though not so much as it distresses Fraser, who meets him repeatedly on the bridge. Like Moon in the novel, Fraser feels that 'there's too much of everything, but the space for it is constant. So the shell of human existence is filling out, expanding, and it's going to go bang.'

Both Moon and Fraser are appalled at the fragility of the chains of economic cause and effect which keep civilization going, and terrified that people might want to stop being dentists, and disgusted that (identical phrasing in both characters) 'the white rhino is being wiped out for the racket in bogus aphrodisiacs'. But Fraser, having climbed high to throw himself off, finds that from this height everything looks 'quite ordered ... From a vantage point like this, the idea of society is just about tenable. ...' (p. 32).

What neither Albert nor Fraser can recognize is that the natural extension of this comfortable but artificial logic is to go so high that nothing can be perceived. As Lord Malquist says to Moon, 'Nothing ... is the history of the world viewed from a suitable distance.'

All of us may know something of what Moon, Albert or Fraser mean, and Stoppard may well be writing of a pressure he has felt personally; but we can't all paint bridges, linger on them, or throw bombs to shock people out of their complacency. In spite of the intellectual attractiveness of the bridge's remoteness, Stoppard presses the claims of ordinary life, giving Albert a pleasant and normal wife and child whom he is virtually deserting and for whom, at the cartoon level of the play, we feel some sympathy.

Another isolated and unreal logic is the County Hall mathematics of the City Engineer, Fitch, on which the play's plot depends. Four men are happily and permanently employed in painting the bridge; Fitch's calculations result in the sacking of three of them, and in the bridge becoming a nasty eyesore—because his paper logic has not considered the time-scale and the rust which will not wait. His re-calculation goes equally logically to the still more ludicrous other extreme, of painting the whole bridge in one day with 1,800 men. But that logic hasn't taken into consideration fundamental laws of physics—the pressures of the real world—and the bridge collapses, which is another kind of reduction to 'nothing' by taking a neat logic to its extreme.

The contrast might almost be seen as that between thinking and caring, where caring is the thinking which accommodates itself to real life and real need. It is a pattern which goes deep in Stoppard's temperament as revealed in his writing: on the one hand the attractions of sheer brainwork, deduction, calculation, order; on the other, the fundamental moral imperatives 'beyond utterance', of diminishing human suffering, responding to human need, and pursuing the good. On the one hand, art for art's sake, and sheer 'style'; on the other, death, chance, real artists being prevented from practising their art in Czecho-slovakia, and, to be sure, the real demands of the box-office.

A look through the plays may illuminate the pattern further. And before that a quotation from an early short story, *Reunion*, not now in print, may be helpful:

'There is a certain word,' he said very carefully, 'which if shouted at the right pitch and in a silence worthy of it would nudge the universe into gear ... a monstrous, unspeakable intrusion after which nothing will be the same for the man who does it. All the things which just miss will just click right, and the mind that heaves and pops like boiling porridge will level off, secretly. .... His mind will have shuddered into a great and marvellous calm in which books will be written and flowers picked and loves complemented. ...

'I nearly got it once. ... We were remembering the dead, supposed to be. At school, in the town church we went to, six hundred of us suspended in the thick of the two-minute silence, and I knocked my prayer-book off the ledge. It hit the floor flat and went off like a pistol shot. I reckon for two seconds everything intrusive to myself flew out of me. ...'

Constance in *M is for Moon among Other Things* is nostalgic for her early childhood.

Everything was so simple then. I thought that each letter only stood for the one word they gave, you know? A is for Apple, B is for Baby, C is for Cat ... M was for Moon. It was ages before I knew that M was for anything else.

In *Enter a Free Man* the contrast is clearly between Riley's inventor's-logic, which is quite excessively selective, and the multiple logics of the real world. Riley's plan for using envelopes twice is excellent provided no one ever tears them open and provided they remain with the sender; his plan for watering indoor plants is fine provided that the rain knows it has to stop when the indoor logic is satisfied.... Persephone and Linda keep Riley alive and comfortable in the real world so that he may continue his inept logical initiatives, and he is sufficiently *innocently* locked in that logic to refuse to draw the dole: 'Let's not have that again. I told you—that's for the unemployed people. You've got to be out of work.' (p. 46).

Glad in *If You're Glad* failed to gain admission to a convent, where she sought 'serenity', and unwisely accepted work for the First Lord of the Post Office for the sake of an ordered existence there. She is trapped, and Frank is unable to release her, but from within she kicks hard against the rigid logics imposed on her, and there is no doubt that she knows they falsify the real. One of her dreams is to sneeze while speaking the time, to 'sneeze the fear of God into/their alarm-setting, egg-timing/train-catching, coffee-breaking faith in/an uncomprehended clockwork—' (p. 24).

Meanwhile it never occurs to Frank to leave his bus timetable—he is as tied to that as Gladys to her clock.

In *Rosencrantz* the arbitrary and self-contained logic is that of Shakespeare's play *Hamlet*; but Ros and Guil feel that they have been, and are, *real* people. Guil is terrified by the loss of chance; to him ordinary life and the law of probability 'made for a kind of harmony and a kind of confidence. It related the fortuitous and the ordained into a reassuring union which we recognized as nature.' (p. 13).

If Ros and Guil's position is to be taken, as some spectators wish to take it, as in any way allegorical of human life, then it is allegory not of existentialism, materialism, or chance, but of a fixed purpose, a logic beyond and outside us which we cannot visualize.

Hound is a farce in similar territory. The play within the play is feeble, all that is worst in stage murder mysteries, but it proves to have monstrous power; its tentacles clutch Birdboot and Moon bodily from their seats and drag them to its maw. Even when Birdboot, once on stage, attempts to apply rationality and learned experience to his predicament, the play is one jump ahead of him—the wheelchair enters from one wing lower down than before and bowls him over (p. 39). Behind the simple contrast of the play's fixed pattern and life's flux, however, we discover in this case that all has been directed by one fanatic logic, that of Puckeridge, the third string. He has evidently decided, rather like Mr Moon in the novel, to do something explosive to break the first-second-third string logic and impose his own. The whole thing is of course a splendid nonsense, and the rationality it travesties is that of 'the supreme example of rational art' (Bigsby), the murder mystery, where equally grotesque chains of grudge and plotting are disclosed in the final moments.

The obvious contrast in *Where are They Now?* is between the fixed logic of school—special slang, artificial rigidities—and the flux of the Old Boys' adult lives. Also obvious is the second contrast, between the Old Boys' dream of the happiest days of their lives, and the tedium and fears of real schooldays. More subtly offered is a third contrast, reversing the second: Gale's fixed image is of school as *all* tedium and fear, but we discover as the play proceeds that he was rather a lively schoolboy and the last sounds are of him, in his schooldays, being 'very happy'.

Finally, in the character of Jenkins, the Old Boy who is at the wrong reunion, we have another preconception ignoring reality. There do happen to be two reunions going on in the same hotel, and there does happen to be a place here for 'Jenkins' (the dead master); but beyond that there is no consistency between Jenkins's recollections and those of the others. He persists, however, in believing that he is the only one in step—until he finds himself, at the end, singing the wrong school song.

Stoppard's finest radio play, *Artist Descending*, abounds in false rationalities and inversions of the expected. The starting-point and finishing-point—the tape of Donner's death—is a piece of real life, chance, accident. Donner fell downstairs while swatting a fly. But the assumption made from the outset is that of murder mystery; and Martello and Beauchamp adhere to it in spite of plentiful 'lateral' clues to the truth. The activities of the artists satirize the self-indulgent false logics of much twentieth-century art: dull pointlessness ('a row of black stripes on a white background') defended because it 'is only when the imagination is dragged away from what the eye sees that a picture becomes interesting'; a gramophone recording of an imaginary ping-pong game ('I'm trying to liberate the visual *image* from the limita-tions of visual *art*'). Ceramic food ('to define the problem' of the luxury of art in a world where peasants starve) is followed by edible art, the previous logic inverted ('it will . . . put taste back where it belongs') and a statue of clichés. Stoppard is fair to this neo-Dadaism by allowing Donner a summary of Dada-ist logic (which *deliberately* puts absurd patterns on life in place of respected patterns it feels to be discredited):

> The war . . . killed it for me. After that, being an artist made no sense. . . . Except for nonsense art . . . We tried to make a distinction between the art that celebrated reason and history and logic and all assumptions, and our own dislocated anti-art of lost faith. . . .
>
> (p. 27)

After Magritte is a farce consisting largely of attempts at deduction. The flux of ordinary life can produce moments which look like manifestations of subversive or sinister systems. In fact there is nothing amiss: the oddest things in the play (apart from Magritte's actual tendency to paint tubas, and Mother's obsessions with tubas and Sir Adrian Boult) are the characters' attempts at explanations. Each person's theory forms its own exclusive logic, denying the possibility of other interpretation at each point of detail; and Stoppard has fun with the tangles into which amateur logicians can get themselves.

The particular game played by this play is one of Stoppard's favourites. The task is to produce a rational explanation of a grotesque circumstance—*or* to make intelligent use of grotesque material. When I was at school (the same time as Stoppard) a commonly set 'composition' was 'Compose a story involving a shoelace, a steeplejack, and a bread roll' or similar; one would like to have seen young Tom's efforts. The composition of Joyce's *Ulysses* is neatly viewed in this way in *Travesties*: 'CARR: Homer's *Odyssey* and the Dublin Street Directory? . . . I admit it's an unusual combination of sources, but not wholly without possibilities' (p. 44) and André Previn presented Stoppard himself with a similar challenge in proposing a play requiring a full-size live symphony orchestra on stage. *Dogg's Hamlet* contrives to make a play out of an idea from Wittgenstein, and the meshing together of this, the fifteen-minute *Hamlet*, and a shortened *Macbeth*, with angry satire on Czech repression, is a particularly fine piece of problem-solving. There is one glorious incidental grace-note as Easy's narrative on p. 20 ('my mate got struck down in a thunderstorm on the A412 near Rickmansworth') when repeated in Dogg-language on p. 71 causes the Hostess to refer to a phrase-book, evidently of the classical kind: 'He says his postillion has been struck by lightning.'

One can imagine Stoppard seeking for years a way of getting that line (the time-honoured parody of phrase-book phrases) plausibly into a play. (See, too, 'I'm going to have to straighten you out when I get you home'—*On the Razzle* p. 46—spoken by Zangler to Melchior who has been folded up inside a screen.)

Jumpers moves from one such conundrum to another; and the explanations are of the Stoppardian anti-surrealist kind which may by now be familiar. The opening sequence turns out to have rational—though distressing—explanations; so do Dotty's apparently dead body on her bed (p. 30), her stomping across the room wearing a goldfish bowl on her head (p. 36), and the George–Bones encounter on p. 43. When Bones finally makes his romantic approach to Dotty (p. 52) Mozart accompanies it; when he raises his head, an elephant's mating-call emerges, and when he drops his vase of flowers on the carpet there is a Goon-show noise as if it had dropped down a long flight of stone stairs. All this too turns out to be explicable—like the blood on the back of the Secretary's coat as she makes her last exit.

Clearly the tape in *Artist Descending* is another example of this kind of problem-solving; so is the corpse-Higgs-Puckeridge connection in *Hound*. A version of the same is McKendrick's laugh against himself:

> My wife said to me—now, Bill, don't do anything daft, you know what you're like, if a blonde knocked on your door with the top three buttons of her police uniform undone and asked for a cup of sugar you'd convince yourself she was a bus conductress brewing up in the next room.
>
> (*Professional Foul*, p. 76)

A rigid view looks at things one way only—at the turning-inside-out of the envelope after use; reality presents opposite possibilities or pressures. *After Magritte* makes as many interpretations as possible of a puzzling glimpse. Guil presents a rather different choice—between one set view, which we assume, and its exact reverse:

> A Chinaman of the T'ang Dynasty—and, by which definition, a philosopher—dreamed he was a butterfly, and from that moment was never quite sure that he was not a butterfly dreaming it was a Chinese philosopher.
>
> (p. 44)

In *Jumpers*, Dotty's assumptions are all smashed. George clings to his, and they carry more of the playwright's sympathy than most, but like the other characters he shuts his mind to flux. Not only does he no longer recognize Dotty's need for him, or his responsibility to her; he fails to see that although a group call themselves 'radical' and 'liberal' they do not necessarily have any of the old-fashioned honour and virtue associated with those terms. He fails to believe they can be evil. Most seriously, in the dream Coda, he fails Clegthorpe.

Jumpers could be said to be about what happens in the flux after moral grids are outworn or discredited. Through the plays Stoppard has shown faith in the flux in spite of intellectual appreciation of the systems. In *Jumpers* even the best of systems seem to have collapsed, and the question is whether all values will collapse in the Dark Ages of Rad-Lib cynicism, or whether George's faith is justified.

In the opening of *Travesties* the game of grotesquenesses rationally explicable is played with language (the opening of *Dirty Linen* is a miniature of the same game). Separate languages; and separate logics. To Joyce art is its own *raison d'être* and the mere events of the world are minor ('If there is any meaning in any of it, it is in what survives as art'). Lenin's mind is equally closed in dedication to his logic ('We shall establish a free press . . . free from bourgeois anarchist individualism!'). As for Tzara, Dada is explicitly illogical as a logical reaction to man's past behaviour—it is, in a way, an attempt to make art out of flux ('It has no meaning. It is without meaning as Nature is. It is Dada.'). Meanwhile the play is set in Switzerland, a neutral country at peace, where the clocks don't strike thirteen and the ground doesn't shift: an ideal fixity, or the normal flux of life? When the rest of Europe is at war, perhaps the flux-normality is war?

These are separate, clashing logics: art, revolution, nonsense; and much of the play's dramatic force derives from the *confidence* of each conflicting advocate. In the structure of the play we have similar creative tension: between the pattern of *Earnest* and the flux of approximately historical action. It says something about the zany nerve of *Travesties* that there are moments when the return to the *Earnest* scheme feels like a return to humdrum normality rather than to the elegant and utterly false logic which it is.

Meanwhile *Travesties* also enjoys minor byplay with the superficial clothing of logical consistency. The mad system of the limerick must complete itself:

JOYCE: When I want to leave things in the air
       I say, 'Excuse me, I've got to repair
       to my book about Bloom—'
       And just leave the room.

(*He has gone. Pause. Low light on motionless* CARR *in his chair.*)
CARR: Well, let us resume. *Zurich By One Who Was There.*

Cecily's knowledge of the poets and Carr's general education have both been strictly in alphabetical order. She has done better than he all round, having reached G in poets and Zimmervaldism ('the last word in revolutionary politics'), where Carr is still struggling with Anarchism. When the logic of Shakespeare's sonnet 18 is cut up arbitrarily by Tzara's scissors, it reassembles itself in a new pattern of embarrassing indelicacy (p. 54).

Language itself, the tool of logic, can betray. Carr comes a cropper in his understandable assumption that Joyce is a woman; but he himself mischievously turns the apparatus of logic to the aid of nonsense ('post hock, propter hock'—p. 36). Ironically, though, the inflexible definitive diagnosis of Marxist theory yields quickly enough to flux when it suits it, and produces an illogicality in the cause of an arrogant logic:

> The Bolshevik line is that some unspecified but unique property of the Russian situation, unforeseen by Marx, has caused the bourgeois-capitalist era of Russian history to be compressed into the last few days, and that the time for the proletarian revolution is now ripe.
>
> (p. 31)

Travesties is a house of cards of tilted, opposing, two-dimensional logics. 'Real life' hardly enters the play—perhaps the most sober moments are the letters of Lenin, and Nadya's memoirs. But the background imagery is of trench-warfare, of the cave-man, of Lenin 'hitting heads'. Round the periphery of the play, as round the borders of Switzerland, are war, revolution, suffering, death—the flux which the elegant and conflicting logics can inadequately treat. The fierce import of the play is its warning against what Lawrence called the 'ghastly obscene *knowers*'; Tzara in the following quotation is taking off from a line of Wilde, but there is the intensity of Stoppard's own perception behind it: 'I am sick of cleverness. The clever people try to impose a design on the world and when it goes calamitously wrong they call it fate.' (p. 37).

To the satyr-play, *Dirty Linen*: here the obvious contrast is between the official version of M.P.s' behaviour and what they actually do. Perhaps more important in Stoppard's mind originally was a contrast between the stereotype dumb blonde secretary and the real alertness, warmth and commonsense of Maddie ('real' in the cartoon terms of this play: her activities defy further belief). A subtle minor contrast is between the page three pin-ups—safely de-humanized, images for the men's club and the men's room, and the actual sight of Maddie losing her clothes. At each 'Strewth!' the M.P.s are seen unconsciously preferring the two-dimensional pin-ups which keep prurience safely in its place.

In *Every Good Boy* we are in a particularly clear diagram. The orchestra vividly represents a set logic, dutifully in time, the State running smoothly. At the end everyone has joined it, except Alexander and Sacha—and Sacha has a different music: a simple lyrical line contrasting with the sophistication of the orchestral sound.

Ivanov has in his head his own logical music, imperceptible to the outside world. As for the State logic, its practitioners have forgotten flux, and Alexander is determined to remind them of it again. 'They lost. And they will have to see that it is so. They have forgotten their mortality. Losing might be their first touch of it for a long time.' (p. 29).

The State logic puts together all prisoners with the same name, and is so certain of its own rightness that all dissent has to be irrational. A complaint becomes, medically, a complaint (p. 26), and when a dissident shows no symptom of disturbance at all that is (since by definition he is ill) 'a pathological development of the personality' (p. 31). The rigidity here becomes literal: prison bars, as in *Cahoot's Macbeth* it becomes a wall. It is also so unresponsive to flux that it becomes stupid:

Incidentally, when you go before the Commission try not to make any remark which might confuse them. . . . The sort of thing I'd stick to is 'Yes', if they ask you whether you agree you were mad; 'No', if they ask you whether you intend to persist in your slanders; 'Definitely', if they ask you whether your treatment has been satisfactory, and 'Sorry', if they ask you how you feel about it all, or if you didn't catch the question.

But Alexander has his own rigidity, of integrity: 'I was never mad, and my treatment was barbaric.'

And perhaps that too ought to yield to flux:

> Stupidity is one thing I can't cure. I have to show that I have treated you. You have to recant and show gratitude for the treatment. We have to act together.
>
> (p. 28)

'act' is of course nicely ambiguous.

Professional Foul is realist in method, but almost all its material still depends on the rigidity–flux tension: in many respects it is Stoppard's fullest and most serious treatment of the subject. The academic philosophy game, which is played verbally, ignores 'simple virtue', truths 'beyond utterance'—and real danger. At the start of the play, Anderson uses his academic wit pedantically and rather ungraciously to object to McKendrick's smoking in a non-smoking area:

> There is a coldness around my heart as though I'd seen your cigarette smoke knock against the ceiling and break in two like a bread stick. By the way, that is a non-smoking seat.
>
> (p. 45)

McKendrick has in fact moved from the front row of the smokers' seats to the back row of the non-smokers' (i.e. forward one row) in order to make a normal human approach to Anderson. At this stage our sympathies are likely to be with McKendrick. When Anderson tells him, a little later, that he has an 'ulterior motive' (pp. 46–7) it is all (especially as finely played by Peter Barkworth) a jolly little don's game. 'You see, if I tell you I make you a co-conspirator.' It does not enter Anderson's head (though it does McKendrick's) that he is travelling to a country where real conspiracy might be necessary. Approached by Hollar, Anderson tells him that 'it would be bad manners' for him to smuggle Hollar's thesis back to England. Manners are a code of conduct, like the rules of philosophy—or like the rules of football. McKendrick, told at the end that he has unwittingly carried out the manuscript, says: 'Jesus. It's not quite playing the game, is it?'

The professional fouler plays the system and chooses to ignore the real: a footballer hacked down in the goalmouth may break a leg, and a penalty is then small consolation: it is small consolation for Hollar that Anderson's ethical fastidiousness would be undisturbed if he refused to take the paper. In deceiving McKendrick and thereby getting the paper out of Czechoslovakia, Anderson has broken the set codes of honesty and honour; the flux of life and need has cried to him and been heard. 'Ethics is a very complicated business.'

Subverting all this uncertainty is the appeal to the ethical sense of a young child, which is spontaneous and judges each case on its merits. The more elaborate the logics on the other hand, the more they may be vulnerable to evil: 'You can persuade a man to believe almost anything provided he is clever enough.'

The false assumptions based on stereotyped thinking, which caused much laughter in earlier plays, are all over the place here. Anderson doesn't think McKendrick would write for a girlie magazine (pp. 48–9). 'Extra-curricular activities' (p. 48) for McKendrick here means political involvement, where Anderson himself means football and thinks McKendrick means sex. See also my examples on pp. 117–19 above. A minor, light-hearted gloss on the play's main theme is the self-absorption of the footballers. Broadbent and Crisp are quite serious on p. 59 in not wishing to discuss dubious football tactics in front of the lift operative, and even in suspecting that the lift may be bugged to catch *their* discussion. And Broadbent is quite serious when, acknowledging how right Anderson proved to be about 'that bloody Jirasek' (p. 86), he adds 'They don't teach you nothing at that place then.'

It is the first time he has any genuine respect for Anderson.

Stone's linguistic analysis, in Anderson's view, is an attempt to find pattern in a natural flux. 'Language develops in an *ad hoc* way. So there is no reason to expect its development to be logical' (p. 63). George in *Jumpers* is less polite than Anderson: McFee's 'clockwork' (p. 72) consists of showing (p. 54)

> that the word 'good' has also meant different things to different people at different times, an exercise which combines simplicity with futility in a measure he does not apparently suspect, for on the one hand it is not a statement which anyone would dispute, and on the other, nothing useful can be inferred from it.

Like Lenin's supporters in *Travesties*, Wagner in *Night and Day* bends his union-logic to suit himself—having reported Milne (according to the code) when it is in his own interests to do so, he then fails to obey the union's directive when it would be against his interests:

> WAGNER: I ought to be there.
> RUTH: Aren't you supposed to be withdrawing your labour?
> WAGNER: (*Snaps at her*) Don't get clever with me, damn you.
>
> (p. 93)

His petty-minded application of the rules (against the *spirit* of reporting) costs him the best story of his life: the Mageeba interview will not see print because of the shutdown he has precipitated.

In the non-realist elements of the play we find the Stoppardian see-saw between a convenient *apparent* reality and the truth. The 'parallel world' of fantasy in which we begin Act Two is tense and beautiful, far from glib: honour and passion nobly engage—it is almost like a piece of Racine. Later we realize it was fantasy, and we are possessed by the realities of death and chance.

Returning to cartoon-worlds, in *Dogg's Hamlet, Cahoot's Macbeth* the systems of *Hamlet*, of school discipline, of *Macbeth*, and of State intrusion continually clash, together with the other systems of language; and the last moments of the play are a race between logics—*Macbeth*, the State, Dogg-language, English—with Easy the hero of flux, able to adjust to almost anything as he has been all evening, and able to survive.

The best overall comment on this insistent pattern in Stoppard comes from George in *Jumpers* (p. 72): 'now and again ... it seems to me that life itself is the mundane figure which argues perfection at its limiting curve.'

It isn't the dogmas, in fact, which imply absolutes, but the flux itself. 'And if I doubt it, the ability to doubt, to question, to *think*, seems to be the curve itself. *Cogito ergo deus est.*'

The doubt, the recognition that dogmas won't do—refusing at the same time to lapse into cynicism, and what one might call the embrace of flux—are summed up a moment later as 'finding mystery':

> McFee never put himself at risk by finding mystery in the clockwork, never looked for trouble or over his shoulder, and I'm sorry he's gone but what can be his complaint? McFee jumped, and left nothing behind but a vacancy.

A AND MINUS A

'Firstly, A; secondly, minus A.' Stoppard made a good deal, in the 1970s, of 'not knowing'. We have seen George, in spite of his academic research into The Concept of Knowledge, still clumsily honest about his confusion ('All I know is that I think that I know that I know ...'); and earlier we have seen Mr Moon refusing to endorse socially acceptable positions until he feels sure they are right. Stoppard's interviews repeatedly show the pattern of reversal, qualification, and uncertainty; see for example the quotations on pp. 15 and 46 above; or his remarks about

> the constantly turning faces of that particular cube which on one side says for example: 'All Italians are voluble' and on the next side says, 'That is a naïve generalization'; and then, 'No, it's not. Behind generalizations there must be some sort of basis.' Tilt it once

more and there's the 'yes, but ...' Then you're back to the original one.

(to Ronald Hayman, 1976)

This 'not knowing' accounts for much of the excellence of Stoppard's work. Even in *Jumpers*, where there is a consistent line of identification with George's thinking, Dotty and Archie are given much wittier and more attractive speeches to the *opposite* effect, George fails signally in the Coda, and, apart from Dotty's final moon-line, Archie has the last word. *Travesties* is the play which most fully and excitingly uses the 'A minus A' pattern; and again we find Cecily's impassioned defence of Marxism *follows* Carr/Stoppard's dismissal of Marx as having 'got it all wrong'. In *Night and Day* we can note five different opinions of the press, its function and its importance, and they are all perhaps partly 'right'—certainly each can draw some of our sympathy in the theatre. 'Ruth', says Carson (p. 47), 'has mixed feelings about reporters'—a characteristically gentlemanly expression, which she promptly flattens:

> No, I haven't. I despise them. Not foreign correspondents, of course [a touch of her own social training emerging?]
> —or the gardening notes. The ones in between ... *Has anyone ever bothered to find out whether anybody really cares?*

Wagner's morality is that of the professional—pride in a job well done—and Stoppard can be expected to sympathize with him.

> I'm known for doing two things well: I can usually find out what's going on in a place while I am in it, and I can usually find a way to get the story back to my office in time to catch the first edition. It's not so much to be proud about, and if I fail nothing happens—not to Kambawe, not to the paper—but such as it is it is my pride.

(p. 54)

Milne accepts all the 'A' arguments and suddenly follows with 'minus A':

> I felt part of a privileged group, inside society and yet outside it, with a licence to scourge it and a duty to defend it, night and day, the street of

adventure, the fourth estate. And the thing is I was dead right. That's what it was, and I *was* part of it because it's indivisible. Junk journalism is the evidence of a society that has got at least one thing right, that there should be nobody with the power to dictate where responsible journalism begins.

(p. 61)

The climax of the play is also the climax of the debate about newspapers: an extended encounter between Wagner and Mageeba, the one hard-bitten but here naïvely unaware, the other machiavellian, well beyond the idealism which he may or may not have expressed 'all those years ago at the LSE'. The aftermaths, the attempts at the last word on the subject, fall over themselves: Guthrie p. 90, Ruth p. 91, and finally Guthrie on p. 92:

I've been around a lot of places. People do awful things to each other. But it's worse in places where everybody is kept in the dark. It really is. Information is light. Information, in itself, about anything, is light. That's all you can say, really.

Stoppard is clearly with Guthrie here—as an ex-journalist, as a keen reader of non-fiction, as an opponent of any force which might inhibit the free passage of information, whether it be a totalitarian State or a union 'closed-shop'. That 'information is light' is worth repeating. The danger is that it makes too slight and comfortable a conclusion to the bitter debate which has preceded it.

LAZINESS?

The most generally damaging criticism of Stoppard's work is that which takes it on its own terms—as thinking as well as amusement—and finds it wanting. The mind *is* very sharp, but perhaps it is at times too easy on itself. Walter Kerr, the New York drama critic, has no doubts about it: 'Busy as Mr Stoppard's mind is, it is also lazy; he will settle for the first thing that comes into his head' (quoted by Kenneth Tynan, p. 115).

It is the misfortune of some very hard-working artists to have their polished product called facile; and people who have worked with Stoppard can testify to his care in choosing even a single word. 'The first thing that comes into his head'—no; that is simply unfair. But to settle for what will 'work' pretty well, that is a constant theatrical temptation. The plays do 'work'; they are funny, exciting, and original. But they often leave us restless, as lesser (and, of course, greater) pieces do not. Kinds of attention are aroused in us which are not in the end fully rewarded.

To base this criticism on the nuts-and-bolts comedies would be unfair. It is fair to note, though, that pieces such as *If You're Glad*, *A Separate Peace*, or *Albert's Bridge*, like the novel *Lord Malquist and Mr Moon*, do tend to dig into our fears or sympathies and then abruptly withdraw. They create pain which is then unresolved, and which the laughter doesn't dismiss. We can also note, though thinking it a little severe, Bigsby's criticism of *Hound* (above, p. 54). The substantial play of this early period is *Rosencrantz*, an immense popular success, which was quickly taken more seriously than Stoppard can have expected. ('There was no doubt in my mind that the novel would make my reputation, and the play would be of little consequence either way.') The links to *Hamlet* and to *Waiting for Godot*, and a tendency to return to the topic of death, led to some very earnest explications. Anthony Callen, describing Stoppard as 'a philosophy graduate', found the play 'Existential', 'baroque', 'nihilistic', and rapped another critic over the knuckles for recognizing that it is in fact 'witty, unpretentious'. He was repeatedly surprised by the 'remarkable' resemblances to Beckett's play, apparently missing entirely the humour of travesty and allusion. Painfully, however, he felt obliged to admit that 'Stoppard seems to doubt the Existential vision'. The audience is permitted

to feel too secure, to enjoy the pleasurable objectivity afforded by dramatic irony and thus to resist the play as a picture of its own condition. This perspective is, moreover, encouraged by Stoppard's somewhat indiscriminate exploitation of the opportunities for comedy.

John Russell Taylor was almost equally toffee-nosed, not so much at Stoppard as at his bourgeois audience:

> for audiences more thoroughly familiar with the more advanced sections of modern theatre than the average National Theatre audience, the play is too long-drawn-out for its material.

Perhaps the truth was that the idea was too good (a thought which might amuse Kenneth Ewing, Stoppard's agent, with whom it originated). 'A conception of genius,' said John Simon in the *Hudson Review*, 'which requires genius to develop it; whereas, in the event, it gets only cleverness and charm.' Similarly, Robert Brustein found it

> a noble conception which has not been endowed with any real weight or texture. The author is clearly an intelligent man with a good instinct for the stage, and his premise is one that should suggest an endless series of possibilities. But he manipulates this premise instead of exploring it . . . in execution, it is derivative and familiar, even prosaic. As an artist, Stoppard does not fight hard enough for his insights—they all seem to come to him, prefabricated, from other plays—with the result that his air of pessimism seems affected, and his philosophical meditations, while witty and urbane, never obtain the thickness of *felt* knowledge. . . .

This, I think, is right enough. The dramatist's offence is to have dared make sport with serious matters. Brustein goes on: 'There is . . . a prevailing strain of cuteness which shakes one's faith in the author's serious intentions.' A faith in his *comic* intentions might have been a better starting-point. John Weightman struggled towards this: 'Perhaps the whole play is just intellectual fooling-around, with occasional stabs at seriousness.' Yes, I think that's about it, though I'd take out the word 'just'. Much of this early criticism of *Rosencrantz* seems to me not exactly wrong, but misplaced.

Nevertheless, Brustein's charge that 'Stoppard does not fight hard enough for his insights' may return disturbingly to our minds as we watch later plays in which Stoppard's intentions are more serious. And there is another observation of John

Weightman's which seems to me shrewd and fair; referring to Guil's 'tongueless dwarf' speech (quoted above, p. 95):

> The bird out of season and the tongueless dwarf are surely *kitsch*, but are we meant to appreciate them as being symptomatic of Guildenstern's camp vibration, or to enjoy them as poetry? I guess Mr Stoppard is hoping for the latter reaction but would settle for the former, and so the former it inevitably is.

This is an aspect of what I called 'the theatrical temptation'. If it works, one way or another, settle for it. This was particularly possible in *Rosencrantz*, the work of a still relatively inexperienced dramatist looking for lively theatre. By *Jumpers* Stoppard was consciously trying to be serious as well as funny, and hoped that

> it makes coherent, in terms of theatre, a fairly complicated intellectual argument.... Opacity would be a distinct failure in that play. I don't think of it as being opaque anyway, and I consider clarity is essential.
>
> (to *Theatre Quarterly*, summer 1974)

What is this 'fairly complicated intellectual argument' which Stoppard reckons to have got clear? I take it to be approximately this: George considers that our ethical debates point in the end not to relativity but to absolute good; and our philosophical debates point in the end to something like God. On the other hand he is naïve about evil, and retreats into soft-liberalism rather than face up to the amoral violence of his country's new rulers; and he fails in his own personal dealings. The knowledge of goodness, in the play, is with the weak-spirited (whereas power has passed to cynics); and his weakness may harm those about him.

Stoppard's sympathies are unmistakably with George. But we have seen a professional philosopher dismiss the climax of George's argument—pp. 53–5—as 'jejune' rather than 'fairly complicated', and C. W. E. Bigsby is probably being fair in saying that George's 'convictions remain nothing more than an expression of faith disguised as logical inferences'.

(Perhaps, however, the same might be said of all intuitionist philosophy.)

John Weightman found the play

> still a bit too scrappy and incoherent for my taste . . . quite a bit of the action did not seem necessary. . . . why has Dorothy gone off sex with her husband? I suspect it is simply because Mr Stoppard wants to make a pun about a consummate artist refusing consummation. And why is the play weighted down at the end with the rather tedious coda? . . . quite a few bits of this play have not been brought into intellectual or aesthetic focus.

(Since Weightman wrote, the Coda has been shortened.) That 'or aesthetic' extends the criticism beyond the play's thinking, to its playing and staging, which would perhaps worry Stoppard more. In 1970, in the early stages of work on *Jumpers*, he wrote to Kenneth Tynan:

> All that skating around makes the ice look thin, but a sense of renewed endeavour prevails—more concerned with the dramatic possibilities than with the ideas, for it is a mistake to assume that plays are the end-products of ideas (which would be limiting): the ideas are the end-products of plays.

He may have been cheered by Bigsby's 1976 judgement that 'the real advance in *Jumpers* is that Stoppard . . . begins to control the resources of theatre with greater confidence and skill than before'. But Weightman's questions need answering. The Coda, then, is there in order to use the jumpers again; to present the final effective trio of set-pieces (Dotty's song, George's agonized donnish rhetoric, and Archie's outrageous cynicism); and as a fantasy humiliation of George, in his failure to speak or act for Clegthorpe. It does in fact advance the argument a little; but if it didn't Stoppard would still want it there as theatre.

Weightman's sense of scrappiness (or indeed the *Theatre Quarterly* word 'opaqueness') may still be shared by many of us, and is not laid to rest by Tynan's claim that he himself, nine days before the premiere, unilaterally made substantial cuts which 'were accepted without demur'. The play, however, is *about* a state of political turmoil, a confused criminal investigation, a disoriented mind, opposing philosophies, and donnish bumbling; and we should hardly be too surprised, or too critical, if it tends itself to be confused at times. It is not a masterpiece of clarity, but one cannot quite imagine how it could have been.

Perhaps the least thought-through element in the play is Dotty. The loose answer to Weightman's question why she refuses sex to her husband must be that her life *in general* was thrown adrift. But we are also meant to recognize a failure of response in George. 'She just went off it. I don't know why'—and we wonder how far he tried to find out. His few efforts at compassion towards her are fairly feeble; his rejections at other times fairly forthright.

Bigsby—oddly, it seems to me—finds them an 'embattled couple', resisting 'the threatened collapse of their world . . . with sporadic displays of affection, humour, and faith'. A moment later he again speaks of their 'faith and lyrical yearnings' (p. 23). But Dotty's philosophy is that 'two and two make roughly four' and heaven is 'just a lying rhyme for seven/Scored for violins on multi-track'. She turns to George for affection or help, as he puts it, 'when all else fails you', and there is nothing in the play to prove him wrong about this. Dotty seems to me to be Archie's creature, without any other 'faith', as George seems immensely alone; I can't see them as an 'embattled couple'. But it has to be said that my further impression is of confusion. 'He can't create convincing women,' Derek Marlowe engagingly told Tynan; but that was said before *Night and Day* and in any case it doesn't seem to me the problem in *Jumpers*. The problem is the jostling of undigested theatrical ideas. Stoppard has said that the play '*breaks its neck* to be entertaining'. The italics are mine.

Perhaps in the end such dissatisfaction with the thinking behind *Jumpers*, as with several other Stoppard plays, should still be notched up to their credit; for where else is such thoughtful disappointment provoked by such successfully slapstick material? 'The perfect marriage between the play of ideas and farce'—it was an extraordinary and perhaps impossible thing to attempt. Nor is it a matter of win-all or lose-all; if the thinking behind a Stoppard play seems, by the expectations it itself arouses, ultimately unfinished, many of the perceptions along the way are still valid and exhilarating. With the possible exception of *The Gamblers*, which I haven't read, Stoppard's plays fail in their thinking rather than in their playing, which is—for an artist—the better of the two evils. If I feel more than usually uneasy about *Jumpers* (though my enthusiasm for many aspects of the play will have appeared earlier) it is because it seems to me *even as farce* to have its dull stretches.

I would back *Travesties* to last better, though it is much more widely criticized. Two aspects of the play particularly upset people: Lenin as cuckoo in a nest of songbirds, and the falsification of history. Those inclined to criticize Stoppard for laziness will tend to suggest that, as in *Rosencrantz*, a brilliant theatrical idea doesn't fully know where to go; and that the dramatist's strategy is to create a fine old flurry in the farmyard, wheel in the scheme of Wilde's *Earnest* as a surrogate structure, and hope for the best: that the play is 'intellectual' in its allusions and characters but not in its dynamic, or indeed that it has *no* dynamic (the charge made by Hayman and by Tynan).

I have argued in more detail above (pp. 31 and 56–7) that the jarring impact of Lenin on the elegant theoretical ball-play on the court of Wilde is right and proper, according to Stoppard's beliefs and intentions. That we step out of Wilde, and even step out of Carr, into direct confrontation with Lenin and his ideas seems to me correctly disturbing. It is an alienation-effect which confirms in the second half of the play a scale and seriousness which Carr's reminiscences of the trenches merely sketch in early on. If it is not a 'marriage' of ideas and farce it certainly and effectively renders the agony of divorce.

The play's dynamic is provided first by the fencing-displays about art and commitment, and later by the tank of Marxist–Leninism bursting into the gymnasium. This is not the conventional 'narrative thrust' the lack of which Tynan laments, but it has intellectual force; and of course it is shaped by two schemes known in advance, the plot of *Earnest* and the preparation, departure and journey of the Lenins to St Petersburg. The second of these, however, never settles well in the play. It is announced in the prologue, with urgency; and then abandoned for the rest of the first Act. Cecily's lecture promises a build-up or count-down which begins in earnest nine pages later (p. 79). Pp. 84–5 are the climax: the train leaves; Carr decides too late to stop the departure, the train noise becomes very loud; and Lenin harangues us.

The harangue actually dates from 1905, so we are told as soon as it has ended. Throughout the play we have to cope with such kaleidoscopic history, as when Tzara himself tells Joyce, in the past tense, of Ball's death in 1927. Soon Nadya is telling us of events in 1919 and 1922: the play almost dies on its feet at this point (the more frenetic the earlier part of the play, the more morose this section seems)—not because the ideas are dark and serious but because the climax has already been passed.

The difficulties Stoppard experienced in handling this material ('I was still looking for answers all the way through') should perhaps be traced to some dubious thinking at base. There are fundamental historical untruths: Joyce's production of *Earnest* took place a year after Lenin had left for St Petersburg and more than two years after the founding of Dada; Carr was a minor official in the British consulate and Bennett was the consul. The deliberate leaping forwards and backwards in the play's allusions are a recognition of the historical approximation, and the play's title, together with Carr's admissions—especially at the end—might be felt to clear the dramatist of any false claim to historical insight. The trouble is that he does in fact want to persuade us that he has the *essence* of the truth: not only of the appalling effect of Lenin, about which he feels intensely, but also about Dada and about Joyce's artistic detachment. Travesty or not, the play urges us to accept a very simplified account of Lenin; even Clive James, a passionate fan of this play, tells us that

Lenin's historical significance doesn't even begin to be reconciled within a scheme that adduces Tristan Tzara and James Joyce as revolutionary exemplars, and by suggesting that it does, Stoppard starts a hare which really never *can* catch the tortoise.

(*Encounter*, November 1975)

More serious, in Kenneth Tynan's view, is an over-simplification of Joyce which never allows us to suspect, during the play, that Joyce—like Leopold Bloom—had socialist and republican sympathies. 'This,' says Tynan, 'is when Stoppard's annexation of the right to alter history in the cause of art begins to try one's patience.' It suits Tynan's general thesis to make much of this; on the other hand Joyce's grand speech (pp. 62–3) is certainly true to the major decisions Joyce took about his own life, and Stoppard's Joyce does distinguish (however disingenuously) between himself as an artist, regarding both sides of the War with equal indifference, and himself as an Irishman. Nor is the play wholly indulgent to Joyce, whose work is excellently and persuasively insulted by Tzara on p. 96 and Carr on p. 97.

Neither should Tynan's sympathies have been too displeased by the play's last words:

Firstly, you're either a revolutionary or you're not, and if you're not you might as well be an artist as anything else. Secondly, if you can't be an artist, you might as well be a revolutionary. . . . I forget the third thing.

Stoppard is clearly the non-revolutionary deciding to be an artist, and his claim for *Travesties* as a serious play would be that its confrontations, however caricatured, together form a 'moral matrix'. In effect, like *Jumpers*, it does not claim to offer profound thinking of its own, but a version of the conflicting thinking of its century. His opponents will always claim that the version, like Carr's reminiscences or George's bumbling, is woollier than he might have made it; or even that it is less than honest.

Reviewing *Enemies of Society*, Stoppard found Paul Johnson in this respect an opponent; he appears to think that because *Travesties* does not present 'real' events in Zurich in 1917, it follows from that that I do not believe in real, truthful history. But I do. My intellect tells me so.

Stoppard continues, in what might almost be an epigraph for this chapter or this whole book:

But art is not the child of pure intellect, it is equally the child of temperament. That is why it is art. And, most of all, that is why it must be distinguished from all other human pursuits. . . .

(*Times Literary Supplement*, 3 June 1977)

By now the pattern is clear: even when the more lightweight plays are set aside, Stoppard is always (except perhaps in *Professional Foul*) liable to be accused from some quarter of slackness in pressing through his ideas. *Every Good Boy* is both funny and moving; and André Previn's original idea of using an orchestra in a play was so good, and so well aimed at Stoppard, that one tends to duck admitting that the attempt is broken-backed. There are two great problems, however. One is common to all attempts to combine speech and music: they operate in modes so different that one always tends to dominate the other. In *Every Good Boy* the music takes second place. The other problem is special to this play, and makes it unsound at the core: the orchestra symbolizes the totalitarian State in which improvization and individual thought are not permitted, yet it tries also to offer a lyrical and intensely sympathetic commentary on the action. There is no way round this problem and the play cannot resolve it.

I have mentioned earlier the inclination of *Night and Day* to let us down rather comfortably with Guthrie's minimal positive; and the fact that the relationship of Ruth's private world to the rest of the play, and especially to the public events and the media of publicity, is not fully sorted out. As with the initial conception of *Rosencrantz*, as with the notion of the Jumpers, Stoppard doesn't do so much with it, and particularly doesn't press its implications so far, as we might hope. He is, as always, unpretentious and clear-sighted about this himself: if the reference to 'myth' in the conversation below seems uncharacteristically lofty, the critical placing of the play itself is quite firm:

STOPPARD: Milne has my prejudice if you like. Somehow unconsciously, I wanted him to be known to be speaking the truth.

GOLLOB: But he gets killed, though, doesn't he.

STOPPARD: That's what happens in myth. That in a sense confirms—not directly, but in some psychological way—the truth which he becomes a martyr to.

GOLLOB: But no, I mean, it depends on the treatment. Take a Christian sort of truth, like the kind you are taking, which is true in a sense essentially *because* it cannot survive—

STOPPARD: (*Interrupting*) The play won't bear that sort of profundity, you see . . . you can follow that line of thought and it would be there in parallel with *Night and Day* and my experience of writing it, but because the play didn't spring from that kind of profound thought it's not that relevant to it. . . .

(*Gambit* interview, 1981)

We may be similarly disappointed in what is made of the Dogg-language notion. In 1974, referring to *Dogg's Our Pet*, Stoppard told Ronald Hayman: 'One of the things I hope I'll do one day is really to make full use of that little idea.'

But in the Preface to *Dogg's Hamlet, Cahoot's Macbeth* (1979), he can still say 'I think one might have gone much further'.

In fact, however, the Dogg joke can already seem overextended, and the significances of the chaotic last fifteen minutes or so are confused. We watch an unsettled mixture of romp and satire, in which the Inspector is, disconcertingly, the most attractive character; and some spectators may indeed feel that the real wretchedness of artists in Czechoslovakia is dishonoured or diminished by the play.

Perhaps we ought to remind ourselves at this point that there is plenty of loose detail, blurred thinking, and undeveloped matter in Shakespeare. . . . Drama that loses sight of showbiz is probably doomed; and showbiz tends to have a lot to do with meeting deadlines, bringing off effects, getting away with short-cuts, and bluffing an audience. Stoppard would probably accept many of the criticisms above, and yet not be too much bothered by them; and although this itself would infuriate some of his critics, and may tend to militate against his earning 'a permanent niche in the dramatic pantheon' (the phrase is Kenneth Tynan's *New Yorker* manner), there is life and health in it. Much of the best of Stoppard is summed up in the testimony made to Ronald Hayman (quoted at length above, p. 15), ending 'I never quite know whether I want to be a serious artist or a siren. It's not a condition of good art that you sit in a brown study.'

This fifty-one/forty-nine split tantalizes Stoppard's audiences and still more his readers, but it is also magic: it is the essence of the *appeal* of his work so far; and it is what makes him uniquely unclassifiable.

Beneath it is not a restlessness but a calm. 'Diffident on the surface', James Saunders told Tynan, 'utterly unworried underneath'. Saunders wants Stoppard—any writer—to be constantly redefining 'the role of the individual ... and ... the role of society: How can it be changed? How *should* it be changed? .... But Tom—Tom just plays safe. He enjoys being nice, and he likes to be liked. He resists commitment of any kind, he hides the ultimate expression of his deepest concerns.'

This is all disapproving, of course. Against it we need to set the puzzled querulous integrity of Mr Moon, and of Stoppard 'not knowing'—he might well say that too many dramatists are only too ready to express their 'deepest concerns' which as a result prove utterly shallow. Against that in turn, however (from minus A back to A, perhaps), we can remember Anderson in *Professional Foul*, finally dropping his elegant scrupulosity in order to respond to real need; and wonder what parallels to draw.

Yet Stoppard's underlying calm is something other than holding back. It is a view of life: the comic/satirical/conservative rather than the angry/visionary/revolutionary. The satirical view is found at opposed extremes of human faith—in cynicism, and in absolute religious assurance; but there may be a kind of middle ground in which it also clings. 'In order to arrive at what you do not know' (this is a Stoppard hero, Eliot, speaking) 'you must go by a way which is the way of ignorance.' Often when Stoppard says 'I just don't know' there is an implication that he is puzzled how others can claim knowledge. Surely, he seems to be saying at times, we must admit our ignorance and accept it? And then, as a direct response to our situation, build 'a system of ethics which is the sum of individual acts of recognition of individual right' (Anderson in *Professional Foul*).

Browning's Abt Vogler comforts himself with a rather bland Victorian faith: 'All we have willed or hoped or dreamed of good, shall exist. . . ./On earth, the broken arcs; in heaven, the perfect round.'

Nowhere in Stoppard is there such a *knowing* optimism as this; but the 'limiting curve' speech of George (*Jumpers*, pp. 71–2) overlaps with Browning's image and offers a view of life which shows every sign of being Stoppard's, not least because it is followed by the defensive 'minus A' line which describes it as 'a mysticism of staggering banality'.

And now and again . . . it seems to me that life itself is the mundane figure which argues perfection at its limiting curve. And if I doubt it, the ability to doubt, to question, to *think*, seems to be the curve itself.

Our lapses, our comic absurdities, the irrationality that keeps the world from becoming 'one gigantic field of soya beans', and our playing—and even our lazy thinking within our playing—these are the mundane figure. And our 'not knowing', the way of ignorance, is the essential wisdom. '*Cogito*,' George continues, the joke and the seriousness folded perfectly together, '*ergo deus est*.'

The bridge from thinking to caring which this implies is explicit in a recent interview (with *Gambit*, 1981):

GOLLOB: Could it be said that in your comic writing you regard man as not being perfectible, and that change should be resisted?
STOPPARD: Nothing could be further from the truth. First of all . . .

the desire to reach perfection and the conviction that it is unattainable are compatible instincts. I think perfection is unattainable because it means different things to different people, but the need to make things better is constant and important. Otherwise you're into a sort of nihilism. . . .

8 · CARING

The main purpose of this chapter is to look through the plays for a last time and see what has I hope already substantially emerged: that Stoppard's clowning is not heartless but is associated with consistent and serious concerns, not least an awareness of mental pain. Before that, I will deal briefly with two fairly often voiced anxieties: that Stoppard is politically reactionary, and that his work is vitiated by its sketchy characterization.

The first of these will not take us long. The *intellectual* orthodoxy of live theatre—in sharp contrast, usually, to the box-office orthodoxy—tends in any age to be radical, and in Western capitalist countries to be socialist. Sometimes this can become doctrinaire. In the otherwise excellent *Theatre Quarterly* interview of 1974 there appears at times, on the part of the interrogating editors, a nudging towards political 'commitment' which Stoppard pushes off briskly and firmly but which would have reduced Cinna the poet to tears. Kenneth Tynan's attractive and interesting essay, *Withdrawing with Style from the Chaos*, based on years of intermittent working with Stoppard, talks in terms of friendship but is constantly trying to shove its subject in the direction of his own Lord Malquist. I hope I have shown that this is distortion. It becomes particularly obvious in Tynan's description of Rad-Lib Britain as 'Stoppard's satiric vision of socialism in action'. Stoppard's own account of the Radical-Liberals is as 'a joke-fascist outfit' (*Theatre Quarterly*).

Stoppard's political sympathies in the last few years have been most engaged, as anybody's might be who had been born in Czechoslovakia, by the difficulties of those campaigning for free speech in Communist countries. Nearer home, he appears to align himself with his friend Paul Johnson (dedicatee of *Night and Day*), a former left-wing journalist who has had a change of heart and is sharply critical of many aspects of socialist thought. Johnson's book *Enemies of Society* (1977) of which Stoppard wrote an appreciation, defends 'Western liberal democracy favouring an intellectual élite and a progressive middle class'. Whether or not one agrees with these sympathies, they are intelligent and far from extreme; there is no reason why they should spoil a playwright's work and no sign at all that they do so. In England in the late 1970s, they amount to a mild and far from doctrinaire conservatism. Some biographical reasons why Stoppard might tend to be conservative in this country were suggested above (p. 153). It may be worth adding here that comic writers in general and satirists in particular tend to be among the mild conservatives of their day.

More widespread, perhaps, is the worry that a writer who so often avoids three-dimensional characterization must be short on human concern. This is no more logical than its converse: plenty of writers, after all, demonstrate talent at psychological realism and also present crabbed and embittered views of humanity. We may well worry when a writer repeatedly *fails* in attempts at realistic characterization, but not when he simply chooses to do something else.

Stoppard's weakest surviving play is *Enter a Free Man*. Dated, second-hand, and not very funny, it makes in the direction of psychological realism uneasy moves which are abortive and embarrassing. As so often, Stoppard's own later judgement is excellent.

It appears to be much more about real people than *Travesties*, which is a huge artifice, but at least I've got a mental acquaintance with the characters in *Travesties*, however much, in one sense, they're two-dimensional dream people. Now *Enter a Free Man* looks as though it's about people as real—at least in terms of art—as the people in *Coronation Street*. But to me the whole thing is a bit phoney, because they're only real because I've seen them in other people's plays.

(to Ronald Hayman, 1974)

The characterization of Riley himself is erratic, without persuading us that the fluctuations are genuinely those of a complex personality. He is pretty well whatever the theatrical drift of the moment would have him be: a music-hall con-man at the outset ('Good Lord, it's my old C.O., isn't it? .... A foaming tankard on the Colonel'), a numbskull a few minutes later ('Gum on both sides of the flap! You see what that means? .... You can use it twice'), an Outsider ('It's not a question of liking or disliking, it's what it does to you ... it's nothing, absolutely nothing. I give nothing, I gain nothing, it is nothing. ...'), a donnish ironist ('attended by haphazard housewives bearing arbitrary jugs of water'), and a figure of pathos ('This little boat isn't the whole sea'). The supporting cast is more predictable but still subject to unconvincing inconsistencies (Linda is a Stoppardian parodist at times and a dim stage-teenager at others). The joke names of Carmen the barman and Able the seaman, and the introductory notes, suggest how little the challenge of characterization interested Stoppard: Persephone is *'matronly, plump, plain, nice'* and so on; Brown is *'almost anonymous'*.

Stoppard never quite knows what he is doing in *Enter a Free Man*. His mature work starts in considerable contrast, with the poised confidence of *Rosencrantz*. One reason for this easy assurance may be that it was written lightly, with nothing to lose; the hard elbow of intention digs the audience less here than in some later plays. There are sections where Stoppard may press a little too much or go on too long; but there is never real doubt about the play's overall ease. It is secured by, and hangs gracefully between, the masterworks of Shakespeare and Beckett with something that now feels like inevitability.

It doesn't necessarily occur to us to think in terms of its characterization. Ros and Guil are, if one does stop to consider it, young men out of 1950s English novels, university-educated, not stuffy but far from being radical either, decent, lonely, bewildered, and—a key word, and Stoppard's—'innocent'. They might well have been found on a CND march but not on a Fair Play for Cuba demo, and if they ever get back to wherever they came from each would be happy with a good woman, a fair-sized garden, a pipe and a junior lectureship. But their special position in a special play makes it unnecessary for them to come from any known context; their idiom of speech is consistent (unlike that of Riley or Linda) and is sufficiently close to that of the average live-theatre audience to pass almost unnoticed. They are, moreover, pleasantly different from each other; and we get a good deal of amusement, and some more thoughtful moments, from the varying drifts of their reactions—Guil's intellectual, abstract, slightly fastidious, Ros's earthier, more blinkered, and more confused. Guil suffers more because he is several jumps ahead in the attempt to diagnose their predicament. Both are much more sophisticated and rational than Beckett's Vladimir and Estragon and it is a mistake to seek to relate the two pairs closely. Stoppard has fun lifting notions from Beckett, but it is very much his play and his pair of personalities. Equally he makes no attempt to relate them to Shakespeare's Rosencrantz and Guildenstern, who are seedy sycophants called in by Claudius to break in, as it were, to the Watergate Building. Stoppard is sympathetic, almost affectionate, towards minor sins of the flesh; but fundamental dishonesty has no interest for him and, unlike many if not most dramatists, he avoids dealing with it.

Not that one would trust the Player all that far; but he is a showman in hard times. Much of the success of *Rosencrantz* is due to Stoppard's creation here of a character adequately consistent with Shakespeare's honest professional and also in the same philosophical-intellectual wavelength as Ros and Guil. He is, of course, one of the last actor-managers, an eloquent old queen; and if there is some doubt whether in modern society he would be running a university drama department or selling tips on a racecourse, that says more about modern society than about the consistency of his characterization. His is a splendid part for an actor, and he and his team provide just the right variation of emphasis in what could otherwise have been an over-simple piece. Just as Shakespeare's Hamlet, acting mad because everyone around him seems also to be acting, has to come to terms with the disconcerting feigning of the 'pro', so Stoppard's Ros and Guil, half aware that they are in a play but anxious not to admit it to themselves, are confronted by the hardened theatricality of the Tragedians, utterly at ease in the 'design' of the play and not at all bothered about its significance.

The characterization in *Rosencrantz* is as three-dimensional as it needs to be and I doubt if any spectator feels dissatisfied by it. Equally I doubt if we are dissatisfied by the figures in the radio plays *If You're Glad* or *Albert's Bridge*, or by the farce-characters in *Hound*, *After Magritte*, *Dirty Linen*, or *On the Razzle*. Here the characters are entirely of a strip-cartoon kind (we can add *Every Good Boy* to the list without denying its 'serious' bite)—and we should remember that the cartoon enables that special poignancy of extension to absurdity: Gladys and John Brown yearning to enter monastic institutions in spite of their religious doubts, Birdboot carrying around a battery-powered viewer and transparencies of his latest review in neon outside the Theatre Royal, Thelma and Harris each thinking that the resident Mother is the other's.

In *Jumpers* the cartoon mode is still pervasive. Archie is—significantly, as Stoppard's only real villain—wholly a fantasy figure: not, as such, at all out of place in the play, but rather commanding its idiom and possibly its action—a Rad-Lib Prospero who introduces the play and ends both Acts. As for Dotty and George, they have a just about plausible past sketched out for them, and we are shown enough of their damaged relationship to feel we approximately understand what the problems are: Dotty unhinged by moon-landings, Rad-Lib jumpings, and Archie's smooth talk of a valueless universe; George hurt by her denial of him, angry at the Rad-Lib take-over, more and more needing to find goodness in theory since it seems to be draining away from the outside world—and consequently rejecting *her*. The play has nothing to do with psychology and the sketched relationship serves most of its purposes, though Dotty's role remains a bit confused. As in *Travesties*, the cartoon mode directs our attention clearly to the arguments. Complex psychology might actually damage these plays; their caring is in the wish to get at truth—even if that is a flux—by pitting persuasive arguments against each other.

The radio play *Where are They Now?* is basically realistic. The slight element of caricature in the characters may tell us about the tendency of the school system to classify people (and language) in caricature terms. The schoolmaster who himself uses schoolboy slang as a matter of course ('Serve the Pom then, Harpo, and do cheer up') is accurate enough; and I can certainly remember teachers like this: 'Nothing wrong with Klim. Fresh from the Ministry of Food's prize herd of Jersey wocs. I have just said something extremely risible—root, boy!' (p. 69).

Vice-Chancellors do not actually talk like Archie; Headmasters, regrettably, do talk like this Headmaster, and Old Boys, met as briefly as we meet them in this play, can seem like caricatures. Gale himself is an entirely serious creation: it is a short play and Gale speaks only in its later pages, but as soon as he is speaking he is not only no kind of caricature himself, but he is trying to get beyond the caricature recollections of others: 'What a *stupid* man! I think we would have liked French. It is not, after all, a complex language' (p. 75).

Gale's longest speech (pp. 76–7) is as delicate as anything in Stoppard. With hindsight we can see that its writer was quite ready (in 1969) to write full-scale realist plays with convincing characters, as soon as he chose. But there were plenty of pressures on Stoppard not to do so, and however much one admires *Professional Foul* and *Night and Day* one may feel relieved that *Jumpers* and *Travesties* were written in the meanwhile.

In his realist plays Stoppard has not yet surprised and excited us as much as in those in the strip-cartoon mode. One should make some exception of the fantasy scene in *Night and Day*, which is a small breakthrough. What can be said about both *Professional Foul* and *Night and Day* is that, as well as being skilfully done, they also prove how well Stoppard writes about caring, about moral enquiry, about things which a mere smart-alec could not handle. This is related, of course, to their persuasive characterization. The genuine good intent of Anderson is coupled with his middle-aged tendency to switch off from the changing world ('Do you know Prague?/Not personally ...') including his own subject—he *ought* to know Chetwyn's work and would be a better thinker if he did. Like most other academics he is naturally frightened of running into trouble with the police state, and his early rationalization, refusing to help Hollar—his professional foul—is most carefully and convincingly shown (pp. 53–7). So is Hollar's anticipation of an underlying moral courage in Anderson ('I did not expect to take it away') which eventually proves justified: a quality Hollar sensed in him as his student years before. McKendrick is vividly characterized, his unawareness of others (he thinks Chetwyn is 'going for the free trip—the social life') and his personal looseness providing swift comedy but also throwing his ethical theory into doubt; his wish to buy shares in any easy virtue that's around is sharply balanced by his squeal of resentment in the last moments of the play. Minor characters are also well drawn: the American linguistic philosopher, Stone, labouring his unremarkable points even at table, is a graceless eater, which allows one of his own theoretical examples to be turned against him. Even the small touch that Chetwyn reads a lot of Dickens feels shrewd and right. Ronald Hayman found 'some sentimentality' in the use of the boy Sacha as interpreter between his mother and Anderson, but this is attributable to the lighting and casting of the scene in the BBC production, which (for once) belied Stoppard's script. In the text Sacha is *'rather a tough little boy'* to whom Anderson tends to speak as if to an adult, and if this guidance is followed each detail seems to me convincing—the boy's premature toughness, his inability to keep it up indefinitely, and—again—Anderson's slowness to become fully aware of those he is talking to.

In *Night and Day* the characters are to some extent types. We may remember Stoppard's remarks to Ronald Hayman about stereotypes which contain truth (quoted above, p. 181). Their language is (see above, p. 106) subtly discriminated. Each character seems to me rounded and convincing, however true to type; the one we may feel least confident of knowing is the least true-to-type, Jacob Milne, because his presence and his ardour disturb the stereotypes; but that doesn't mean that either he or the stereotypes are unreal. Such disturbances occur in any environment, often. As for Ruth, of all the characters in Stoppard she is the most known.

We are back to cartoon in *Dogg's Hamlet, Cahoot's Macbeth*, with no lack of theatrical energy or comic ingenuity. What the play does lack is a central point of focus. Easy is a link man and the likeliest repository of our sympathy; but he is offstage for half the evening. The stage is stolen, in *Cahoot's Macbeth*, by the Inspector, who is also the villain. The burden of opposition to him is shared by Cahoot, 'Macbeth' and the Hostess and there is no question of any of them being much developed. Part of the reason for this central vacancy is the way the play was put together. The effect is a probably unintended coldness, a loss of caring. One almost worries more at the end about what the Inspector is going to say to his chief than about the future of the hounded actors. We survive almost as unruffled as Easy.

Whether strip-cartoon or three-dimensional, within their plays Stoppard's characters can surprise us with the sharpness of their own sense of values. Guil's *'rage and fright'* at the Player's clumsy bawd-work (p. 20) is unnecessary to the action of the play but important to Stoppard's conception of his bewildered decency. Ros is caught out, late in the play, trying to make Guil happy by letting him win every guessing game. Even the Player can refer, not entirely ironically, to his troupe's 'integrity', and offer the perception, in the last minutes of the play, after his mock-death, that 'For a moment you thought I'd—cheated.'

Albert too rejects cheating, very early in his play: 'tickle it into the corner, there, behind the rivet. . . . No one will see that from the ground; I could cheat up here. But I'd know. . . .' (*Albert's Bridge*, p. 8).

And a moment later, defining his yearning for a single logic: 'Now that's something; to keep track of everything you put into the kitty . . . there are no consequences to a coat of paint . . . a factory man . . . doesn't know what he's done, to whom' (p. 9).

His obsession makes him a poor husband, but never knowingly an unkind one, and at the end of the crockery-throwing scene he can still murmur: 'I never had any regrets, but I did want her to be happy too' (p. 28).

The state Albert aspires to, though the aspiration is unwise, is not unrelated to 'happiness as a state of being', which Gale (*Where are They Now?*) last experienced at the age of seven:

> I remember walking down one of the corridors, trailing my finger along a raised edge along the wall, and I was suddenly totally happy, not elated or particularly pleased, or anything like that—I mean I experienced happiness as a state of being: everywhere I looked, in my mind, *nothing was wrong*.
>
> (p. 77)

Obviously George in *Jumpers* cares about things being right or wrong; so, as we shall remind ourselves in a moment, does Donner in *Artist Descending*; and each character in *Travesties*, except possibly Carr, the uncommitted chorus, cares with dogmatic passion. The two 1977 plays about Communist countries show no interest in the stock material of behind-the-Iron-Curtain drama—escape, deception, armed intervention, and so on; instead they are intensely interested in matters of integrity and principle—the struggle between 'Don't be rigid' and 'One and one is always two'. As for *Night and Day*, the whole play is about values—those of the press, and those of private conduct:

> thinks I hop into bed with strange men because I hopped into bed with a strange man. . . .
> Post-coital remorse. Post-coital ruth. Quite needlessly—I mean, it's a bit metaphysical to feel guilt about the idea of Geoffrey being hurt if Geoffrey is in a state of blissful ignorance—don't you think?

MILNE: No.
RUTH: No....
Which page is it on?.... This thing that's worth dying for....

In *Lord Malquist and Mr Moon*, Moon's hysteria originates in feeling locked into moral search and universal awareness, however little he likes it. It is 'something to do with no one being *good* any more' ... 'I don't know a single person who is completely honest, or even half honest'. Near the end of the book, he explicitly challenges Lord Malquist:

> I mean, you can't dismiss it all—the Tibetans and everything, and yourself—you can't compare everything awful with something bigger.... I mean, it's all *people*, isn't it? That's what the world *is*.
>
> (p. 188)

There is a telling moment earlier, as reality breaks into his whimsy:

> He took off all his clothes and wrapped himself in the towel and stood in front of the mirror with the towel round his body and over his head. He looked at himself.
> *I am very fine saint, my goodness yes. I will not break my fasting I tell you till the British give me back my country, esteemed sir.*
> That was a mistake. He shook for forty million potbellied starvlings, and pulled the towel over his face....
>
> (p. 73)

One of Stoppard's more extraordinary abilities, at his best, is to render through grotesque comedy real pain, and a yearning for the good. The pain in *Jumpers* is almost pervasive, the laughter rarely at ease. If we can brush away Dotty's first failure to remember her song, and treat as amiable slapstick Crouch's being knocked headlong by the swinging Secretary, we can hardly do the same with the '*sudden obliterating fury*' of Dotty's 'It's my bloody party, George'. A moment later the jumper dies '*pushing himself up against Dotty's legs ... He crawls up her body. His blood is on her dress.*' He is to become a comic prop, swinging into view every time the bedroom door is shut, but it is black comedy. It is hardly too much to say that Dotty and George are both in misery throughout the play, and the ludicrousness of their circumstances, most notably in the deaths of Thumper and Pat, rob their wretchedness of the dignity and consolation of tragedy. Archie's glittering smile over all is the ultimate bitterness.

Less well-known, but a remarkable achievement, is the presentation of pain, heightened again by ingenuity and irony, in the radio masterpiece, *Artist Descending*. Sophie, the blind girl, has relatively little to say, and yet her suicide (p. 50) is by then plausible. It is not her blindness itself which makes her agony, but the way she is treated—the lack of straightforwardness of her lover Beauchamp when she herself has consistently manifested a straightforwardness which enables her to see potential humour in her handicap. By the day Beauchamp and Martello are leaving her, however, this humour is on the breath of agony: 'Perhaps he was going to leave me a note on the mantelpiece. As a sort of joke' (p. 33).

In effect, we are to feel, Beauchamp's departure is as callous as such a 'joke' would be. Perhaps still more impressive is the pain of Donner. At the start of the play Donner is dead; in the cumulative flashbacks and flashforwards we gradually discover his decency, goodness, and integrity by comparison with his two companions. In the earliest scene of the play (1914—pp. 42–7) Donner is the least frivolous of the three, able to send himself up where the others have grander pretensions: 'Donner, why are you trying to be an artist?' 'I heard there were opportunities to meet naked women,' telling the bald truth about their 'picturesque' walking tour ('I'm bitten all day by French flies and at night the mosquitoes take over. I nearly drowned trying to cross a laughing torrent . . .'), being the first to recognize the reality of the war and expressing his fear in terms of fundamental value ('I don't want to die *ridiculously*').

In the 1920 scenes, at Sophie's first introduction, Donner is the most restrained and tactful, but it is also clear that he is the one who *did* notice Sophie the previous year when she visited their exhibition before losing her sight. By 1922 Donner is offering his love to Sophie when she is rejected by Beauchamp and Martello. He goes downstairs to see them off—and she throws herself through the upstairs window to her death.

The time-gap is then very large. In the 'last week' scenes Martello is making his Dada-ist sculpture of clichés. Donner is equally stuck in the Dada-ist groove, but his art is preoccupied with suffering. 'The war . . . killed it for me. After that, being an artist made no sense.' Now, he has tried ceramic food, but 'The question remained: how can one justify a work of art to a man with an empty belly?' His solution—appropriate both to the grotesque comedy of the play and to his characterization as the man of compassion—is 'make it edible'. The conversation with Martello is amiable enough until he discovers that the cliché-statue is supposed to be Sophie. His weeping remembered passion is mocked by Martello's relish of its clichés. An echo of Archie and George begins to be heard, and in the second 'last week' scene the echo becomes much stronger:

MARTELLO: Fifty years ago we knew a nice girl who was due for a sad life, and she jumped out of a window, which was a great shock and certainly tragic, and here we are, having seen much pain and many deaths, none of them happy, and no doubt due for our own one way or another, and then we will have caught up on Sophie's fall, all much of a muchness after a brief delay between the fall of one body and another—
DONNER: No, no, each one is vital and every moment counts—what other reason is there for trying to work well and live well and choose well? I think it was a good life lost—she would have been happy with me.

(p. 51)

The moral dignity is starker even than George's. Appallingly, Martello now suggests that it was really Donner Sophie loved, and thought she lived with for two years, all those years ago. It is an almost insupportable cruelty. Donner's repeated 'Oh my God' is a kind of hieroglyph of grief, of astonishing pain as acute as anything in a realist play, a blade drawn across our nerves which have been made open and vulnerable by the preceding laughter and the sound-conundrums. In the 'two hours ago' scenes Donner has renounced a lifetime's Dada-ism to return 'to traditional values'. At the beginning and end of the play he is dead.

Travesties, of course, develops a sketch in the early pages of *Artist Descending*. The personal pain of the radio play drops away, apart from Carr's skids into trench-memory which are an effective reminder of the suffering raging outside Switzerland's borders; and what is projected large is the difficulty of relating the values of art to immediate human need. In *Every Good Boy* the pain is expressed in Swiftian understatement: 'I thought this really wasn't fair'; 'a conventional girl who died uncontroversially in childbirth'; 'To put this another way, a girl removing her nail-varnish smells of starvation'; 'They did this to me for ten days in a row, and still my condition did not improve.' Nothing in *Professional Foul* (where we actually *see* some of the violence of the State) is as powerful as this dryness, though one's breath is caught by Hollar's 'I mean, it is not safe for me' and Stoppard does give him a 'theatrical' exit line perfectly balancing bitterness and civility: 'I forgot—welcome to Prague'. (Hollar is showing 'good manners'.)

The pain in *Night and Day*—Ruth's pain, pervading the play—is of a different order, moral and psychological, and no doubt minor by comparison with the nightmare of the trenches, the 'medical' treatment undergone by Alexander, or even the magnesium flare of suffering to which Martello exposes Donner. But Stoppard's study of Ruth's pain is most carefully made, and the steadiness of his hand as he reveals the wounds more than confirms his range as a dramatist. The slip in London, with Wagner, was a bad one, but Ruth could reasonably expect to keep it safely behind her, in a 'separate moral universe'. Guthrie's revelation, very early in the play, that 'I've come to meet Dick Wagner' is numbing. *'Ruth remains perfectly still.'* From here on, though immensely poised, she is in a state of alienation, not less disturbing if, as we suspect, it is an all-too-familiar state (Carson seems to know it well). Cleopatra-like, she resents Guthrie, the bringer of the bad news, more than Wagner, the news itself (see pp. 18, 19, 44, 45). With Wagner she tries to live dangerously, attempting to be the suave scarlet woman whose lovers regularly turn up to have drinks with her husband—but panics quickly: '"RUTH": Don't get cheeky, Wagner. He's not stupid.' (p. 45).

A moment later she is shouting 'Get out of this house!' No one, except the audience, can hear. The 'Ruth' convention takes us into her alien state.

Stoppard delays as late as possible the meeting of Ruth and Milne. It is their only true meeting and it lasts for five or six minutes. The old word 'exquisite', implying acuteness both of pleasure and pain, may describe it. Ruth can survive, in her alienation, in the company of hard men, cynical men, or men of few words: but Milne is too much—a glimpse of an idealism, a humour and energy, and a youth and beauty for which she might judge the world well lost, particularly when so estranged from it. It is he who cuts short the meeting, after she begins to make a pass at him. And that is it. She intends to get up early, to see him off; and is an hour late. 'I went peculiar. I lost my view of myself. I was unembarrassable' (p. 69).

Once one has grasped what is going on, the opening scene of Act Two is the most painful in Stoppard: a whispered walk along nerve-endings. Studying the fantasy conversation in the text afterwards we can see the significant points at which Ruth is the directing force:

We seem to have got off the subject

(p. 66)

Carry on from there

(p. 67)

No. Fresh start. Hello!—had a good trip?

(p. 68)

You say something

(p. 69)

But her fantasy is too vivid, too real: it includes Milne's goodness. She wants Milne no other way than he is, and the way he is he will not accept her. The best of her—let no one say Ruth lacks moral awareness—fleshes out his refusal in the most convincing detail. He turns her name on her; later, she turns it on herself—not, we can be sure, for the first time. The best of her allows Milne to leave. The worst of her steps out of her dress and walks naked offstage after him.

And then, the real-life pain: blazing:

> 'Where's Jacob?/In the jeep./In the jeep? What's he doing there?'
> [In our memories: 'Was it dark or daylight? On a bed? On the floor? Long grass? In the jeep? (*Pause*) It was in the jeep . . .']
> 'GUTHRIE: (*Sharply*) Don't turn him over—he'll come away in your hand.' (p. 86)

Stoppard is uneasy about having his work viewed overall: there is a tendency to pay disproportionate attention to minor commissions and bits of fun, and so to undervalue the full-length plays. Critics, on the other hand, may feel that the minor pieces are done so well that they cannot be put aside, and that they illuminate the more deliberately 'substantial' pieces; possibly, too, that the serious plays stop short of full commitment.

There is also in art a cumulative dimension. The overall force of Stoppard's drama is to me more significant than the success of single plays. It has to do with a view of life as well as with theatrical and verbal brilliance. The caring in Stoppard is not a matter of scorched primal emotions or of impassioned social comment. Throughout his work Stoppard returns to concepts of order and of goodness, and to characters whose sins are not those of destruction, repression, or meanness; and in spite of the hysteria glimpsed in Mr Moon, in Fraser (*Albert's Bridge*), in the projected Rad-Lib future, or in the frenzied building-race at the end of *Cahoot's Macbeth*, his import repeatedly seems to be a faith in life. Most people, too, are fundamentally innocent, including the conventionally guilty: it is, like the vision of the great comic writers, strangely like a priest's view.

Most of Stoppard's people, whether cartoon-figures or realistic characters, mean the world and others no harm and if possible a bit of good. It isn't just that he avoids villains. He also makes little of the grand Insufferables of the comedy of humours, on whom so many comic writers rely; they do appear, at least in the early plays, but treated with affectionate restraint: the Chairman and Fitch in *Albert's Bridge*, Lord Coot in *If You're Glad*, Lord Malquist himself, Dobson in *Where are They Now?* Everyone except Maddie in *Dirty Linen* is potentially Insufferable, but the generosity of Stoppard's humour makes us like them all. None of these really wishes ill to anyone else: it is an interesting contrast to, say, the world of Ben Jonson, where almost everybody is malevolent or avaricious most of the time, or to that of Oscar Wilde where even when in love the characters are spikily scoring points off each other. Petty deceptions related to sins of the flesh are in Stoppard manifestations of sin so Original that it is essentially innocence, and actually endears the characters to us: Linda on pp. 57–8 of *Enter a Free Man*, Ros tricked by the Player (p. 47), Albert and Kate (*Albert's Bridge*, pp. 15–20), Birdboot in *Hound*, Carr's schoolboy humour and sexual fantasy (*Travesties*, pp. 24–5, 78), Gwendolen's inadvertent completion of Tzara's limerick (*Travesties*, p. 35), the men in *Dirty Linen*, Anderson and the girly magazine, Anderson and the football match; and Wagner and Ruth (though theirs is a more complex case). 'Innocent' is a key word in Stoppard and it is significantly applied not only to Ros, Guil, George, and 'the late Herr Thumper', but also to Maddie in *Dirty Linen*, whose *'whole attitude in the play is one of innocent, eager willingness to learn'*.

This pattern of characterization throughout the plays amounts to a moral statement more significant than anything explicit, especially when endorsed by the corresponding cold-heartedness of the few able to talk themselves urbanely out of any situation: Archie, and to some extent Mageeba. To the minor sinners above should be added the bumbling official-dom—not resented, in Stoppard, but positively crying out for our sympathy: the pontoon-booted Inspector Hound, the slack-bowelled Inspector Foot, Inspector Bones with bouquet and gramophone record, the Czech Inspector with his henchmen Boris and Maurice, even the Doctor in *Every Good Boy*

('We have to act together') ... and even the men searching Hollar's flat, who sympathize with Anderson's missing the football match and arrange for the radio to be turned on ('Is good. O.K.?'). But *not* the fluent English-speaking 'Man 6' who then appears, the Jumper of the State machine, and who is a manifestation of rigidity where the others, reassuringly and comically, are of flux.

Travesties looks like something of an exception to this epic sequence of innocents. Every character in the play, except Nadya, is more urbane and confident, even arrogant, than almost any other character in other Stoppard plays, except Archie. Perhaps Carr and Gwendolen are still essentially innocents, in spite of their poise. But Tzara, Joyce, Lenin, Cecily and of course Bennett pride themselves on their knowingness: each is sure he or she *has it right*. Yet, with the possible exception of Bennett, they show no inclination to Jump about: their fervours are in every case those of passionate commitment and the dramatist wants their causes to be heard and considered.

He wants them heard and he wants us to care: about the horror of the trenches, about the commercial and political amoralities that led to that horror, about 'the natural right of the people to the common ownership of their country and its resources', about the 'false premise ... that people are a sensational kind of material object', about the absurdity and gratuitousness of art, about its commercialization, and about its necessity and immortality. But in the beginning and the end, and in the brief refuelling stop at the end of Act One, our only grounding is in Carr: there is little risk of our identifying with these 'knowers'.

It is common observation that the main historical figures in *Travesties* were revolutionaries; what may less often be considered is the view that all three were failures. About Tzara this may be widely agreed. About Joyce readers will always disagree; Stoppard is clearly fascinated by Joyce's ennobling of art and dedication to it, but the only judgement he allows us to hear is the shrewd epigram of Tzara: 'as an experience it is like sharing a cell with a fanatic in search of a mania'. About Lenin Stoppard has no doubt: he sees the man not as a Jumper, but as a sincere moral pervert, who believed he acted in the interests of his people, of life and flux, and who in fact brought them rigidity and terror, and the most powerful totalitarian State there has ever been.

We are close to saying that for Stoppard 'not knowing' connects vitally with caring, as well as with wisdom (see p. 195 above): that the man who 'knows' is the man who 'thinks he's God' (Glad talking about the First Lord of the Post Office) or (Alexander's phrase in *Every Good Boy*) has 'forgotten his mortality'. Out of context this could evidently be misunderstood as a licence for apathy, or even for Jumping ('Do not despair—many are happy much of the time. . . . Hell's bells and all's well.'). The view of men as innocent, of life as generally *less* strange than it may seem to be, and of ideas as constantly reversible, may lead Stoppard sometimes into sentimentality or excessively comfortable short cuts; but it also leads him to most of what is best and most distinctive in his work.

STUDY-GUIDE

BIBLIOGRAPHY

Texts

Stoppard's three early short stories (*Reunion, Life, Times: Fragments*, and *The Story*) were published in 1964 in *Introduction 2* by Faber.

The novel *Lord Malquist and Mr Moon* was published in 1966 by Anthony Blond and in 1974 by Faber.

The published plays are listed and summarized below, pp. 217ff.

Articles by Tom Stoppard

'The definite maybe' (Stoppard describes early setbacks and success as playwright.) *The Author*, vol. LXXVIII, no. 1, Spring 1967.

'Something to declare' (Stoppard discusses 'why I write' and concludes 'because I love writing, really'.) *Sunday Times*, 25 February 1968.

'*Orghast*' (Stoppard watched a rehearsal of Ted Hughes's play, interviewed Hughes, and produced this sympathetic but cautious study.) *Times Literary Supplement*, 1 October 1971.

'Playwrights and professors' (A funny, well-founded and good-tempered dismissal of most academic theatre criticism, especially of his own work.) *Times Literary Supplement*, 13 October 1972.

'The face at the window' (Stoppard describes his visit the previous week to Russian dissidents. Dry, bleak, quietly angry.) *Sunday Times*, 27 February 1977.

'But for the middle classes' (a highly sympathetic review of Paul Johnson's *Enemies of Society*. 'Truth is objective. Civilization is the pursuit of truth in freedom.') *Times Literary Supplement*, 3 June 1977.

'Prague: the Story of the Chartists' (Stoppard's account of Charter 77 in Czechoslovakia—its antecedents and its fate.) *New York Review of Books*, 4 August 1977.

'The Czech trials' (of, amongst others, Vaclav Havel—see p. 12 above) *New Statesman*, 28 October 1977.

Interviews with Tom Stoppard

The most substantial and valuable are:

—with Giles Gordon, *Transatlantic Review*, no. 29, Summer 1969, reprinted in *Behind the Scenes* (ed. Joseph McCrindle), Pitman 1971.

—with the editors of *Theatre Quarterly*: 'Ambushes for the audience: Towards a high comedy of ideas', *Theatre Quarterly*, vol. IV, no. 14, May–July 1974.

—with Mark Amory, 'The joke's the thing', *Sunday Times*, 9 June 1974.

—with Ronald Hayman, 12 June 1974 and 20 August 1976, transcribed in *Tom Stoppard* by Ronald Hayman, Heinemann 1977.

—with Joost Kuurman, March 1979, *Dutch Quarterly Review of Anglo-American Letters*, vol. 10, 1980/1.

—with David Gollob and David Roper, *Gambit*, vol. 10, no. 37, 1981.

Other interviews include: *Guardian*, 12 April 1967, 10 December 1971, and 21 March 1973; *Observer*, 17 December 1967; *Times*, 11 November 1972; *Plays and Players*, April 1973.

Criticism of the plays

A recommended selection from what is becoming a large field.

IN BOOKS

'Waiting for Hamlet', pp. 149–53 of *The Third Theatre* by Robert Brustein, Cape 1970.

Tom Stoppard by C. W. E. Bigsby, Longman for British Council 1976, enlarged 1979.

Tom Stoppard by Ronald Hayman, Heinemann 1977; second, enlarged edition 1978.

'Example 12, Stoppard, *Travesties*, 1974', pp. 245–62 of *From Writer to Reader: Studies in Editorial Method* by Philip Gaskell, Oxford 1978.

Beyond Absurdity: the Plays of Tom Stoppard by Victor L. Cahn, Fairleigh Dickinson U.P. 1979.

'Withdrawing with style from the chaos', pp. 44–123 of *Show People* by Kenneth Tynan, Weidenfeld 1980. (This essay was first published in *The New Yorker* of 19 December 1977 and has been reprinted in *Gambit*, vol. 10, no. 37, 1981.)

IN NEWSPAPERS AND PERIODICALS

'Mini-Hamlets in limbo' by John Weightman, *Encounter*, vol. XXIX, no. 1, July 1967.

'Theatre chronicle' (on *Rosencrantz*) by John Simon, *Hudson Review*, vol. XX, no. 4, Winter 1967–8.

'A metaphysical comedy' by John Weightman, *Encounter*, vol. XXXVIII, no. 4, April 1972.

'Love among the logical positivists' by A. J. Ayer, *Sunday Times*, 9 April 1972.

'The zealots of Zurich' by Richard Ellmann, *Times Literary Supplement*, 12 July 1974.

'Count Zero splits the infinite' by Clive James, *Encounter*, vol. XLV, no. 5, November 1975.

'Philosophy and Mr Stoppard' by Jonathan Bennett, *Philosophy*, vol. 50, 1975.

'Who are the Dadas of *Travesties*?' by Margaret Gold, *Modern Drama*, vol. 21, 1978.

'Faith in Mr Stoppard' by Eric Salmon, *Queen's Quarterly*, vol. 86, no. 2, Summer 1979.

'Stoppard's critical travesty, or, Who vindicates whom and why' by Craig Werner, *Arizona Quarterly*, vol. 35, no. 3, Autumn 1979.

'*Jumpers*: a happy marriage' by Tim Brassell, *Gambit*, vol. 10, no. 37, 1981.

GUIDE TO THE PUBLISHED PLAYS

'P. 1' refers to the first page of the published play; '1' to pages in this book.

Enter a Free Man

Published by Faber, 1968.

Stage right is the living-room of George Riley's house, left the bar of his local pub. The play moves between these as Riley does, and within each area adopts generally realist methods. In nicknaming the play 'Flowering Death of a Salesman' Stoppard recognized its debt to two 1950s successes, Robert Bolt's Flowering Cherry *and Arthur Miller's* Death of a Salesman; *but it also owes much to 1950s radio and television comedy scripts such as those written by Alan Simpson and Ray Galton for Tony Hancock.*

*Riley is middle-aged; he left the family business to become an inventor, working at home in a house inherited from his father, and kept by the shop jobs first of his wife and later of his teenage daughter. None of his inventions succeeds; the ones we hear most about are an envelope gummed on both sides of the flap and an arrangement to bring rain indoors to water house-plants. His wife Persephone (a caricature of Linda in Miller's play) humours and loves him; his daughter—Stoppard's Linda—gives her father pocket money but during the play is losing patience with him and embarks on an abortive elopement, deceived by an already married boyfriend. (*PERSEPHONE: *How—how far did you let him go?/*LINDA: *Northampton.)*

In the bar Riley's regular cronies are Carmen the barman, who tries, like Persephone, to humour him and prevent his being hurt; Able the young seaman, 'almost gormless'; and Harry, a flashy type a good deal younger than Riley, who kids him into delusions of grandeur. At the end of the play Harry humiliates Riley in the pub; Linda comes back depressed from Northampton; and the floor is flooded by the indoor rain. Linda gives her father more pocket-money, and the circle of collusion is re-established.

use of two stage-areas   47
characterization   198–9
names   124
role of Riley   44
inconsistency of speech-register   103
rigidity and flux   170

p. 13 'A man is born free and everywhere he is in chains.' The correct answer to 'Who said that?' is given on p. 18: Jean-Jacques Rousseau (1712–78). 'Houdini' was an 'escapologist', good at getting *out* of chains.

p. 23 echo of Tony Hancock 37
p. 32 comic use of cliché 110
p. 33 comic deflation 86
p. 55 'Gretna': just over the border in Scotland, it was once the scene of English runaway marriages.
p. 57–8 innocence 212
p. 73 'Hey, what's Harry's other name?' 124

If You're Glad I'll Be Frank

Published in one volume with *Albert's Bridge*, Faber 1969.
Published alone, Faber 1976—page-references are to this edition.

Gladys is the voice of the telephone speaking clock—not a tape, but a trapped person. She unwisely volunteered, after being turned down by a nunnery because of her religious doubts—what she really wanted was 'serenity . . . that and the clean linen'. Frank, her husband, is a bus driver, who recognizes her voice on the speaking clock and attempts to liberate her whilst still keeping to his bus schedule. The First Lord of the Post Office manages to defeat Frank's efforts and stave off Gladys's breakdown. At the end she has resumed her automatic chant and Frank has lost her; but her mental independence has to some extent survived: the last words of the play are her contemptuous comment on the First Lord: 'He thinks he's God.'

original notion 167
self-contained logics 170, 201
use of radio medium 67
characterization and speech-registers 103, 107, 201, 214

pp. 8–9 speech-registers, and Lord Coot's name 86, 107, 121
p. 31 'He thinks he's God' 16, 214

A Separate Peace

Published in *Playbill Two* (edited Alan Durband), Hutchinson 1969.

John Brown wanted to join a monastery for the same reasons as Gladys (above) wanted to join a nunnery; and was rejected for the same reasons, too. Now, as second best, he hires a room at a private hospital ('clean linen') though he is not ill. He forms a friendship with his nurse Maggie, and trusts her with a few memories, which she relates to the doctor—and this leads to the tracing of Brown's relatives. Maggie makes up for this by allowing Brown to leave the hospital quietly the night before the relatives arrive.

What Brown wants is to contract out of the 'wide-open' scene of the world which appals Mr Moon in the novel. 'Fire, flood, and misery of all kinds, across the world or over the hill, it can all go on, but this is a private ward.' Mr Moon worries about the possibility of failure in the chain of supply; Brown is impressed by hospitals because 'they've all got their own generators. In case of power cuts. And water tanks. I mean, a hospital can carry on, set loose from the world.' Earlier he has used the phrase which recalls Gladys and anticipates George's view of McFee (Jumpers, p. 72): 'Like clock-work. Lovely.'

Maddie's name 121

p. 116 'Your complaint'—compare *Every Good Boy*, p. 26.

Rosencrantz and Guildenstern Are Dead

Published by Faber 1967; re-set 1968 (page-references are to 1968 edition).

The context is the action of Shakespeare's Hamlet *(of which a close knowl-edge is here assumed) or just offstage of it. So, for example, we see onstage a telling scene which Shakespeare—because it is silent—deliberately sets offstage so that he can describe it to us (it is also more enigmatic offstage, like the offering of the crown to Julius Caesar)—Hamlet's 'unbraced' intrusion to Ophelia's closet. Ros and Guil know they have been summoned, but can remember nothing more of their past. They while away their time before their entrance into* Hamlet *(the first of many jokes about theatre, though all the time they are not actors but* characters) *spinning coins, which always fall heads. The law of probability seems to have been suspended; they seem part of a predetermined action; and it worries them. They are joined by the Players or Tragedians, due to perform at court, who have been reduced to the lowest of 'theatrical' money-raising: bawdy sketches and perhaps prostitu-tion. The Players are more at ease in the predetermined action than Ros and Guil, who are not even sure of their own names.*

Fragments of Hamlet *itself cross the stage; but mostly the play consists of Ros and Guil's quasi-philosophical speculations about why they are here and what their deaths will be like: the Players are particularly good at acting deaths, and throughout the play we* know *and Ros and Guil suspect that they will be jettisoned when their usefulness is over. As in* Waiting for Godot, *which Stoppard echoes affectionately and frequently, we are free to see parallels with our own lives if we wish.*

The play is in three acts, the first ending as Hamlet makes his first contact with Ros and Guil, the second ending just before the embarkation for England, the third (mostly) occurring on board ship. In the third act (which was added later, on a commission) we are already beyond the action of Hamlet *and there is more forcing of the comedy, though Stoppard contrives to bring back the Players (who have stowed away in a hasty escape from the King's displeasure at their play), and there is good slapstick at the expense of one of Shakespeare's most blatant plot-mechanisms, the encounter with the pirates. Stoppard also handles skilfully the problem of how to end. Ros and Guil discover the letter to the English King in its form as rewritten by Hamlet, ordering their deaths. They cannot question their dramatic destiny. The Players die stage deaths which this time seem real; Ros and Guil fade out; and the play ends with the final tableau of* Hamlet, *and Horatio's speech fading into darkness and music. (The early version ended with a fresh pair of attendant lords being woken in a fresh dawn.)*

Albert's Bridge

Published in one volume with *If You're Glad*, Faber 1969.
Published alone, Faber 1970—page-references are to this edition.

Albert, a philosophy graduate, is a vacation employee of the Clufton Council, one of a team employed painting the Clufton Bay Bridge. When one end is reached the other needs repainting. The City Engineer, Fitch, produces a scheme to save money by using a paint that lasts eight years and therefore will need only one painter. Albert accepts the job: he likes the distance it gives him; the clutter of the everyday world looks like a neat pattern, and the bridge itself has a self-contained logic—'the whole thing utterly fixed by the rules that make it stay up'. He has worked on the bridge, living away from home, every university vacation; when he does spend a few days at home (his father is a local captain of industry) he gets the maid, Kate, pregnant. He at once marries her and genuinely wishes her and the child well, but he himself has time only for his bridge; even on family holiday in Paris he spends his time on the Eiffel Tower—an even more magnificently self-contained logic than his bridge. Back at work in Clufton he is joined by a would-be suicide, Fraser, whose attitude and lines are lifted substantially from Mr Moon in the novel; Fraser is appalled by the enormous disorder of life, but, like Albert, finds it looks reassuringly ordered from the height of the bridge, and once up there no longer wishes to die.

After two years three-quarters of the bridge need repainting: Fitch's logical calculations are seen to have ignored the initial transition period. An opposite logic is then operated: 1,800 men are hired, to paint the bridge in one day. Albert and Fraser, both on the bridge, are horrified as the army of painters approaches: Albert feels 'they're moving in on me, the dots are ganging up'; Fraser fears 'they have finally run out of space, the edges have all filled out and now there is only up'. The marching painters are too trapped in their logical tramp to recognize the logics of physics: they fail to break step and the bridge collapses.

The Real Inspector Hound

Published by Faber, 1968.

A one-act farce parodying country-house who-dun-its and jaded theatre reviewing, the play has no intellectual pretensions but is a pleasant gloss on the reality/illusion anxieties of Ros and Guil, or on Pirandello. The two reviewers, Birdboot and Moon, sit in the front row of the stalls in a fictional theatre: they are upstage, facing us, but even their whispers are clearly audible to us. Birdboot is an old hand, given to liaisons with up-and-coming actresses whom he will lavishly praise; Moon is a second-string reviewer longing to step into the shoes of the first-string, Higgs. The play they are watching starts with a char, Mrs Drudge, and continues with caricature who-dun-it characters and lines. The 'third Act' starts with the phone ringing on stage. Moon gets up from his seat, steps on 'stage' and answers it: Stoppard is borrowing from the anecdote about the American critic Robert Benchley, who is said to have responded to a similar moment by getting up saying 'That's for me' and leaving the theatre. Characteristically, Stoppard twists the joke a shade further—the call is not for Moon but for Birdboot. It is his wife. He has just pacified her when the action of the 'play' resumes around him, with dialogue from 'Act One' trapping him in the role of Simon, the male lead. Birdboot discovers that the corpse is that of Higgs. Moon joins him and 'Simon' and 'Hound' take their places as critics. Birdboot is shot; a new Inspector Hound appears, denounces Moon as the murderer, and shoots him. As Moon dies he recognizes the 'real' Hound as Puckeridge, the third-string reviewer for his newspaper.

After Magritte

Published by Faber, 1971.

The merest skeleton outline is offered here: the play defies summary. The point to grasp is that everything has a rational explanation. The opening tableau shows furniture barricading the street-door of a half-lit room; a possible corpse or sedated victim stretched out on an ironing board; a man in waders and dress trousers, but naked to the waist, puffing at a lamp above his head; and a woman in a ballroom gown but barefoot, on her hands and knees, sniffing. A police-constable stares in, transfixed, at the window.

The ensuing dialogue is based in heated debate about different interpretations of a grotesque sight the Harrises and Mother saw while out driving. Later the police constable (Holmes) returns with his superior (Foot of the Yard), who bursts in confident of interrupting a sensational crime. But by then the room has been restored to normal. Unnerving interrogations follow, at the end of which it becomes clear to the audience though not to anyone on stage that the grotesque spectacle glimpsed by the Harrises and Mother, which has been reported to the police and which the Inspector is investigating, was in no way criminal and was in fact the Inspector himself.

Before and during this revelation a second absurd stage tableau has gradually developed, again for innocent and fairly rational reasons:

Thelma in underwear, on hands and knees, sniffing; Harris wearing Thelma's ballroom gown over full evening dress, with a cushion cover over his head to blindfold him, arms outstretched, standing on one leg, counting aloud; Foot with one bare foot, wearing dark glasses, eating a banana; Mother standing on one foot on a wooden chair which is on the table, a woollen sock on one hand, playing the tuba; the basket of fruit slowly rising to the ceiling; the central light slowly descending to the table; and P.C. Holmes in the doorway looking even more baffled than by the opening tableau.

The play has passed from absurdity to normality and back to a different absurdity; and everything can be explained. The dialogue has offered at least seven explanations of a grotesque sight seen earlier in the day, the last of which is not advanced as an explanation but as another topic—though it is in fact the correct explanation.

Surrealist painting shows, amongst other things, strange juxtapositions. Its general import is that the psyche, and perhaps reality itself, are stranger and less stable than we like to think. The oddity of surrealism appeals to Stoppard, but his import is in some respects the opposite: the strangest things can have simple explanations, and we must not mistake the delights of diversity (Mother's enthusiasm for the tuba, for example) for dangerous instability. A simpler more obvious message is that things are often not what they appear to be; and in this sense the play itself is 'after' Magritte in the sense of following Magritte's thinking.

rational explanations of apparent irrationality   37, 48, 76, 89, 172
the innocence of truth   172
Foot—as echo of Goons etc.   41
    —his name   121
    —crying to our sympathy   212
characterization   201

title: René Magritte (1898–1967) painted strange juxtapositions; he regarded his work 'as an instrument of knowledge, though knowledge not reducible to conceptualization' (*Oxford Companion to Art*). The play's events occur 'after' a visit to a Magritte exhibition, and its ideas are 'after' (along the lines of) Magritte's.
p. 22 'She's *your* mother!'   201
p. 24 entrance of Foot   82
p. 27 'Not—' Thelma would like to believe the constable is *Sherlock Holmes*.
p. 36 'Maigret' is the police detective hero of Georges Simenon's novels. Magritte and Simenon were both Belgian.
p. 38 'Sir Adrian Boult'—born 1889, doyen of British orchestral conductors.

Where are They Now?

Published in one volume with *Artist Descending*, Faber 1973.

'The play is set almost entirely in two inter-cut locations: School Dinner (1945) and Old Boys' Dinner (1969). Part of the idea is to move between the two without using any of the familiar grammar of fading down and fading up; the action is continuous' (Stoppard's note). Predictably, the Old Boys

sentimentalize their schooldays—all except Gale, who makes the opposite
error. He is silent for most of the meal and eventually, when the company
stand in memory of a recently dead master, refuses to stand and mutters a
poignant outcry against the man's cruelty. Soon after this we find out which
of the schoolboys he was, and it proves to be one of the more cheerful and
extrovert; Gale himself goes on to recall from his prep school days a moment
of 'happiness as a state of being'; and the play ends with (for the first time) a
cross-fade into the past:

'on an open windy field, GALE is playing some sort of game with a few
other boys. . . . It is a day he has forgotten, but clearly he was very
happy.'

Extra interest is added by the Old Boy Jenkins, who has accidentally
come into the wrong re-union (one school and its Old Boys are evidently much
like another's) and taken the name-place allotted to the dead master,
Jenkins.

The play is relatively realistic, and there are no doubt fragments of
Stoppard's own schooldays embedded in it.

use of radio medium   68–9
names   121, 123
as travesty of school   151
rigidity and flux   171
characterization   202, 212

p. 63 'Eurgh!'   68
p. 65 'Ivory Coast'—the old Colonial name
p. 69 'Nothing wrong with Klim'   202
p. 76 'Fat Owl of the Remove'—Billy Bunter, in the fantasy public-
        school stories of Frank Richards.
        'Steerforth'—David Copperfield's idol at school
        'Mr Chips'—hero of James Hilton's popular novel about a long-
        serving schoolmaster.
pp. 76–7 Gale's speeches—discussed on 202, 205.

Jumpers

Published by Faber, 1972.

The Radical-Liberal party has taken over Britain by a landslide victory at a
General Election, which it would not be beyond its members to have rigged.

('*Archie says it was a* coup d'état *not a general election.*') *The play, which observes the Unities of time and place, though hardly that of action, takes place in a Mayfair flat. Overhead, jets scream in a victory fly-past; outside, soldiers and crowds parade. On the moon Astronaut Oates has been marooned by Captain Scott (their crippled space-capsule will carry only one man, and in a savage reversal of the famous altruism of the Oates on Scott's Antarctic expedition,* this *Scott knocks his fellow-man to the earth, or rather to the moon, and takes off). The whole thing is seen by the populace on television, and by the audience in the theatre on a large screen.*

The flat belongs to George and Dorothy Moore. Dorothy has already become unhinged by the moon-landings (like Penelope in Another Moon Called Earth*); she has broken down and retired prematurely from a brilliant career in musical comedy. The collapse may have been aided by the dubious attentions of Sir Archibald Jumper, Vice-Chancellor of the university in which George is professor of Moral Philosophy; Archie (philosopher, doctor, coroner, athlete, and—in this case—psychiatrist) visits Dotty (as she is appropriately known) in bed each morning and leaves 'looking more than a little complacent'. Since the moon-landings Dotty has not allowed her husband to make love to her. George stands apart from the logical-positivist thinking of Archie and his fellow academics, and refuses to join Archie's only-too-symbolic acrobatic troupe of dons, the Radical-Liberal Jumpers. His own disabilities are incoherence—some funny parodying of the donnish manner at its most rambling—and withdrawal into the comfort of the abstract. Exasperating as Dotty is, he is still guilty of failing her at crucial moments (see, for example, the bottom of p. 41/top of p. 42). He shows a foolish tolerance of Rad-Lib barbarities (see the 'carefully reassuring himself' speech on p. 36); and in the phantasmagoric Coda he fails to lift a finger to save the unfortunate Clegthorpe from murder: all he does is mutter 'Well, this seems to be a political quarrel. . . . Surely only a respect for absolute values . . . universal truths—*philosophy—*'. He is silenced by the gunshot which kills Clegthorpe. He will stand up to the amoral only in the shelter of his thesis.*

The play opens late at night at a Rad-Lib celebration party in the flat. George refuses to join in, and continues to attempt to work on his paper to be delivered at a Symposium the following evening. As the Jumpers perform, a bullet is fired from the gloom and one Professor McFee is killed. Dotty is left, more or less deranged, in her bedroom with the corpse. George does not know of the murder, and next morning he and Dotty talk at cross-purposes while the corpse itself hangs behind a door, always unseen by George. Elements of

*parody who-dun-it develop, particularly in the person of Inspector Bones,
who assigns himself to investigate the case because he is a fan of Dorothy
Moore (he arrives carrying a bouquet, and a record for her to autograph).
Archie and the Jumpers return and remove the corpse while George and the
Inspector are inspecting the rest of the flat. In the second half of the play
Dotty traps the Inspector in an apparently compromising position and Archie
smoothly persuades him, in return for his good name, to drop the case.*

*The murdered man was a linguistic philosopher due to read a paper at the
Symposium; indeed George's paper is intended as a reply. George seeks to do
nothing less than argue for the existence of moral absolutes and of a God
behind them, which makes him a lone and archaic voice in a world of
Rad-Lib relativism; and George's drafting of his paper is the ground-bass of
the play.*

*The audience is clearly meant to sympathize with George's argument, but
the play's action does not. Towards the end we learn that McFee had
undergone, just before his murder, an astonishing change of faith; had begun
like George to believe in altruism and was even planning to enter a monastery. His murder, which we have tended to associate with Dotty's dementia,
now looks more like the vindictiveness of a Radical-Liberal not wishing
McFee to give his revised lecture; and there are hints that the murderer may
be George's secretary, who was McFee's mistress until ditched by his change
of faith. Certainly George seems surrounded by ruthlessness; very late, he
learns of McFee's murder; and, in a tragi-farcical denouement he also learns
that—as a result of one of Dotty's wild cries early in the play—he himself
has unwittingly killed an innocent friend (his tame hare, Thumper); where-
upon he equally unwittingly kills his only other friend, a tame tortoise. The
play ends with a dream Coda: the new Rad-Lib Archbishop of Canterbury
(an agnostic vet.) is called on to speak at the Symposium on the 'goodness,
badness, or indifference of man' and is then shot as the Becket to Archie's
Henry II, while George fails to intervene. Archie's own speech is mocking
gibberish; Dotty's testimony is a pop song denying the existence of heaven and
categorizing men as 'some ain't bad and some are revelations'; and George's
despairing but eloquent final statement is superseded by the bland cynicism of
Archie, who has the impudence to parody one of Stoppard's own artistic
heroes, Samuel Beckett. It is a very dark comedy.*

opening sequence   36, 81, 86, 160, 206

pp. 19–20 discussed   115

p. 21 —death of McFee   206

p. 22 Scott–Oates   76. Oates, a member of Scott's expedition to the Antarctic (1910–12), became crippled by frostbite and walked out into the snow to die rather than be a burden on his starving comrades. His last words were 'I am going out now. I may be gone for some time.' Oates's death is often instanced as an example of human altruism—see *Jumpers*, p. 80.

p. 23ff. Dotty's cries   115

p. 24ff. 'Russell': Bertrand, 3rd Earl Russell (1872–1970) was joint author of *Principia Mathematica* (1910) and of much subsequent rationalist philosophy. Russell's 'Theory of Descriptions' is a way round the absurdity of 'Is God?'; he argued that to talk of something existing is to *describe* it, and that 'God' is not a proper name but a descriptive term summing up a number of attributes ('predicates') which may or may not include existence. 'Is God?' is not questioning a predicate which is certain.

p. 25 'Professor Ramsay.' He was not a professor and his name was spelt F. P. Ramsey: a contemporary of Russell's, who published *The Foundations of Mathematics* in 1931.

p. 26 'quiver of arrows . . .' etc.   37, 87

p. 27 'Cantor': George Cantor (1845–1918) worked on these topics of number and infinity.

'Zeno' the Eleatic was a contemporary of Socrates (fifth century B.C.).

'Saint Sebastian' is painted in Renaissance times transfixed with arrows.

p. 28 'our cave': a reference to the allegory of the cave by Plato (427–347 B.C.). At the mouth of the cave is the fire; man sits in the cave with his back to it, perceiving it by its flickers on the cave wall.

'Aristotle' (384–22 B.C.) taught that all matter is potentially alive and striving to attain its particular form: there is a whole series from the simplest kind of matter to the perfect living individual, behind which there must be a supreme source: the Unmoved Mover.

p. 29 'Unmoved Mover'—see A. J. Ayer's comment on   163

'tumbler'   86

'St Thomas Aquinas' (1225–74) developed Aristotle's Unmoved Mover into a Christian divinity.

Zeno's paradox is about *Achilles* (the legendary athlete) and a tortoise. George splendidly muddles this with Aesop's fable about a hare and a tortoise. Russell deals with the fallacy of Zeno's paradox in *Our Knowledge of the External World*.

'the point of a converging series': an infinite *series* does not make infinity.

The arguments of this page are discussed on   161

p. 30 'revealing the corpse'   91–2, 160, 206

'*The Naked and the Dead*'   115, 173

p. 31 'Mao Tse-tung' (1893–1976) was leader of the Chinese people from 1949 till his death. Russell occupied himself considerably in later years as a would-be international peacemaker, including contacting Mao when few could do so.

p. 35 'Ryle'—Gilbert Ryle, author of *The Concept of Mind*, was a behaviourist philosopher.

'Ayer'—A.J., now Sir Alfred, Ayer, author of *The Problem of Knowledge* is Professor of Logic at Oxford and the best-known English logical positivist philosopher. He enjoyed *Jumpers*, and an extract from his review of the play appears on   163–4.

p. 37   'The Thirty-Nine Articles' of Religion are a statement of doctrine
        of the English Church.

p. 44   'dem bones, dem bones, dem dry bones'—refrain of a popular
        spiritual

p. 48   McFee's ethical relativism owes a good deal to Ayer.

        'logical positivists' teach that the only meaningful statements are
        those which can be validated by sense-experience. The meaning
        of a statement is the method of its verification.

p. 50   'Benthamite Utilitarians': Jeremy Bentham (1748–1832) taught
        that what is good is what will make the greatest pleasure or
        happiness for the greatest number. Self-interest (rather than
        altruism) can lead to general good.
        Immanuel Kant (1724–1804) was the pioneer of much modern
        thinking.
        'empiricists' teach that all concepts are derived from experience
        and that all statements claiming to express knowledge depend for
        their justification on experience.

p. 51   'Behaviourists' explain all behaviour in terms of conditioned
        responses. Like all the others in George's list they would not
        subscribe to his 'intuitionist' faith in moral absolutes.

        'Hobbes'—Thomas Hobbes (1588–1679), author of *Leviathan*,
        was a materialist who might well have given the answer imagined
        here.

Ayer's most popular book is
        Language, Truth and Logic.

p. 63   'Bedser' and p. 66 'Bradman' were cricketers of the 1940s and

50s. The datedness of the references tells us something about George.

p. 64 'an ice-pick in the back of the skull' alludes to the murder in 1940 of Leon Trotsky, one of the leaders of the Bolshevik revolution, who was dismissed from office in 1925 after failing to persuade his colleagues back to what he thought was the true path.

p. 66 'a cry for help'   113

p. 67 G. E. Moore (1873–1958) published *Principia Ethica* in 1903. Stoppard's George Moore is a travesty version, but their beliefs are similar.

p. 69 'Darling!'   113

p. 70 innuendoes   78

p. 72 'the limiting curve'   181, 195
'McFee never made that mistake'   181
'*Cogito ergo deus est*' (I am thinking, so God exists) is a travesty of René Descartes's (1596–1650) '*Cogito, ergo sum*' (I am thinking, so I must exist).

p. 74 'Meccano Magazine'. Meccano was an educational toy: a kit from which varied mechanisms or structures could be invented, and its magazine recorded some of the more elaborate. What George suggests is that the rationalism of Archie and Dotty is mechanical, cold, and perhaps also childish.

p. 75 Nicholas Copernicus proved, disturbingly in the early sixteenth century, that the planets revolved round the sun. Similar upheavals in twentieth-century thought are associated with Albert Einstein (1879–1955) and his theories of relativity.
Ludwig Wittgenstein (1889–1951) was a linguistic philosopher whose explorations of language interested Stoppard (and generated, the year before *Jumpers*, *Dogg's Our Pet*).
The Wittgenstein anecdote is quoted on   76; see also *Jumpers* pp. 60 and 78.

p. 77 the George–Crouch conversation is discussed on   117

pp. 79–81 the Archie–Crouch conversation, and the Secretary's actions, are discussed on   84–5

p. 81 the blood: 85, 174
deaths of Thumper and Pat   49, 85, 160

p. 83 the Coda   42, 55, 187
'Mr Crouch, ladies and gentlemen': a few threads in Archie's deliberately tangled speech: *nucleic acids* are crucial to the

fundamental chemistry of life; *random tests* may be a scientific method but the *testes* are the testicles, storing seeds of life; *universa vice* is a pun on 'vice versa'; the saying is that 'necessity is the mother of invention'; *Voltaire* was an 18th century rationalist; *Darwin*'s study of evolution is 'Origin of Species'; and for the last bit of nonsense, see the note above on Descartes's *Cogito, ergo sum.*

p. 85 'My lord Archbishop ...' Archie becomes Henry II and Clegthorpe Thomas à Becket, whose assassination is supposed to have resulted from Henry's saying 'Will no one rid me of this turbulent priest?' George's failure to defend Clegthorpe is discussed on 88, 163, 187.

p. 87 George's speech 163
Archie's speech 74, 151
George here bundles together St Augustine with St Thomas Aquinas, and Jesus Christ with G. E. Moore.
Archie's 'One of the thieves was saved' comes from St Augustine via Beckett's *Waiting for Godot*: Christ was crucified between two thieves.
'At the graveside the undertaker ...' is a travesty of a crucial image in the late pages of *Waiting for Godot* ('they give birth astride of a grave ... the gravedigger puts on the forceps').
Beckett's Christian name is Sam.

Artist Descending a Staircase

Published in one volume with *Where are They Now?*, Faber 1973.

The play works in a V formation of flashbacks followed by flashes forward to regain the present at the end. It may be helpful here, however, to summarize its events in true chronological sequence.

In 1914 three young artists, Beauchamp, Donner, and Martello, take a walking tour in France ignoring the threats of war. They are upper-middle-class, bantering, Rupert-Brooke-like figures, but Donner is less frivolous than the other two: he is irritated by their continuing foolery as the machinery of war arrives around them. ('I don't want,' he says, 'to die ridiculously.') After surviving the war in the army the three become avant-garde painters, still fundamentally fooling around; and in 1919 hold a joint exhibition, Frontiers in Art, consisting of a series of pictures of fences and barbed wire, which is visited by Sophie Farthingale ('with spectacles and a long pigtail'). The artists are photographed for a magazine with pictures they have painted,

*and Sophie, whose sight is failing, takes a liking to the one standing in front
of a border fence in the snow.*

*In 1920, now totally blind, Sophie meets Martello and is taken to tea with
the others, and from her description they decide that the artist she found
personally attractive was Beauchamp. A liaison develops between Sophie
and Beauchamp. By 1922 Beauchamp is tired of her; the three artists are to
move into new lodgings, abandoning Sophie, but Donner (who adores and
pities her) stays behind. As the other two leave and Donner is downstairs
seeing them off, Sophie kills herself by hurling herself through the first-floor
window.*

*A large time-gap follows, to 'last week'. The three artists, senile, still live
together, still playing at Dada-ist art long out of date; and Martello discloses
to Donner that for many years he has suspected that they all made a mistake
in identifying which painter the nearly sightless Sophie had liked.
Beauchamp's picture was indeed of a border fence in the snow; but Donner's
was of a thick white fence with black gaps between it. . . . Donner's pain is
extreme; yet in a way he ceases to be embittered and disappointed and
becomes again, terribly belatedly, a committed artist, a man capable of love
and of being loved. He takes up traditional brushwork and starts on a
painting of Sophie naked in a garden with a unicorn (remembering something
she said in 1920, newly blind: 'If I hear hoofbeats, I can put a unicorn in the
garden and no one can open my eyes against it and say it isn't true.')
Beauchamp's present obsession, meanwhile, is surrealist tape-recording ('the
detritus of audible existence') and by a macabre chance, when he and
Martello are both out, he gets a tape of Donner's death, falling downstairs in
attempting to swat a fly. The tape, with which the play begins and ends,
suggests, however, that Donner and Martello are each convinced that the
other is the murderer. The audience realizes, at the end, the innocent truth (cf.
After Magritte) but the characters do not, and we are left to speculate on
what Sartrean hell they will now enjoy together.*

*The play actually unfolds like this: now; a couple of hours ago; last week;
1922; 1920; 1914; 1920; 1922; last week; a couple of hours ago; now.*

use of radio medium   66, 69–71
ambiguity   69, 76, 82, 171–2
twists of plot   75, 174
moves into past and back   90
names   123
fixed logics   171–2
treatment of pain   207–9

p. 15 'Augustus John' was an English painter (1878–1961).
'Edith Sitwell' was an English poet (1887–1964).

p. 16 'Grundig' is a make of tape-recorder. See 43, 77.

p. 20 'Wyndham Lewis' was a painter and writer (1884–1957).

p. 21 The 'Queen Mary' was an ocean liner, named after the Queen.

p. 22. 'symbolism ... post-object': a list of fashions in twentieth-century visual arts. 'Venus de Milo'—famous classical sculpture. 'post-Pop'=of the here and now (early 1970s). 'Pre-Raphaelite' was a mid nineteenth-century style imitating the simple naturalism of Botticelli and contemporaries. 'Dada': see *Travesties*, pp. 56–6 for an excellent summary.

p. 23 'Tzara'—see *Travesties*.

p. 24. 'Max' Ernst (1896–1976), 'André' Breton (1896–1966) and 'Marcel' Duchamp (1887–1968) were Dada-ist or surrealist painters. One of Duchamp's paintings, *Nude Descending A Staircase* suggested the title of this play. 'Praxiteles' was a classical Greek sculptor; and Auguste 'Rodin' (1841–1917) was an outstanding sculptor of recent times.

pp. 25–7 discussed 208

p. 26 'Le Penseur' (the Thinker) is Rodin's best-known sculpture.
'Pablo'—after the other name-droppings, we are meant to assume (wrongly) that Pablo Picasso (1881–1973) is meant.

pp. 28–9 statue of clichés 110

p. 31 J. M. W. 'Turner' (1775–1851) was one of the greatest English painters. Edwin 'Landseer' (1802–1873) was a celebrated traditional painter, particularly of animals.

p. 33 'Perhaps he was going ...' 207

p. 35 'But I am—blind as a bat ...' 90

p. 36 'Lloyd George' was Prime Minister at the time.

p. 39 'I believe we exchanged a look!' 207

p. 41 'Jack Dempsey' was a famous boxer.

p. 42 'Donner, why are you trying ...' 207

p. 43 'I nearly drowned ...' 207

p. 50 Sophie's suicide 208

p. 51 'Fifty years ago ...' 97, 208

p. 52 'Oh my God ...' 208

Travesties

Published by Faber, 1975.

The following summary of background material may be of use. During the First World War (1914–18) Switzerland was neutral. Stoppard's play concerns three famous men who lived in Zurich at that time (though they were not in fact acquainted): the novelist James Joyce, the Rumanian poet who called himself Tristan Tzara, and the Russian revolutionary Vladimir Ulyanov (Lenin). To these Stoppard added one little-known but equally real figure, Henry Carr, a British consular official in Zurich after being invalided out of the trenches.

As an erratic, vague socialist (an aspect of his thinking which Stoppard chooses to suppress) Joyce felt that ordinary men were dying because of the rivalries of imperialist states; and as an exceptionally dedicated artist he regarded his work as far more important to him than the war. Tzara was a leading figure in the Dada-ist movement (succinctly summarized within the text of Stoppard's play, pp. 56–61) which regarded traditional art itself as tainted by the inhumanity of the societies which had created such war, and as a commodity within such societies. Lenin was a Marxist political theorist, certain that Communist revolution would come but not necessarily expecting it in his own lifetime. Clearly here was an opportunity for a play debating different revolutionary views of the twentieth century, neatly set in a No Man's Land around which the worst horror of the century raged.

In 1918, a year after Lenin and his associates had returned to Russia to take power, Joyce presented in Zurich an amateur production of Oscar Wilde's The Importance of Being Earnest, *with Henry Carr as Algernon. They bickered afterward about costs, and Joyce pilloried Carr in a scene of his novel* Ulysses. *Reading of this in Richard Ellmann's definitive biography of Joyce, Stoppard was attracted by the idea of using the Wilde play as a basis for his own Zurich play. His success with the off-stage scenes of* Hamlet *will also have been in his mind. The intensity of the self-confidence of the three Zurich revolutionaries—all of whom were fanatic 'knowers' of the kind Stoppard never wants to be—would clash creatively with the detached amorality of Wilde's drawling time-wasters.*

Certain liberties with history were necessary (and indeed the play's title firmly disclaims any attempt to portray the characters fairly). Carr became Consul, not assistant, and the name of the real Consul—Bennett—was transferred to his fictional subversive butler. More important, the Earnest *production was brought forward at least a year, so that it could take place before Lenin left for Russia—a piece of forcing necessary to the whole caprice of the play, yet inextricably connected with its most suspect area: its uncertainty how far to make a clown of Lenin as clowns are made of Joyce and Tzara.*

In The Importance of Being Earnest, *Jack Worthing is a foundling adopted by a wealthy gentleman who, at his death, left Jack as guardian of his daughter Cecily at his country house. In order to get up to London Jack has invented a brother Ernest, under whose name he lives in London, becomes engaged to Gwendolen, and is a friend of Gwendolen's cousin Algernon. Cecily is 'a little too interested' in the wicked brother Ernest. Algernon appears at the country-house passing himself off as Ernest. Jack returns and dare not expose him. Gwendolen arrives, being nosy, and has a fine passage at arms (itself a travesty of Molière in* Le Misanthrope) *with Cecily, since both young women believe themselves engaged to 'Ernest'. Lady Augusta Bracknell, Gwendolen's mother and Algernon's aunt, enlivens proceedings and trips the denouement in which it appears that soon after Jack's birth he was accidentally exchanged for the manuscript of a three-volume novel, and that he is in fact Ernest Moncrieff, Algernon's brother.*

Stoppard's play is not about Joyce's production of the Wilde play: it is a travesty of the Wilde itself, with Carr=Algernon, Tzara=Jack and Joyce =Lady Bracknell—this last ludicrous of course, but madly logical in the apparent femininity of Joyce's surname and in the fact that for the Zurich production he was *the overbearing Gorgon. (Of two extraordinary coincidences of name Stoppard was not at the time aware: that the actor who played Jack in Joyce's production was indeed called Tristan, and that Joyce himself had actually been christened in error James* Augusta. *These coincidences Stoppard has described as 'almost like little signs from God that you're on the right track'). Cecily is librarian of the Zurich Public Library, where she has come to know Tristan Tzara as 'Jack' Tzara (Carr/Algernon later flirts with her as 'Tristan') and where she has become dedicated to Lenin's work and convictions. Gwendolen is Carr's sister and he has inadvertently agreed to her being chaperoned by Joyce, believing the name to refer to a middle-aged* woman; *she has in fact become Joyce's amanuensis.*

The prologue (pp. 17–21) caricatures Joyce, Gwendolen, Tzara and Lenin at work in the Library, hissed at occasionally for silence by Cecily. Nadya, Lenin's wife, comes to tell her husband of the revolution in St Petersburg.

The stage is then Old Carr's, reminiscing (pp. 21–6). On p. 26 he becomes young Carr/Algernon and we begin repeated attempts to parallel the opening scene of Earnest. *Tzara/Jack enters on p. 32 but he is a 'Rumanian nonsense' quickly followed by Joyce and Gwendolen and a crazy limerick sequence. On p. 36 there is another attempt at the Jack–Algernon dialogue early in* Earnest: *this time Tzara is impeccably English. The Wildean scene disintegrates but a third attempt is made on p. 41 and this time we quickly gain the subject of Cecily. Carr discovers that Tristan has passed himself off to Cecily as 'Jack' Tzara (Stoppard here cheerfully muddles the roles of Wilde's Gwendolen and Cecily). On p. 47 Gwendolen and Joyce/Lady Bracknell appear. We depart from Wilde's scheme, ironically in order to introduce Joyce's idea of producing* Earnest *with Carr as Algernon. Carr and Joyce (like Algernon and Lady Bracknell in Wilde) leave Gwendolen alone with Tzara/Jack, and courtship develops through a patter of Shakespearean allusion and the chance reshuffling of Shakespeare's sonnet 18. Joyce/Lady Bracknell interrupts their embrace (p. 55) and proceeds to interview Tzara/Jack, travestying the 'handbag' interview in Wilde and also the dry catechetical tone of the penultimate section (Ithaca) of* Ulysses. *The content of the interview, meanwhile, is an effective exposition of Dada, relieved towards the end by a casual conjuring act from the travesty Joyce. The act ends with further Old Carr reminiscence.*

Act Two opens, disconcertingly, well away from Wilde, with a humourless lecture by Cecily on Marx and Lenin. Carr/Algernon turns up in the Library masquerading as 'Tristan' Tzara; three attempts at Wildean amorous conversation are made, the third of which goes quite excessively well and results in Cecily's dragging Carr down behind her desk (p. 79). We fall away from Wilde again as Nadya and Lenin appear, and for the next five pages (79–84) the stage is most uneasily shared by the Wildean travesty and the Lenins' plans to join the Russian revolution. The uneasiness is of course deliberate. On p. 84 the Lenins' train leaves for Russia, its noise becomes very loud, and 'everything goes black except a light on Lenin'. He harangues the audience, after which we have four dark pages of extracts from Lenin's letters and Nadya's memoirs. We have lost Wilde and lost laughter. The dark section ends with the sound of Beethoven's Appassionata *sonata swelling to fill the theatre. Absurdly it turns into a double-act song, Mr Gallagher and Mr Shean, travestying the Gwendolen–Cecily teatime passage-at-arms in Wilde. Pp. 93–7 correspond in a neatly telescoped way to the last Act of* Earnest. *The baby–handbag swop in Wilde here becomes the inadvertent swop of two folders, Lenin's and Joyce's, in the Library. The pairs—Cecily–Carr, Gwendolen–Tzara—are briskly united and there is a short dance sequence ('a complete dislocation of the play'). The play ends with Old Carr, joined now by Old Cecily, admitting that the whole thing has been historically inaccurate.*

This is the dramatic sequence. At least as interesting, however, is the actual content of the dialogue, which is often eloquent and impassioned debate about art, politics, and human values.

pp. 17–21 (Prologue)   26–7, 36, 49, 101, 175
p. 18 'Eel ate ...' Tzara's 'random' poem is in fact, by a private Stoppardian joke, the play's first limerick—in *French*. It goes something like this:

Il est un homme, s'appelle Tzara	He is a man called Tzara
Qui des richesses a-t-il nonpareil (?)	who has unparalleled talent
Il reste à la Suisse	He stays in Switzerland
Parce qu'il est un artiste	Because he is an artist
'Nous n'avons que l'art', il déclara.	'We have only art,' he declared.

'Deshill holles eamus'—what Joyce is dictating is the opening of chapter XIV of *Ulysses*.

pp. 20–1 limerick: 26, 107

p. 22–8 Carr's ramblings are full of pun and parody, which it would be grotesque to attempt to annotate in detail here. It is suggested as a game for a fairly erudite reader confined to bed with a temperature.

p. 23 'in short a liar and a hypocrite . . .'   107

pp. 26–32 (Carr–Bennett sequence)   27–8

p. 32 'Quel pays sanguinaire . . .' Far from being from La Rochefoucauld, this is simply a translation of Carr's earlier line 'What a bloody country even the cheese has got holes in it!'

p. 34 'H.M.G.'=His Majesty's Government (Carr's employer).

p. 35 'I thought he was going to say . . .'   107

pp. 33–6   27–8, 107

p. 36 'Well, let us resume . . .'   175–6

'Benthamite'—see note above to *Jumpers*, p. 50.

'Stoical' and 'Epicurean': Tzara refers to the popular conceptions of Stoic and Epicurean philosophies as recommending, respectively, gloomy self-denial and self-indulgence.

'Post hock . . .' *Post hoc, propter hoc* (after this, therefore because of this) is a formula of causality.

p. 38 'Narcissus'—the legendary youth who fell in love with his own reflection.

p. 39 the argument is compared to G. B. Shaw on   96

p. 40 'My God, you little Rumanian wog'—the first of four such outbursts which form a pattern (the others are on pages 47, 62, and 77)—discussed on   27

p. 44 'Homer's Odyssey . . .'   173

p. 46 discussed   28

p. 47 discussed   29, 30

p. 50 'The Prime Minister'   83

p. 51 'Gomorrahist'—Carr's spontaneous invention to avoid the word 'sodomite' in Gwendolen's hearing. Sodom and Gomorrah (Old Testament) were twin cities of corruption.

p. 53 'GWEN: (*Absently*)'   114

p. 54 the cut-up sonnet—   78, 176. Every spoken word on p. 54 is from Shakespeare: what is not the sonnet is a collage of quotations from other sonnets or the plays, including *Julius Caesar*, *Hamlet*, *As You Like It*, *Much Ado About Nothing*, *Othello*, *I Henry IV*. Another game for the literary invalid.

Dirty Linen and New-Found-Land

Published by Faber, 1976.

The setting for both plays is 'an overspill meeting room for House of Commons business in the tower of Big Ben'. Dirty Linen shows the preliminaries and proceedings of the Commons Select Committee on Promiscuity in High Places, a committee formed in response to newspaper stories of a 'mystery woman' who is 'going through the ranks' of M.P.s 'like a lawn-mower in knickers'. The mystery woman, Maddie Gotobed, turns out to be the secretary of the Select Committee, and we quickly gather that each of its members has been having a clandestine affair with her; this includes Mrs Ebury, the lady member, but not Mr French, the new member. French is the only one inclined to press for a tough investigation. In the main part of Dirty Linen the M.P.s' evasions are punctuated by their scanning of pin-ups in tabloid newspapers; as each pin-up is scrutinized Maddie herself appears as a pin-up to the audience (she steadily loses articles of clothing through bizarre accidents) but the M.P.s are always engrossed in their newspapers. The climax is when, while the M.P.s' evasions crumble and give way to admissions, Maddie is reduced to bra and panties and the M.P.s simultaneously discover a double-page pin-up spread of Maddie herself. She launches into a triumphant chant of names of her associates, which frightens away all of the committee except of course French. She inveigles French offstage with her just as the two characters of New-Found-Land *enter to begin their play.*

The title is taken from Donne's Elegy on his Mistress Going to Bed ('O my America, my New-Found-Land') and thus cleverly refers to America, Berman's land of origin, to Britain, his newly-found home, and to the erotic excitement of gradually undressing a mistress. Two Home Office officials, one very senior, the other very junior, are preparing to discuss with the Home Secretary Berman's application for naturalization; and they distract themselves into monologues. Bernard, the very senior official, has an anecdote developing absurdly the old gag line 'my father knew Lloyd George'. He has obviously bored Arthur and probably many others with the anecdote before; yet it is clear that he himself has never got the real point of it, which is that Lloyd George bluffed his way into a lady's bedroom. The bluff turns on being able to see Big Ben, but again Bernard does not notice that his present location is ironically appropriate. The anecdote refers to 'French' but this turns out to be Sir John French of the First World War. Arthur's longer monologue opens with the Donne line, not giving its context, and proceeds to comprehensively send up tourist travelogues about America; it is a separate set-piece of its own with excellent opportunities for the right actor. The monologue is abruptly interrupted by the return of the Select Committee.

A squabble starts over which meeting is entitled to the room. The Home Secretary, arriving importantly, is all set to pull rank but abruptly changes his mind as he too recognizes Maddie; he forthwith signs the naturalization order and makes a hasty escape. We now gather that French has had a change of heart during the adjournment, and if we have any problem guessing why, we have only to wait a few minutes till the end of the play, where he pulls out from his breast-pocket, to mop his brow, the knickers which Maddie was seen to be wearing at the beginning of the play. The Committee rapidly agree on a report saying that what Members of Parliament do 'in their own time, and with whom, is between them and their conscience, provided that they do not transgress the rights of others or the law of the land'.

The evening disappoints some spectators, particularly those expecting *intellectual stimulus; it is a satyr-play, a romp, not too choosy about its jokes (at one point we are invited to laugh because 'Noes' is written on a blackboard as 'Nose') and it is patently beamed at the business-men's evening-out lowbrow West End audience. Stoppard would undoubtedly say that it is an honest piece of showbiz (its only dishonesty, perhaps, is selling itself as a full evening when it is really too short). I would go further: not only is the play theatrically original and deft, its glancing points are humane and tend in the general direction of wisdom: the dumb blonde turning out to have far more sense than her masters; the real tiresomeness, and sometimes worse, of the Press in fussing out the private life of public figures; echoes, amongst the innocent nonsense, of the sinister nonsense of Senator Joseph McCarthy brandishing his supposed list of Communists in the State Department (is it accident that Maddie's gleeful outcry at the end of Part One travesties the hysterical crying-out-of-the-names of the girls in Arthur Miller's The Crucible?); and the truly 'moral' point that the M.P.s fail to notice Maddie's real undress because they are chortling over newspaper pin-ups.*

Ed Berman   51
names   121
sound-patterns   100–1
'ideas'   86
underwear   37
'blue' jokes   76, 77, 80
characterization   201, 212
'Strewths'   51, 89, 91, 177

opening   101, 175
p. 19 'Gregg's' and 'Pitman' are methods of shorthand.
p. 23 'when the smoke has cleared'   110
p. 25 'Caxton Hall'—the most well-known London registry office.
p. 27 Withenshaw's puns   77
p. 30 'Mrs Grundy'—traditional figure of a prude.
p. 49 'I was sick on her shoes'   83
pp. 49–50 discussed   100
p. 50 'Don't talk to me about voluptuous'   80
pp. 51–2 discussed   101
pp. 60–5 discussed   43
p. 70 'How do you do? My name's Jones'   85
p. 72 'Finita la Commedia'   101

Every Good Boy Deserves Favour

Published in one volume with *Professional Foul*, Faber 1978.

There is a full-scale symphony orchestra and conductor on stage. There are three acting areas, separate but small—the Cell, the Office, the School. In the Cell are (1) (Alexander) IVANOV, *a lunatic obsessed with the idea that he has a symphony orchestra (in which he plays triangle) and that music is a disgrace of madness which nevertheless everyone shares (the obvious parallel is sexuality, and Ivanov is allowed some comic Freudian slips), and (2)* ALEXANDER(*Ivanov*), *a sane man put into a mental hospital for saying that sane people are put into mental hospitals. In the School is (3)* SACHA (*Alexander Ivanov*), *Alexander's son, a small boy who plays triangle in the school band and is victimized by his teacher because of his father's notoriety. These are the only named characters; that they all have the same, John-Smith-type name is of course characteristic Stoppard, but also a satirical snap at the depersonalizing State. It is the idea of the Colonel who runs the 'hospital' to put in the same cell prisoners of the same name.*

In the Office the Doctor interviews Ivanov and Alexander from time to time; at other times he has a back desk in the violin section of the orchestra. Alexander has been moved to this 'hospital' from the Arsenal'naya, the Leningrad Special Psychiatric Hospital, where he was on hunger strike. Clearly he has won and the State has decided to release him, but has to do so without losing face. The Doctor tries to persuade Alexander to recant, and to show gratitude for his treatment. Later Sacha is brought in to add his poignant plea to his father to 'Be brave and tell them lies. If they're wicked, how can it be wrong?' ALEXANDER: 'It helps them to go on being wicked.'

Alexander's release is eventually contrived by the Colonel's deliberately confusing him with Ivanov, who is also released. The three representatives of the State in the play are not fanatics; they merely go through the motions expected of them (which is very much what Vladimir Bukofsky, for whose release Stoppard had campaigned the previous year, and who watched a rehearsal of this play, says Russia is like). At the end the Teacher, the Doctor and Ivanov join the orchestra. Alexander and Sacha go out, cutting through the middle of the orchestra. Sacha sings—to his own music, not that of the orchestra—'Everything can be all right!'—but the phrase is learnt from the State's indoctrination, and it is a very ambivalent ending.

A substantial amount of the performance time is occupied by music without action, and a good deal of the dialogue is accompanied by the orchestra. One gathers that Previn's music, which is relatively accessible, contains a number *of ironic or poignant allusions to Russian symphonies. There is an obvious case for issuing the play as a record: reading the text one tends to forget the much fuller texture supplied by the music.*

fundamental inconsistency 192
Title: a mnemonic for the lines of the treble clef (upwards: EGBDF)
staging 51–2, 173, 192
rigidity and flux 177–8
televized 73
names 124
characterization 201
values 205
Absurdism of the State 88
Sacha 52, 91

pp. 16–18 Ivanov's puns 77–8
p. 17 'A harpist . . .'—the original Pope line is 'And fools rush in where
angels fear to tread'. Angels traditionally play harps. . . .
'Heifetz'—famous violinist; 'Sousa'—writer of military marches
(which go oom-pah oom-pah). 'Jew's harp'—not, of course, an
orchestral instrument, but included here for its ironic appropriateness to the Soviet Jews who have difficulty getting permission to leave Russia. 'Verdi' and 'Puccini' were, of course, com-
posers.
p. 19 'Turgenev' wrote the classic novel *Fathers and Sons*, here a title
chosen with bitchy sarcasm by the Teacher.
p. 23 Alexander's monologue 73, 102, 209
p. 26 'A plane area bordered by high walls' 91
'I have a complaint' 79
p. 27 'Yes, he has an identity problem' 81
p. 30 Tchaikovsky's '1812' Overture celebrates Russia's victory over
Bonaparte, also part of the material of Tolstoy's *War and Peace*.
p. 31 'Look, if you eat something' 91
'Archipelago'—Alexander Solzhenitsyn's metaphor for the scattered 'islands' of gulags (forced labour camps) throughout Russia.
p. 32 'Euclid': pioneer Greek geometrician.
pp. 36–7 freeing of Alexander and Ivanov: this is still sometimes misunderstood by readers and audiences as being the Colonel's *error*.
Stoppard did not intend any ambiguity: the Colonel is *pretending*

to make an error, as a face-saving way of ridding himself of the two prisoners.

p. 37 ending 52

Professional Foul

Published in one volume with *Every Good Boy*, Faber 1978.

Anderson (J. S. Mill Professor of Ethics at Cambridge) travels with McKendrick and Chetwyn (philosophy lecturers at other universities) to a Colloquium Philosophicum in Prague. In the first scene, on their aircraft, we learn that Anderson has accepted the invitation not primarily for the philosophy (the prospect of which appears to bore him) but for some other reason. We are led to suspect that this might be some action on behalf of 'persecuted professors'; Chetwyn has already written letters to The Times *on the subject. In Prague the philosophers are sharing a hotel with the England football squad, and we discover that Anderson has a ticket for their match against Czechoslovakia the following day. At the hotel however, he is approached by Pavel Hollar, who studied under him in England but is now a lavatory cleaner and under police surveillance. Hollar has written a paper concluding that 'there is an obligation, a human responsibility, to fight against the State correctness'. He expects Anderson to smuggle the paper to England where another Czech, Volkansky ('He didn't come back. He was a realist.') may publish it. To his surprise and dismay Anderson refuses: 'it's just not ethical'. This is Anderson's 'professional foul', excusing himself from hazardous involvement by relying on the letter not the spirit of the 'rules' he works by. He does however agree to keep the manuscript overnight and return it to Hollar's flat next day on his way to the match.*

The following day Anderson leaves the Colloquium after a polite but dismissive comment on the linguistic philosophy of an American, Stone. 'The importance of language is over-rated . . . The important truths are simple and monolithic. The essentials of a given situation speak for themselves.' He arrives at Hollar's flat to find it being searched by plain-clothes police, and he himself is detained, missing the match. He is allowed to listen to it in Czech on the radio, and hears the first goal, scored by the Czechs from a penalty after a 'professional foul' by an English player when a goal was otherwise certain. (In a 'professional foul' the letter of the rules is accepted—the fouler expects the penalty to result—but the spirit *is flagrantly ignored.) The police plant and 'find' contraband money in the flat. Hollar has already been arrested. Anderson retains Hollar's manuscript.*

In the evening at the hotel the philosophers discuss meaning and ethics. We learn in passing that Chetwyn also played truant from the Colloquium in the afternoon; he was 'meeting some friends'. McKendrick attempts to explain his ethical relativism (I find his explanation—pages 77–8—incomprehensible: I hope this is Stoppard's intention). The contrast is briefly but clearly made between this and, on the one hand, Chetwyn's 'classical' beliefs in absolutes of goodness and beauty and, on the other, Anderson's theory of 'fictions'—the theory that if goodness and beauty do not exist we need to invent them for ourselves and then treat them as if they were absolutes. Chetwyn also discloses that he often tries ethical dilemmas out on his eight-year-old son—'a good rule'.

Hollar's wife and son come to the hotel and ask Anderson to give Hollar's manuscript to 'Jan' at the Colloquium the next day. They warn Anderson that he is now likely to be searched at the airport. Anderson borrows a journalist's typewriter and rewrites his paper for the Colloquium.

The paper is soon challenged by the Chairman because it is not the one which has been circulated in advance. Anderson perseveres. His new paper points out the agreement of the American and Czech Constitutions on certain fundamental rights of the individual, and develops Chetwyn's hint that a small child's sense of natural justice may be important. 'There is a sense of right and wrong which precedes utterance . . . the implications are serious for a collective or State ethos which finds itself in conflict with individual rights.' The Chairman stages a fire alarm and the Colloquium breaks up.

This summary omits a good deal of byplay with England footballers, football journalists, and in particular with McKendrick—excellent stuff, leavening the darker story but also relevant to it. McKendrick is not unlikeable but he is insensitive, boorish, fundamentally unaware of ethical issues. In the final scene of the play, on the aircraft flying out, we learn that Anderson has smuggled out Hollar's manuscript in McKendrick's briefcase ('they were very unlikely to search you'). McKendrick, in his sublime unawareness, was the perfect carrier; and the ethical dubiety of what Anderson did—a foul of a different order, breaking the letter to follow the spirit—is arguably the sort of action McKendrick's confused theory has recommended. A further appropriateness is that McKendrick has announced himself, in the opening scene, ready to assist with such 'extra-curricular activities' at a time when Anderson had no thought of them. The amused satisfaction we may feel at the ending is darkened not only by our memory of the Hollars or of the Czech oppression in general, but also by our having seen, moments earlier, Chetwyn stopped at the customs and found to be attempting

*to smuggle out papers relating to another dissident. Chetwyn, who all along
has seemed more consistently honourable than Anderson, was not devious
enough—would not stoop to a foul of any sort.*

genesis   12–13
use of television medium   71–3
rigidity and flux   156, 178–80, 213
inadequacy of language   79, 94–5, 108–9, 162
philosophy   156, 162, 164–6
characterization   104–5, 203

p. 43 brochure/magazine   72, 86
p. 44 'I wasn't sure it was you'   79
        'A lot of chaps . . .'   108–9
p. 45 'There is a coldness'   178
        'Do you know Prague?'   113
p. 46 'Letters to *The Times*'   118
pp. 46–7 'ulterior motive'   178
p. 48 'I see you like tits and bums'   86
        'extra-curricular activities'   179
        'You mean you write for—?'   117
p. 50 McKendrick's misunderstanding   80, 118
p. 52 Thomas Paine (1737–1809) and John Locke (1632–1704) were
        classic liberal philosophers. Locke turns up again on p. 88.
p. 54 'bad manners'   178–9
p. 54 'not a safe conclusion'   118
p. 57 'I did not expect . . .'   203
        'I forgot—welcome to Prague'   209
p. 59 Anderson advising footballers   86–7, 104
        'maybe the lift's bugged'   179
p. 60 G. W. F. Hegel (1770–1831) was a pioneer rationalist
        philosopher.
        W. V. O. Quine (born 1908) is a modern rationalist philosopher.
        'empirical' = based on sense-*experience*.
        'epistemological' = to do with philosophical *theory* of knowledge.
        McKendrick's gaffe   104
p. 61 'I knew his face'   72
p. 62 'Do you ever wonder . . .'   109

Night and Day

Published by Faber, 1978.

The set is basically realistic, but the house, of which we see the verandah, the living-room and part of the study, moves about in the first act according to whether we are in the open air or indoors. The prologue is done on an empty stage, with a real jeep. The second act takes place entirely within the house, at night. We are in Kambawe, a fictitious former British Colony in Africa, in the home of Geoffrey Carson, who runs the business side of the local mining industry. Guthrie, an internationally celebrated press photographer, has come to the house to meet Dick Wagner, a 'big-name roving reporter' of the kind the boy Stoppard idolized. Their paper, the Sunday Globe, has advised them to meet at the Carsons' house (without telling the Carsons) because it has a telex machine. The country is divided in incipient civil war between President Ginku Mageeba (educated at Charterhouse and the London School of Economics) and Colonel Shimbu of the Adoma Liberation Front.

The play starts in Guthrie's nightmare: very loud helicopter noise, darkness, a jeep's headlights, a spotlight from the helicopter, very loud machine-

gun noise. Guthrie jumps from the jeep, shouts 'Press!' but is gunned down. When the lights go up the house is on stage; Guthrie is asleep outside on a long garden chair. Ruth Carson wakes him. She is taken aback to hear that Dick Wagner is coming to the house, but manages to conceal the fact that a few days earlier in London, where she was picking up her son from prep school, she slept with Wagner in a hotel. She is offstage when Wagner arrives; he fills Guthrie in with what he knows about events in Kambawe. He says he has been in the capital, Jeddu, for ten days (p. 21); either he is lying or Stoppard has made an error: today is Thursday (p. 22), Ruth left London on Friday last (p. 44) after sleeping the previous night with Wagner (pp. 51–2). Either way, this is not noticed in the theatre.

Wagner has been 'scooped' by an unknown correspondent to his own paper, Jacob Milne, who now turns up with Carson himself. Young, attractive, idealistic, Milne was previously employed on a provincial evening paper but lost his job for objecting to a 'closed shop'. Wagner, further exasperated, talks heavily about 'worker solidarity' and telexes his.union leader in London to protest at Milne's employment.

Ruth and Wagner are introduced and show no signs of having met before, though he teases her sotto voce *and some of her thoughts can be heard by the audience—a convention Stoppard has briskly established at the start of the play. Carson is preoccupied with political manoeuvres, attempting to fix a secret meeting at the house between Mageeba and Shimbu. He makes a plan to 'use' the reporters next day as messengers to Shimbu. Wagner discovers (from the Carsons' son, who has learnt it from Ruth) that Mageeba is coming to the house the following night (Friday–Saturday); he keeps the knowledge to himself and allows Milne and Guthrie to go to Shimbu. In three duet scenes—with Carson, with Wagner, and with Milne—we gain insight into Ruth's personality and state of mind: she is underemployed and restless in her marriage with Carson, she is upset by her own misconduct in London and still more by Wagner's turning up at her home in Africa; and she is now fiercely attracted by the boyish Milne. The first act ends not with darkness but with 'night into day'—the departure of Milne and Guthrie early the next morning: the jeep on stage again. Guthrie is appalled by Milne's naive choice of army-type clothing and insists on his changing.*

Act Two (late on Friday, early on Saturday) opens with Ruth waiting in darkness for Milne's return; she has dressed to kill. He appears quietly. In a tense, delicate verbal wrestling Ruth attempts to seduce him; he admits himself attracted but holds back on principle. He leaves. Ruth disappears momentarily behind a sofa (or tree growing in the house) and when she reappears undoes her dress, steps out of it, and is naked; she follows Milne into the dark. Carson appears and watches her go. We then discover that Ruth is still in the room. Now, or later, we are meant to realize that all these first minutes of Act Two have been entirely Ruth's fantasy, and the naked figure following Milne offstage was a fantasy Ruth. It is one in the morning but the reporters have not returned. Carson thinks Ruth has 'got dressed-up' for Mageeba, who 'may not come for hours'.

Wagner horrifies Carson by turning up to meet Mageeba. 'Be careful if he laughs,' Carson warns him. Mageeba arrives with a 'convincing' toy machine-gun for the Carsons' son. He is suave, cynical, several jumps ahead of Wagner who grossly underestimates him and attempts to ingratiate himself. Mageeba plays with Wagner like a cat with a mouse; at last 'throws back his head and laughs', then suddenly 'brings the weighted end of his stick down upon Wagner's head' and shouts at him. This climax immediately breaks into another: Guthrie arrives with the news that Milne is dead, gunned down before they could reach Shimbu. It is clear that Shimbu will not come to meet Mageeba and that the war will now escalate. Mageeba leaves; Carson prepares to follow him, taking Guthrie. A telex arrives: a full strike will take place at the paper in London as a result of Wagner's news that Milne is a 'scab'. This means that Wagner's 'scoop' interview with Mageeba cannot be printed. Carson leaves, and Ruth and Wagner will spend the night together. In her head, not audible to Wagner, Ruth sings 'The lady is a tramp'.

names   64, 121, 124
critique of Press   60, 62, 182–3, 205
as realist writing with departures   57–66, 97
psychology   18, 61–6, 209–11
characterization   57–8, 93, 105–6, 203–4, 212
moral enquiry   62–6, 203, 205
Ruth   61–5, 85, 166, 204

title: is that of a classic pop song. There is also a loose thread of idea, as
   follows: p. 15 (stage-directions), p. 61 (Milne's long speech and
   also the stage-direction at the bottom), p. 62 (stage-direction at
   top), p. 67 (Milne's 'Sharply' speech) and perhaps p. 92 (Guthrie's
   speech).

opening   37, 58
p. 17 'RUTH *remains perfectly still*'   58, 209
pp. 18–19 'Boy about this high'   59, 80

Dogg's Hamlet, Cahoot's Macbeth

Published by Inter-Action Imprint, 1979; and by Faber, 1980. Page-references are to the Faber edition.

The script adapts the earlier play Dogg's Our Pet *and the* 15-minute Hamlet *and adds a shortened* Macbeth *thrown into chaos by police interruption and a recourse to Dogg-language.* Dogg's Hamlet *is dedicated to 'Professor Dogg' (Ed Berman) and* Cahoot's Macbeth *to Pavel Kohout, a Czechoslovak playwright whom Stoppard met on his visit to Prague in June 1977. In 1978 Kohout wrote to Stoppard about the 'Living-Room Theatre' group formed in Prague by actors banned from public performance: Kohout had adapted* Macbeth *to be performed in private flats. Stoppard makes it clear in his preface, and by the travesty spelling 'Cahoot', that* his Macbeth *is 'not supposed to be a fair representation of Kohout's elegant seventy-five minute version'.*

Dogg's Our Pet *derived from an idea in Wittgenstein whereby two different languages could for a short time be happily coincident. (See Stoppard's preface.) Schoolboys are preparing for a Speech Day which will include a shortened* Hamlet. *Their Dogg-language (the Headmaster's name is also Dogg) is—to us—ludicrous, very much in the manner of schoolboy humour, though they are innocent of it. Thus 'Have you got the time please, sir?' addressed to the Headmaster is 'Cretinous pig-faced, git?' (It is not amongst Stoppard's subtler humour.) As in the later plays* Travesties *and* Dirty Linen, *it is some time before we hear intelligible English, and it appears in the form of the opening lines of* Hamlet, *in which the boys test each other for words: ironically, it is clear that the lines are scarcely intelligible to the boys. The boys' names are Able, Baker, and Charlie; the Headmaster is Dogg and the other identified pupil (he wins all the prizes) is Fox Major. The missing initial letter in this sequence is supplied by a lorrydriver, Easy, though in every other respect he is a misfit: he speaks English not Dogg and there is considerable reciprocal confusion between him and the Dogg-speaking characters as an innocent word in one language proves abusive in another. Easy and the boys erect a platform of blocks, planks, slabs and cubes (this was Wittgenstein's actual example).*

Some of the blocks have letters painted on them and form a wall, saying MATHS OLD EGG. *Dogg enters, reads it, and knocks Easy through the wall. A second attempt at the wall produces* MEG SHOT GLAD; *Dogg again knocks Easy through the wall. A Lady appears and gives 'nicely' a short speech full of clashing Anglo-Saxon monosyllables, which happens to make in English a summary of the awfulness of kids (the opposite of what is expected on a Speech Day). She lapses into Latin for her conclusion: 'Mens sana in corpore sano'—Stoppard mixing in another strange language (he is to do the same again with the Inspector's 'Wilco zebra over' later in the play). Fox Major collects his prizes, Mrs Dogg gives a (nauseating) vote of thanks, and the Lady's exit line is* '(with energy and charm) *Sod the pudding club!'*

The wall now says GOD SLAG THEM. 'Easy looks at Dogg. Dogg looks at the wall. Easy dutifully hurls himself through the wall which dis-integrates.' *The wall is reassembled to read* DOGGS HAM LET *and the fifteen-minute* Hamlet *follows. It is a genuine potted version, preserving the outline of the plot and a few famous lines, but not much else, and also parodying school plays in general—the Guards are 'costumed for a typical Shakespeare play except that they have short trousers'; Ophelia pulls down her own gravestone. After the fifteen-minute version, 'Encore' signs appear and there is* another *run-through of the story, this time in thirty-eight lines.*

The action of Cahoot's Macbeth '*takes place in the living-room of a flat'. The shortened* Macbeth *runs smoothly and reasonably until 'Didst thou not hear a noise?', when a police siren is heard approaching. Shakespeare's famous knocking leads to the entry not of the Porter but of the Inspector. After a considerable interruption and hostility between himself and the actors, he takes a seat in the audience. At the 'interval' he gets up ('So nice to have a play with a happy ending for a change') and cautions the actors on the subversive nature of Shakespeare; he lets it be known that he has the flat bugged, a list of the audience's names and occupations, and two henchmen (Boris and Maurice) at the door. He leaves. The performance continues. Where Shakespeare supplies a third Murderer (greeted with suspicion by the first two), Stoppard supplies a bewildered Easy, again delivering blocks, now talking in Dogg language. The Hostess leads him off, but he returns a moment later and unwittingly plays Banquo's ghost ('Macbeth does his best to ignore him'). The play staggers on as far as the news that 'Macduff is fled to England', then Easy returns and insists on attention. He has a 'lorry load of wood and timber'. The play resumes briefly, but at 'Bleed, bleed, poor country,' the police siren is again heard, and at 'See who comes here? /My countryman, but yet I know him not' the Inspector re-enters: Stoppard's irony at its fiercest and best. The time the audience is told to 'stay where you are and nobody use the lavatory', but the Inspector's plan for a swift clean sweep is thrown into chaos by Easy's Dogg-language. The actors decide to perform Act Five of* Macbeth *in Dogg: it is the funniest use of Dogg in the play since most theatre audiences are familiar with Shakespeare's words and can recognize the rhythms being travestied (e.g. 'Dominoes, et dominoes, et dominoes'). Easy's lorry is opened and he and the actors start building a platform for Malcolm's coronation. The Inspector's henchmen appear and hand in their own 'grey' slabs with which they build a wall across the proscenium opening. Malcolm completes the play of* Macbeth, *standing on the platform. Easy ends Stoppard's evening, speaking into the telephone: 'Well, it's been a funny sort of week. But I should be back by Tuesday.'*

On the Razzle

Published by Faber, 1981.

Zangler the provincial grocer plans marriage to Madame Knorr, who runs a Viennese fashion house. He informs his counter-clerk, Weinberl, and his apprentice, Christopher, that he is promoting them, to partner and chief sales assistant respectively. Although he has no other employees in the shop, they feel gratified; yet they also become aware of 'a sense of . . . grief'. 'Beyond the door is another room. The servant is the slave of his master and the master is the slave of his business.' The middle-aged Weinberl dreams of being able to 'look back on a day when I was fancy free, a real razzle of a day': he must 'acquire a past before it's too late'. On impulse, he and Christopher (traditionally in Austria played as a 'trouser-role' by an actress) nip off to Vienna.

Zangler—whom in a series of farcical near-misses they keep almost running into—is in Vienna both to dine with his fiancée and to chase his niece and ward, Marie, who has eloped with the fortune-hunter Sonders. Zangler has brought with him his brand-new manservant, Melchior, an amiable wriggler who does not know Weinberl or Christopher by sight (and can therefore be allowed, by the rules of farce, to encounter them frequently).

The emergencies and instant improvizations in which Weinberl and Christopher in true farce tradition become entangled include hiding in Scottish plaid capes in the fashion house, being obliged to escort to dinner Madame Knorr and her ladyfriend in the same restaurant in which Zangler awaits Madame Knorr's arrival and at which Sonders and Marie also dine, being arrested in mistake for Sonders and Marie (Christopher having donned a woman's coat to escape the preceding predicament) and being finally embroiled in a frenetic, silent-movie-like sequence at the house of Zangler's sister-in-law, Miss Blumenblatt, where Zangler has intended to confine his niece. One of the best moments in these late pages finds Sonders and Weinberl being introduced as each other to each other. Weinberl and Christopher contrive to travel back to the provinces on the roof of Zangler's coach and—by means of the cellar trapdoor and the goods shute from above—to be just opening up the shop as Zangler knocks on the door. News arrives that Sonders has come into an inheritance and Zangler now agrees to his marrying Marie. Melchior recognizes Weinberl and Christopher from their razzle in Vienna but is full of admiration for it and will not give them away. The play ends with Weinberl's employing (at no actual pay!) a solemn and ludicrously well-spoken ragamuffin to be Christopher's junior: the sequence of respectable employment and promotion re-establishing itself.

On the Razzle *is sizzling traditional farce enriched exceptionally by Stoppard's quickfire verbal slapstick. Many of its jokes are weak puns to be delivered in clusters at top speed—a particularly English tradition, this; but there are also really stylish stage set-pieces, such as Zangler's employing of Melchior (pp. 13–19) or Weinberl's cod toasting of the merchant class (p. 21) punctuated by Christopher's licking of a stamp on cue. The numerous minor roles are rewarding, and the play is likely to establish itself as a perennial for amateurs.*

OTHER GROVE PRESS DRAMA AND THEATER PAPERBACKS

Quare Fellow, Richard's Cork Leg, Three One Act Plays for Radio) / $4.95

E784   BENTLEY, ERIC / Are You Now Or Have You Ever Been and Other Plays (The Recantation of Galileo Galilei; From the Memoirs of Pontius Pilate) / $12.50

B60   BRECHT, BERTOLT / Baal, A Man's A Man, The Elephant Calf / $1.95

B312   BRECHT, BERTOLT / The Caucasian Chalk Circle / $2.95

B119   BRECHT, BERTOLT / Edward II: A Chronicle Play / $.195

B120   BRECHT, BERTOLT / Gal'leo / $2.45

B117   BRECHT, BERTOLT / The Good Woman of Setzuan / $2.95

B80   BRECHT, BERTOLT / The Jewish Wife and Other Short Plays (In Search of Justice, The Informer, The Elephant Calf, The Measures Taken, The Exception and the Rule, Salzburg Dance of Death) / $1.95

B89   BRECHT, BERTOLT / The Jungle of Cities and Other Plays (Drums in the Night, Roundheads and Peakheads) / $3.95

B108   BRECHT, BERTOLT / Mother Courage and Her Children / $1.95

B333   BRECHT, BERTOLT / The Threepenny Opera / $2.45

B193   BULGAKOV, MIKHAIL / Heart of a Dog / $2.95

B147   BULGAKOV, MIKHAIL / The Master and Margarita / $4.95

E773   CLURMAN, HAROLD / Nine Plays of the Modern Theater (Waiting for Godot by Samuel Beckett, The Visit by Friedrich Durrenmat, Tango by Slawomir Mrozek, The Caucasian Chalk Circle by Bertolt Brecht, The Balcony by Jean Genet, Rhinoceros by Eugene Ionesco, American Buffalo by David Mamet, The Birth day Party by Harold Pinter, and Rosencrantz and Guildenstern Are Dead by Tom Stoppard) / $11.95

B459   COWARD, NOEL / Plays: One (Hay Fever, The Vortex, Fallen Angels, Easy Virtue) / $7.50

B460   COWARD, NOEL / Plays: Two (Private Lives, Bitter-Sweet, The Marquise, Post Mortem) / $7.50

B461   COWARD, NOEL / Plays: Three (Design for Living, Cavalcade,

E679	IONESCO, EUGENE / Man With Bags / $3.95
E589	IONESCO, EUGENE / Rhinoceros and Other Plays (The Leader, The Future Is in Eggs) / $4.95
E485	IONESCO, EUGENE / A Stroll in the Air and Frenzy for Two or More: Two Plays / $2.45
E496	JARRY, ALFRED / The Ubu Plays (Ubu Rex, Ubu Cuckolded, Ubu Enchained) / $7.95
E697	MAMET, DAVID / American Buffalo / $3.95
E778	MAMET, DAVID / Lakeboat / $4.95
E709	MAMET, DAVID / A Life in the Theatre / $3.95
E712	MAMET, DAVID / Sexual Perversity in Chicago ad The Duck Variations: Two Plays / $3.95
B107	MOON, SAMUEL, ed. / One Act: Eleven Short Plays of the Modern Theater (Miss Julie by August Strindberg, Purgatory by William Butler Yeats, The Man With the Flower in His Mouth by Luigi Pirandello, Pullman Car Hiawatha by Thornton Wilder, Hello Out There by William Saroyan, 27 Wagons Full of Cotton by Tennessee Williams, Bedtime Story by Sean O'Casey, Cecile by Jean Anouilh, This Music Crept By Me Upon the Waters by Archibald MacLeish, A Memory of Two Mondays by Arthur Miller, The Chairs by Eugene Ionesco) / $7.95
E789	MROZEK, SLAWOMIR / Striptease, Tango, Vatzlav: Three Plays / $12.50
E650	NICHOLS, PETER / The National Health / $3.95
B429	ODETS, CLIFFORD / Six Plays of Clifford Odets (Waiting for Lefty, Awake and Sing, Golden Boy, Rocket to the Moon, Till the Day I Die, Paradise Lost) / $7.95
B400	ORTON, JOE / The Complete Plays (The Ruffian on the Stair, The Good and Faithful Servant, The Erpingham Camp, Funeral Games, Loot, What the Butler Saw, Entertaining Mr. Sloane) / $6.95
E724	PINTER, HAROLD / Betrayal / $3.95
E315	PINTER, HAROLD / The Birthday and The Room: Two Plays /

$3.95

E299   PINTER, HAROLD / The Caretaker and The Dumb Waiter: Two Plays / $2.95

B402   PINTER, HAROLD / Complete Works: One (The Birthday Party, The Room, The Dumb Waiter, A Slight Ache, A Night Out, The Black and White, The Examination) / $6.95

B403   PINTER, HAROLD / Complete Works: Two (The Caretaker, Night School, The Dwarfs, The Collection, The Lover, Five Revue Sketches) / $6.95

B410   PINTER, HAROLD / Complete Works: Three (Landscape, Silence, The Basement, Six Revue Sketches, Tea Party [play], Tea Party [short story], Mac) / $6.95

B464   PINTER, HAROLD / Complete Works: Four (Old Times, No Man's Land, Betrayal, Monologue, Family Voices) / $5.95

E411   PINTER, HAROLD / The Homecoming / $4.95

E764   PINTER, HAROLD / The Hothouse / $4.95

E663   PINTER, HAROLD / No Man's Land / $3.95

E606   PINTER, HAROLD / Old Times / $3.95

E350   PINTER, HAROLD / Three Plays (The Collection, A Slight Ache, The Dwarfs) / $4.95 [See also Complete Works: One by Harold Pinter, B402 / $3.95 and Complete Works: Two by Harold Pinter, B403 / $6.95]

E744   POMERANCE, BERNARD / The Elephant Man / $4.25

B467   RATTIGAN, TERENCE / Plays: One (French Without Tears, The Winslow Boy, The Browning Version, Harlequinade) / $5.95

E497   SHAW, ROBERT / The Man In the Glass Booth / $2.95

E757   SHAWN, WALLACE / Marie and Bruce / $4.95

E763   SHAWN, WALLACE, and GREGORY, ANDRE / My Dinner with Andre / $5.95

E686   STOPPARD, TOM / Albert's Bridge and Other Plays (If You're Glad I'll Be Frank, Artist Descending a Staircase, Where Are They Now? A Separate Peace) / $3.95

E684   STOPPARD, TOM / Dirty Linen and New-Found-Land: Two Plays / $2.95

Critical Studies

GROVE PRESS, INC., 196 West Houston St., New York, N.Y. 10014